D0433916

NINJA

www.**transworldbooks**.co.uk

Also by John Man

Gobi
Atlas of the Year 1000
Alpha Beta
The Gutenberg Revolution
Genghis Khan
Attila
Kublai Khan
The Terracotta Army
The Great Wall
The Leadership Secrets of Genghis Khan
Xanadu
Samurai

NINJA

1,000 YEARS OF THE
SHADOW WARRIORS

JOHN MAN

BANTAM PRESS

LONDON • TORONTO • SYDNEY • AUCKLAND • JOHANNESBURG

TRANSWORLD PUBLISHERS
61–63 Uxbridge Road, London W5 5SA
A Random House Group Company
www.transworldbooks.co.uk

First published in Great Britain
in 2012 by Bantam Press
an imprint of Transworld Publishers

Copyright © John Man 2012

John Man has asserted his right under the Copyright,
Designs and Patents Act 1988 to be identified as the author of this work.

A CIP catalogue record for this book
is available from the British Library.

ISBN 9780593068113 (cased)
9780593068120 (tpb)

This book is sold subject to the condition that it shall not,
by way of trade or otherwise, be lent, resold, hired out,
or otherwise circulated without the publisher's prior
consent in any form of binding or cover other than that
in which it is published and without a similar condition,
including this condition, being imposed on the
subsequent purchaser.

Addresses for Random House Group Ltd companies outside the UK
can be found at: www.randomhouse.co.uk
The Random House Group Ltd Reg. No. 954009

The Random House Group Limited supports the Forest Stewardship
Council (FSC®), the leading international forest-certification organization.
Our books carrying the FSC label are printed on FSC®-certified paper.
FSC is the only forest-certification scheme endorsed by the leading environmental
organizations, including Greenpeace. Our paper procurement
policy can be found at www.randomhouse.co.uk/environment

Typeset in 11.5/15pt Sabon by
Falcon Oast Graphic Art Ltd.
Printed and bound in Great Britain by
Clays Ltd, Bungay, Suffolk

2 4 6 8 10 9 7 5 3 1

MIX
Paper from
responsible sources
FSC
www.fsc.org   FSC® C016897

CONTENTS

A NOTE ABOUT TRANSLITERATION

Except for Japanese names and words common in English (e.g. Tokyo, Kyoto, shogun), Japanese has been romanized according to the 'revised Hepburn' system, with a macron on ō and ū to indicate long vowels.

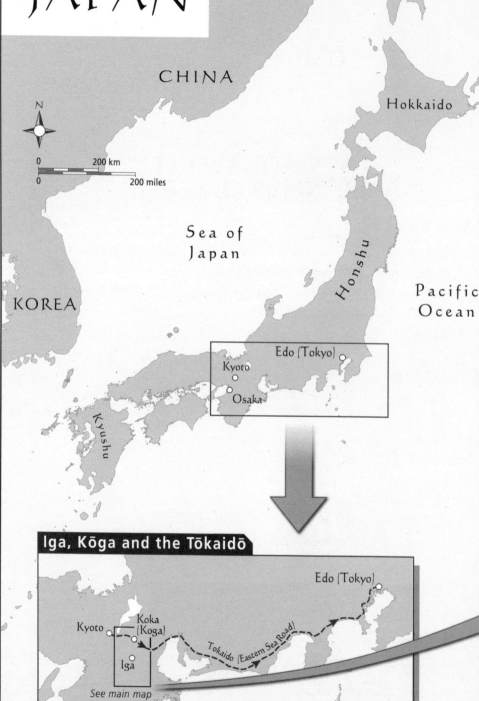

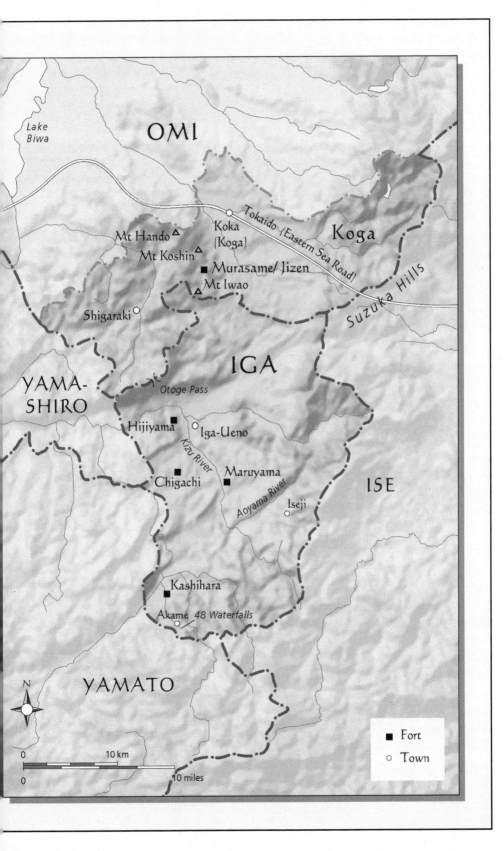

INTRODUCTION:
GHOSTS OF THE SHADOW
WARRIORS

*Once you get the details and layout of the castle or the camp,
all you need to do is get back with the information as soon as
possible.*

Ninja instructional poem

THE RESTAURANT OWNER, IN HIS MID-70S BUT AS FIT AS SOMEONE
half his age, was talking about his ninja ancestors. A firm
gaze behind huge glasses, a ready laugh, a torrent of words:
Mr Ueda's ninja blood had kept him youthful and exuberant.

'But how do you know all this?' I asked, because ninjas
were famous for leaving few written records.

'It's in the family. My grandmother was a Momochi.' A
famous name, an eminent family, one of several hundred who
used to share these forested hills and steep-sided valleys. 'She
used to talk to me about the past, when I was helping her on
the farm and when we went away on holiday.'

It was from her, with her childhood memories of her grand-
parents – his great-great-grandparents – that he had learned
about Iga's ninja families, about the way they had worked
together to build an early form of democracy, keeping themselves independent of power-hungry lords. Did people where

I came from know about this? No, I said, it would be news to them, because most people thought ninjas were comic-book creatures.

He had much more to tell, but I was short of time, and interrupted with a glance at my watch and an abrupt question. Was there anything else? I was hoping for another swift bullet-point that I could follow up at leisure, and was utterly unprepared for what came next.

'I would like to show you what I inherited from my grandmother.'

How could I refuse, without seeming impolite? He led the way past tables, pushed aside boxes and revealed a narrow door into the roof space, for like most countryside buildings in this earthquake-prone country, the restaurant was a single-floor structure, with a loft for storage.

'Be careful,' he said, carefully stepping over a mat on the floor. 'That's to catch rats. Very sticky. If you step on that, you will not get off.'

The stairs rose steep and shoulder-width into shadows. I followed, with a twinge of anxiety at the delay, wondering how on earth I could beat a graceful retreat.

Above and ahead, he stooped clear of the sloping roof along a little space too small to be called a corridor, and led the way into a gloomy attic packed with, of all things, what looked like tailor's dummies. It took my eyes a few seconds to get used to the half-light before I realized what I was looking at: suits of ninja armour.

There were ten of them, slung over simple wooden cross-pieces, lined up among piles of empty cardboard boxes. They were nothing like the theatrical creations favoured by samurai, with segmented breastplates and garish face-masks and exotic helmets. These were austere, dark, cloak-like things for medieval hoodies, the ghosts of shadow warriors. When I got up close, they turned out to be chain-mail doublets made of minute metal rings. From a metre away they looked more like material than metal, hardened versions of the black peasant costumes that are nowadays considered traditional ninja garb.

Downstairs, he had regaled me with family memories which may have been no more than folklore. These were the real things, direct links back centuries to a time when ninjas were ordinary farmers until called upon to defend, not some lord, but themselves, fighting for their families and villages against armies that had to be opposed with covert, night-time operations because to engage with them in open, daylight conflict would be suicidal.

Nothing could have brought home more powerfully something I had hardly glimpsed until that moment: that I was dealing with a tradition both very Japanese, yet completely different from the more obvious, better-documented traditions of the samurai. To learn about ninjas, I would be peering into shadows, and it would take a good deal of help and luck to discern underlying truths.

Before starting on this book, I thought I would be engaging mainly with cartoon turtles, invisibility, flying and other such nonsense. I was wrong. The ninjas, for centuries the secret agents acting for their communities and their employers, had remarkable qualities – among them an extraordinary ability to inspire myths – but there was nothing magical about them. If ninjas ever mastered the art of invisibility (the subtitle of at least one book about them), they did so by being masters of disguise and camouflage.

I found instead a complex subject, rooted in real events, real people and a charming region, little known to outsiders, of steep, forested hills, hidden valleys, mountain streams and patchworks of paddy fields. Here, in the two areas that used to be the provinces of Iga and Kōga (and are now parts of

Shiga and Mie prefectures), the ninjas were part of life for centuries, and still are, because they are an essential tourist attraction. I got to know a little about a way of life – ninjutsu – that had less in common with martial arts than with the arts of survival. And I learned something of the mystical traditions which the ninjas shared with those who sought to gain power, by undertaking rigorous mind-and-body training regimes in sacred mountains. The true ninjas were, it turns out, not only masters of exotic fighting skills: they were men who sought 'right-mindedness' for their work as spies, mercenaries, police and soldiers.

What was going on here? What was it about Iga and Kōga and the late Middle Ages that suited the development of the ninja way of life? In the 1970s, the evolutionary biologist Richard Dawkins suggested that ideas take root and spread in the same way as genes. He called the intellectual equivalent of a gene a 'meme'. Perhaps ninjutsu started as a recessive 'meme' in ancient China and Japan, evolved into a dominant one because it proved useful to its hosts, and was then spread to outlying areas by carriers, who in this case were mercenaries. It seemed there was much to explain: Why then? Why there? Why did ninjutsu in the end cease to be so effective?

Perhaps most surprising to me was the realization that the ninjas had been around in Japan for 700 years before the word 'ninja' appeared, and remained a thread in Japanese history long after the 'real' ninjas had been deprived of almost all relevance by unification in 1600. The ninja ethos resurfaced, remarkably, in World War II as the very opposite of mainstream Japanese militarism: these ninjas (though not named as such) were no less loyal to the emperor, but imbued with a spirit of generosity, creativity and internationalism utterly at odds with the arrogance and xenophobia that typified the armed forces until they went down in defeat in 1945.

There have been several 'last of the ninjas'. In fact, ninjutsu seems to have found its final and most extraordinary expression in the career of the soldier who held out for 30 years in the Philippines, Hiroo Onoda. In his commitment to survive, in the techniques he used to do so, and in his humanity, Hiroo – who, as I write, is still going strong at 90 – is in many ways the *real* last of the ninjas.

1

ORIGINS

*Make yourself resolute with the idea that you will win when-
ever you go on a ninja mission, and you can win even if it is
not so realistic.*

Ninja instructional poem

JAPAN'S 'SHADOW WARRIORS' ROSE TO FAME AT A PARTICULAR
time, roughly 1400–1600, in a particular region, and in
particular circumstances. But they did not spring into
existence fully formed. To find their roots, look far away and
long ago, to China, almost 800 years earlier.

In the early seventh century, Tang dynasty emperors emerged
as rulers of a great empire and a great culture. The Japanese,
precariously united under their own ambitious emperors,
wanted to know its secrets. Court officials, students, teachers,
monks and artists visited, were vastly impressed, and
returned with the 'new learning', which was in effect all the
main elements of Chinese civilization – Confucianism,
medicines, textiles, weaving, dyeing, the five-stringed lute,

masks, board games, and whole libraries of books on scripture, history, philosophy and literature, all in Chinese.

One thing China knew a lot about was war. For centuries, it was war that divided the nation, yet it was war – and ultimately conquest – which, in 221BC, brought peace and unity. China's military wisdom had been summarized some 100 years earlier (or more, no one knows for sure) by the great military theoretician, Sun Zi (Sun Tzu as he is in the old Wade-Giles orthography). His *Art of War* was already one of the great classic books. Sun Zi was a professional through and through. He spelled out the 'five fundamentals' – politics, weather, terrain, command and management – and went on to analyse details like the cost of entertaining envoys and the price of glue. He was not interested in glory; he was interested in fast and total victory, for, as he said, 'There has never been a protracted war which benefited a country.' Only by quick victory can more war be avoided. Today's generals study him. Politicians ignore him at their peril. George Bush might have had second thoughts about invading Iraq, let alone boasting of 'mission accomplished', had he pondered one of Sun Zi's aphorisms: 'To win victory is easy; to preserve its fruits, difficult.' The lessons were clear: don't engage unless sure of victory; don't take risks; better to overawe your opponent than fight. But if you have to fight, do it my way! Learn the rules of military leadership, logistics, manoeuvring, terrain and, in particular – he saves this for last – deception.

This is the chapter which interests us, and these are the crucial words:

All warfare is based on deception. Therefore when capable of attacking, feign incapacity; when active in moving troops, feign inactivity. When near the enemy, make it seem that you are far away; when far away, make it seem that you are near. Hold out baits to lure the enemy. Strike the enemy when he is in disorder. Prepare against the enemy when he is secure at all points. Avoid the enemy for the time being when he is stronger.

Only in this way can you gain the essential – speedy victory.

Of all the weapons vital for a speedy victory, the most vital is information. 'The reason a brilliant sovereign and a wise general conquer the enemy ... is their foreknowledge of the enemy situation ... this foreknowledge cannot be elicited from spirits, nor from gods, nor by analogy with past events, nor by astrologic calculation. It must be obtained from men,' namely spies.

There are five types of spies, he says: native, internal, double, doomed and surviving. In brief, your own people, the enemy's people, double agents, expendables, and ninja-like spies who can penetrate enemy lines, do their job and return. All these men are vital for victory. None should be closer to the commander and none more highly rewarded, and of all matters none is more confidential than spy operations. He who is not sage, wise, humane and just cannot handle them, 'and he who is not delicate and subtle cannot get the truth out of them. Delicate, indeed! Truly delicate,' for if plans are divulged prematurely, the agent and all those to whom he spoke must be put to death.

An example of what he was talking about occurred when King Zheng of Qin, the First Emperor, was halfway through unifying what would in 221BC become the heart of modern China. The First Emperor, brilliant, ambitious and utterly ruthless, was the target of several assassination attempts. Like many a head of state today, he took care to protect himself at all times. When travelling he was particularly vulnerable, as we know from an archaeological find made near his tomb mound close to Xian, and also near the tomb's greatest treasure, the several thousand life-size soldiers that make up the Terracotta Army.

In 1980, archaeologists working at the western end of the First Emperor's tomb mound found a pit divided into five sections, in one of which were the remains of a wood-lined container, crushed beneath the fallen earth. Inside lay what have become the crown jewels of the Terracotta Army museum: two four-horse, two-wheeled carriages, in bronze, half life-size, complete with their horses and drivers. The carriages had been smashed into fragments, but after eight years' work they were restored to full working order, perfect down to every rein and harness and free-spinning axle-flag.

One chariot is an outrider, with a driver standing on a canopied platform. The other is the emperor's. It has a front section for a charioteer and a second, enclosed, section for the emperor, with a roof of silk or leather waterproofed with grease. In the windows there is mosquito netting – all this being rendered in bronze, of course – and, on the side windows, a little sliding panel so the emperor can see out, get air in and issue orders without his august person being seen.

But his chariot is not exactly a tank. It had to be relatively lightweight for easy movement, and was therefore vulnerable to heavy-duty arrows or swords, such as might be carried by would-be assassins. The solution, as Sun Zi knew, was deception, which meant exactly the same solution as adopted by many a head of state today: decoy vehicles. The emperor travelled in any one of several identical carriages. At least one assassination attempt failed because the assailant attacked the wrong carriage. Possibly, another four decoy carriages remain to be found, so that a would-be assassin had only a one-in-five chance of attacking the right carriage.

So to get at him, a conventional approach would be useless. What was needed, in effect, was a ninja.

They got half a ninja, in what became one of the best known incidents in Chinese history, one that has become a popular subject for film and TV dramatization (most effectively in the 1998 epic *The Emperor and the Assassin*, directed by Chen Kaige). The source is the Grand Historian Sima Qian, whose account, written a century after the event but based (he says) on eyewitness accounts, is as vivid as a film synopsis.

Prince Dan is the heir apparent of Qin's neighbour-once-removed, Yan. Dan lives in fear of King Zheng, because he was once a hostage in the Qin court, where he was so badly treated that he fled. A Qin general, Fan Yuqi, defected, and is now under the protection of Prince Dan. The general needs all the protection he can get, for Zheng has offered a reward of a city plus 250 kilos of gold for his head. Qin troops are massing on Yan's border, and the only way to stop Zheng's meteoric rise is to find an assassin to kill him. A young adventurer named Jing Ke is chosen for the task. He is an ice-cool character of high intelligence, who likes 'to read books and practise swordsmanship' – in brief, the essence of the true ninja. He refuses to quarrel: if offended, he simply walks away. Jing Ke is too smart to agree at once, but his reluctance is overcome by being made a minister and given a mansion.

Knowing he has no chance of getting close to Zheng without a good excuse, he approaches the renegade Qin general, Fan, with an extraordinary suggestion: if only he can have the general's head, he will go to Zheng offering Yan's surrender, with the head as a sign of good faith. He will also have a map of Yan territory. These two items will gain him access. Inside the rolled-up map he plans to conceal a poisoned dagger, with which he will stab Zheng. The general finds this an excellent idea – 'Day and night I gnash my teeth and eat out my heart trying to think of some plan. Now you have shown me the way!' So saying, he obligingly cuts his own throat.

Head and map gain Jing Ke and an accomplice entry into the court, and an audience with the king. At this moment the accomplice has an attack of nerves, leaving Jing Ke to go on

Ninja: the Word Explained

English-speakers are often puzzled that the word *ninja* is sometimes rendered *shinobi*. How can two such different words in English be the same in Japanese? Here's how:

From the seventh century, Japanese took on Chinese culture as the foundation of their own. This included writing with Chinese signs, despite the fact that there is no connection between the two languages. This script – *kanji* – is used in combination with two other scripts, both of which are syllabic. The two syllabic scripts are relatively easy to learn, but in practice they are not much use without knowing several hundred *kanji* signs as well. It's a struggle, and frankly, for non-Japanese, a nightmare.

The *kanji* signs have two pronunciations: mock-Chinese, which, being more scholarly, has high status, and real Japanese. For example, a mountain in Chinese is written 山 and pronounced *shān*, the line over the *a* [*ā*] representing a level tone of voice, as opposed to a rising [á], falling [à] or falling-rising [ǎ] tone. In the Japanese version of the Chinese, that becomes *san*. But in proper Japanese 'mountain' is *yama*. The Japanese use both, with *san* as the higher status: hence Fuji-san for their most famous mountain, rather than Fuji-yama, which is favoured by foreigners. One sign, two utterly different pronunciations.

The same system applies to the signs and words usually transcribed in English and many other languages as 'ninja'. In Chinese, the signs 忍者/ *rěn zhě* mean 'one who endures or hides'. Japanese uses the same signs. But in the Japanese pronunciation, the term is distorted into *nin sha*, usually transliterated as *ninja*. In spoken Japanese, the word for 'one who endures or hides' is *shinobi mono* ('enduring or hiding person'), usually shortened to *shinobi*. The 'nin' part of ninja consists of two elements, 'blade' (刃) placed above 'heart' (心) in the wide sense of intelligence, soul, life. By tradition, the two suggest a hidden meaning. Perhaps a ninja is someone who has a sword-blade hanging over him, ready to end his life if anything goes wrong; perhaps he is someone who knows how to make his intelligence as sharp as a blade.

Until quite recently, Japanese were happy to use both terms indiscriminately, because they have the same signs and mean the same thing, except that the mock-Chinese version is higher status. Since early contacts between foreigners and Japanese were at a high social level, 'ninja' became the preferred version in both foreign languages and Japan.

alone. Watched by a crowd of courtiers, Jing Ke unrolls his map, seizes the dagger, grabs the king by the sleeve, and strikes. The king leaps back, tearing off his sleeve, and Jing Ke's lunge misses its mark. Zheng flees with the assassin in pursuit, while the unarmed courtiers stand back, appalled, watching their lord and master dodging around a pillar, trying in vain to untangle his long ceremonial sword from his robes. A doctor has the presence of mind to hit Jing Ke with his medicine bag, which gives the king a moment's grace.

Even as Jing Ke comes at him again, the king manages to untangle his sword, draw it and wound Jing Ke in the leg. Jing Ke hurls the poisoned dagger, misses, and falls back as the king strikes at him, wounding him again. Jing Ke, seeing he has failed, leans against the pillar, then squats down, alternately laughing hysterically and cursing the king. The crowd moves in and finishes him off.

Would it be fair to call Jing Ke a forerunner of the ninjas? Hardly. True, he gained entry to the emperor by means of a trick. But the plot demanded that he operate in public and be prepared to die. Ninjas operated in secret and planned for survival. If there are lessons in this story, they are that rulers should be more careful and that secret agents should up their game. There's no point in half a ninja.

The incident, along with much of China's recorded history, became familiar to the Japanese from their embassies. Scholars knew about the First Emperor and were familiar with the 'Five Classics', among them Sun Zi's *Art of War*, known in Japan as *Shonshi*, a Japanese version of 'Sun Zi'. In theory, therefore, they knew about Sun Zi's admiration for the dark, covert arts of deception and spying. In addition, a number of wealthy Chinese fled the war-torn mainland in the early Middle Ages (10–12th centuries), many travelling through the Japanese heartland to the court and some settling along the way, emphasizing to their Japanese hosts the importance of Chinese culture, including the techniques of covert warfare. The famous Takeda family, which rose to prominence in the 16th century, owned at least six of the Chinese classics, including those by Sun Zi, Confucius and Sima Qian (the Grand Historian who told the story of Jing Ke), proof that the fundamentals of ninjutsu, the 'art of invisibility', are Chinese in origin.

In fact, the idea of deception has well-established Japanese roots, as two stories reveal. They appear in Japan's most ancient surviving book, the *Kojiki*, the 'Record of Ancient Things'. The *Kojiki* was one of two works produced for Emperor Temmu, who in AD682 commanded his princes and nobles to 'commit to writing a chronicle of the emperors and also of matters of high antiquity'. Produced for the court thirty years later, the *Kojiki*'s amalgam of written and oral tales purports to explain the origin of the nation, from the beginning of heaven and earth, 'when the land was young, resembling floating oil and drifting like a jellyfish'. From three gods sprang the islands of Japan and eight million – 'eight hundred myriad' – other gods, among them Amaterasu, the sun goddess, ancestor of the royal family. In a slurry of myth, song, legend, pseudo-history and history, the 149 brief chapters reveal how, over 1,200 years, 34 emperors imposed their wills on rival clans as Japan's divinely ordained ruling family.

Two stories tell of a young hero called Wo-usu, later renamed Prince Yamato the Brave, who still wore his hair up on his forehead in the style of a teenager. He was (supposedly) the younger son of the 12th emperor, Keikō of Yamato, which in the second century AD was one of the five provinces of central Honshū, the heartland of the almost-unified nation. The words in quotes are from the original as translated by Donald Philippi.

The Wiles of Prince Yamato

Emperor Keikō tells the elder of his two sons, whose name is Opo-usu, to bring him two beautiful sisters to marry. Instead Opo-usu marries the sisters himself. Then, in embarrassment, he avoids coming to eat morning and evening meals with his father.

The emperor tells the younger son, Wo-usu, to summon his brother.

Five days later, Opo-usu has not appeared.

'Why has your elder brother not come for such a long time?' says the emperor. 'Is it perhaps that you have not yet admonished him?'

'I have already entreated him,' replies Wo-usu.

'In what manner did you entreat him?'

'Early in the morning when he went into the privy, I waited and captured him, grasped him and crushed him, then pulled off his limbs and, wrapping them in a straw mat, threw them away.'

Wo-usu's ruthlessness strikes the emperor as a pretty rough

punishment for skipping a few meals. He instantly finds a mission that will suit his son's 'fearless, wild disposition'.

'Towards the west,' he says, meaning the southern part of Japan's southern island, Kyūshū, 'there are two Kumaso-takeru' – *kumaso* being a word for the aboriginals of that part of untamed Kyūshū, and *takeru* meaning 'brave'. If this were an English fairy tale these aboriginal chieftains would be ogres, and Wo-usu a Japanese Jack-and-the-Beanstalk. Anyway, says the emperor, 'They are unsubmissive, disrespectful people. Therefore go and kill them.'

Before departure, Wo-usu's aunt, who in other versions of the story is a high priestess of the sun goddess, gives him two items of clothing suitable for a woman, an 'upper garment' and a skirt. Why? Because very soon they will become vital to the story, and he has to get them from somewhere. Armed with a small sword, which he tucks into his shirt, he sets off.

When Wo-usu arrives at his destination, he finds the ogre brothers inside a newly built pit-house, for in olden days aboriginals often lived in houses hollowed out of the ground. There is much noise, for the ogres are preparing a feast to celebrate the completion of the house. Wo-usu waits, walking around until the feast day. Then he dons a ninja-like disguise. He combs his hair down in the style of a young girl, puts on the robe and skirt given him by his aunt, hides his sword under his costume, mingles with the women and enters.

The two ogres take one look at this vision of loveliness and command the 'maiden' to sit between them.

When the feast is at its height, Wo-usu draws his sword, seizes the elder ogre by the collar and plunges the sword into his chest.

The younger ogre, seeing this, takes fright and flees, with Wo-usu in pursuit. At the foot of the stairs leading out of the pit-house, Wo-usu catches up with his victim, seizes him by the shoulder and stabs him in the rectum.

'Do not move the sword,' says the ogre. 'I have something to say.' At this the action, as if in a dream, comes to a dead halt, giving the ogre, to whom it has now occurred that the 'maiden' is no maiden, time to ask, 'Who are you, my lord?'

Wo-usu launches into a long explanation of his origins, naming his father the emperor. Hearing that 'you [ogres] were unsubmissive and disrespectful, he dispatched me to kill you'.

Then the ogre, still ignoring the sword up his backside, says politely, 'Indeed this must be true. For in the west there are no brave mighty men besides us. But in the land of Yamato there is a man exceeding the two of us in bravery. Because of this I will present you with a name. May you be known from now on as Yamato the Brave.'

Then, at last, Wo-usu, now Yamato-takeru, Yamato the Brave, killed his long-suffering victim, 'slicing him up like a ripe melon'.

In the next chapter, Yamato the Brave comes to an old province in south-western Honshū, intending to kill the ruler, Idumo the Brave, otherwise known as Many-Clouds-Rising. To do this, he uses two deceptions. First, he pretends to be Idumo's friend, then he makes an imitation wooden sword.

The two 'friends' go to a river to bathe.

Yamato comes out first, and says, as a friend might, 'Let us exchange swords!' Idumo agrees, and straps on Yamato's wooden sword.

At this Yamato issues a challenge, but of course Idumo can do nothing with the imitation sword and falls an easy victim to Yamato, who exults in his unsporting victory with a song:

> The Many-Clouds-Rising
> Idumo the Brave
> Wears a sword
> With many vines wrapped round it
> But no blade inside, alas!

*

After my visit to the restaurant owner and his collection of ninja armour, we – my local guide Noriko and I – had gone south in a small, swaying train to Akame, to explore a beauty spot known as the Forty-eight Waterfalls. We were on a paved path, walking up a gorge beside a river that fell over rocks and trees brought down by a typhoon a few days earlier. Japanese of a certain age strolled ahead and behind. Walking shoes, backpacks and jackets with many pockets: these were people prepared for a serious day out, the ladies shielding themselves with parasols from the late summer sun filtering through the near-vertical forest. I wanted to see the falls because the mountain from which they flow was a place once favoured by ascetics who practised Shugendō, Japan's ancient folk religion. The practitioners, uncounted generations of them coming here for over a thousand years, included warrior farmers who would eventually be known as ninjas, for they wanted to share in the knowledge and skills that gave the 'mountain ascetics' – the *yamabushi* – their power. That was why I was interested in this extraordinary tradition.[1]

They came for two reasons. The first is that mountains have a particular significance in Japanese religious thinking. In old Japan, existence depended on rice, which grew in patchworks of fields that had to be created and managed with expertise and hard work. Men and women needed to be in control. The landscape was flat. Water must flow gently in and out, at the right time. Mountains are the opposite of all this. They are steep and forest-covered (not rocky eminences, like the Alps), and home to wild and dangerous things, like bears and snakes and the supernatural beings called *tengu*, with their red faces and long noses and scaly

---

[1] *Yamabushi* is sometimes translated as 'mountain warrior', because *bushi* means a warrior. In this case, not so. This *bushi* has a different sign, and derives from a word meaning 'to prostrate oneself'. A *yamabushi* is one who 'prostrates himself on a mountain'.

forearms. Mountains were uncivilized, untamed places, where the souls went after death, and where countless deities lived. They were the sources of life-giving water, of the spirits that cause disease, and of the medicinal plants that can control the spirits and cure the diseases. In short, they were places of power. The only way ordinary people could respond to the world of spirits was with subservience, expressing gratitude, or awe, or contrition to the spirits that came and went from the mountains.

But you could be less subservient, more proactive. That was what it took to develop what ninja sources call 'correct mind'. For 'shadow warriors' were – in principle, at least – more than the traditional idea of warriors, as one of my advisers was keen to make clear. Toshinobu Watanabe, a remarkably fit 70-something from the ninja base of Koka (or Kōga, as it used to be), will appear several times in this book, guiding us here and there, but here he is a guide to the state of mind sought by the ideal ninja. 'You Westerners often think of ninjas as men of darkness who only knew how to assassinate. Completely wrong! The records, every single one of them, insist in their first lines that you need the correct mind.'

'What does that mean?'

'Do no evil! The ninjas believed in peace. They gathered information in order to avoid as much war as possible. They were dedicated to the idea of killing only if necessary, and to their own survival. They practised martial arts only for self-defence. Of course, not all ninjas were like this. That is why the sources emphasize the need for "correct mind". But most of the time they did their best.'

If you wanted 'correct mind', if you wanted power over your own life, over others, over events, and over the world of spirits, you would go to the mountains, find yourself a master and subject yourself to rigorous physical, mental and spiritual rituals. This was and is today the practice known as

Shugendō, the Way of Mountain Asceticism. You walked the sacred spots, the groves, the exposed rocks, the ancient trees, the waterfalls, the streams. You fasted, you purified yourself by sitting under waterfalls, you hardened your body with feats of endurance, you got to know the spirits of the mountain, and because the spirits might object to your presence on their territory, you learned how to propitiate them. Having done this, you became a *yamabushi*, a mountain ascetic. Moreover, you got a certificate from your master to prove you were not a fake.

'And there were plenty of fakes,' said one of my advisers, Tullio Lobetti, an Italian expert in Shugendō at London's School of Oriental and African Studies. He is a graduate of one of Japan's most famous training centres, on Mt Haguro in Yamagata prefecture, and thus one of the few Western *yamabushi* ('though I have only the lowest form of certificate'). 'How else do I show I am not a fake? By being able to perform supernatural feats. Like being able to stay in a cauldron of boiling water.' He saw my raised eyebrows. 'Being boiled – really!'

'You have actually seen this?'

'Yes. It was not much water, but still – it was hot.'

'Do you know how it was done?'

'I know the rituals, but not the mechanism. I didn't ask. It's not the kind of thing they want to talk about. Also walking on swords.'

'You've seen that too?'

'I have done it. Anyone can. It's not hard. You just have to know the right technique. It's all part of proving you have the right credentials and are part of an established group.'

Perhaps, if you were an advanced adept, you would become a priest. That was the equivalent of an MA or PhD. But at the very least you would emerge with a technical and professional qualification – knowledge and skills and power to cure diseases, exorcise evil spirits and perform rituals essential for ordinary people, like funeral rites and the breaking of new ground for building a house. You would be respected, and people would pay for your services.

As a ninja, the advantages of Shugendō training was obvious. Miyake Hitoshi, a pioneer in Shugendō studies, explains why:

Especially remarkable among the activities of the *shugenja*, or *yamabushi*, in the Kamakura and Muromachi periods (1185–1573) were those in time of war – performing magico-religious rites, acting as messengers or spies, and practising the martial arts. The *shugenja*, who knew the mountain trails and through their travels were familiar with conditions all over the land, were well qualified to undertake these activities. Before battle, they blessed horses, arms and armour and prayed for the defeat of the enemy. Their intercessory rites were called for when camp was set up or broken . . . Then too there were significant links between *shugenja* and the ninja masters of Koga (Omi province), Iga and Negoro. So skilled were the *shugenja* at stealthy appearances and disappearances that they were compared to the legendary mountain creatures called *tengu*, who were said to inhabit the very mountains where the *shugenja* had their centres.[2]

I asked Tullio about the training. In summary, this is what he said:

In Japan, mind and body are not separate. In the West, we often say it doesn't matter how you are outside, it is the inside that matters, the mind. But in Japan, that is not true. How you are outside matches how you are inside. If you are tall, strong,

[2] *The Mandala of the Mountain*, pp. 67–8.

beautiful and rich, that is how you are inside. If you are weak, bent, diseased, that is how you are inside. You want to achieve some inner benefits? Well, you can do it by improving your body.

The idea is that whatever you do, it should take physical effort. When you walk from sacred spot to sacred spot, it's sort of like a pilgrimage, but harder. You can walk 20 or 25 kilometres a day over mountains, over rocks. There are often no paths. You may have a rope to climb down to worship a sacred spring or rock. It's not a matter of imposing pain for its own sake, but of doing something hard, and the harder it is, the greater the reward. So if it is done in winter, so much the better. You know, there is energy within us that we do not use. If you sit under a waterfall and it is minus 10 degrees, what you feel is a surge of heat. That's the way your body reacts, if you don't die.

There is a whole universe of lore – religious, philosophical, literary – that you can do in advanced Shugendō, and an encyclopedia of magical gestures to be mastered and then performed hidden by clothing. Take the reading of the texts, which is mainly in *kanji*. But there is also a secret reading, with special Shugendō pronunciation, which is meant to be more powerful. Then you have Sanskrit mantras. In the Heart Sutra, for instance (he started a rhythmic, low-voiced chant, *Ya-te-ya-te-para-ya-te-parasan*[3]), the sutra says in effect, 'Now I will teach you the greatest spell of all, the spell that conquers all passion, the spell which says, "Form is emptiness, emptiness is form, there is no ear, no nose, no eye . . ."' Ultimately, this high-level esoteric practice is all about being reborn at ever higher levels until you become a Buddha and achieve enlightenment and enter Nirvana.

[3] Wikipedia quotes one translation: 'Gone gone, gone beyond, gone altogether beyond, O what an awakening, all hail!' However, it comments, the string of words resists analysis and, like most mantras, is not a grammatical sentence.

Well, no ninja, surely, would be interested in this. How would it help with spying and fighting and survival? But one thing is certain: if you, as a warrior, undertook even part of the training, you would emerge tougher in mind and body. Tullio knows why because he has been through it. 'You become completely estranged from everyday life. You are so exhausted you do not think any more. You do not remember where you are from. This is the point at which you can rebuild yourself in a different way.' Tullio chose a computer analogy: 'The experience *resets* you. I was told by a friend who had joined the SAS that an SAS training course has the same effect. You emerge rebooted, refocused, ready for battle.'

Why would you, as a would-be *yamabushi* or shadow warrior, come to one mountain as opposed to another? Because it had a tradition of being sacred, a tradition that was guaranteed by an oral history (or in rare cases a text) that led from master to master, right back to the time the mountain was 'opened' by the very first religious adept to come there, the one who marked out the sacred spots. The more ancient the opening and the more eminent the opener, the better. The most eminent of all was and is Shugendō's semi-mythical eighth-century founder, En no Ozunu, also known as En no Gyōja, En the Ascetic.

En is a vital figure in Shugendō, because he was everywhere, or so countless traditions claim. 'He's a sort of a wild card,' as Tullio Lobetti put it. 'If you issue certificates to qualified *yamabushi*, you have to legitimize your practice. You do this with an impressive foundation narrative, and there is no one more impressive as a founder than En no Gyōja. That's why he is everywhere. Well, obviously he cannot possibly have been to all these places, although he is imagined as running and jumping from one to another. That doesn't matter. What matters is the impressiveness of the claim.'

So who opened the Forty-eight Waterfalls? Why, En no Gyōja, of course.

So the future ninjas joined the *shugenja* (as those who practise Shugendō are called) and other would-be curers and warriors and priests. They came here to train on the mountain ways – in effect, marking out commando routes and running and climbing them at speed and subjecting themselves to endurance tests, but also aiming to acquire purity of mind, with the hope of achieving magical skills, medical powers and longevity.

It wasn't just here, either; and it wasn't just then; and it wasn't any one sect or religion. Japanese religion is a unique mixture of Buddhism, introduced from Korea and China, and the native Shinto practices, with their assumptions about a parallel universe of spirits – *kami* – which had to be worshipped, propitiated and befriended so that their powers could be used. (The mixture also includes traces of Daoism and Confucianism. Japanese culture has integrated religious ingredients like a kitchen blender.) The two – Buddhism and Shinto – were only seen as separate in the 18th century, when scholars became interested in identifying the (supposedly) original, indigenous Japanese traditions. Though formally separated in the late 19th century, they still co-exist, with Shinto gates leading into Buddhist temples, and Buddhist temples displaying Shinto charms. Shugendō, as much Buddhist as Shinto, is alive and well, practised by many groups all over Japan, as my guide Noriko was happy to tell me, because as mentor and fixer for films and TV channels she had explored many training areas, entered more temples and shrines than I knew existed and met uncounted priests, martial artists and ninja experts.

'My grandfather did Shugendō. He died from sitting under a waterfall.'

'*What?*'

'It happens all the time.' She sounded really casual.

'But *what* happened?'

'I don't know. It was long before I was born. He was forty-five. My father was five.'

'But . . .' I stuttered. 'Did he drown? Or catch a cold?'

'Well, it was December.' She was speaking to me as if surprised at my surprise. 'It's religious training! If you don't believe in the religion, don't do it. It has to be tough, so obviously it was winter. If you go under a waterfall in summer, it's not training, it's called "nice".'

That was half a century ago, but the traditions are still strong. My hosts in Kōka took us to a Shugendō fire festival, where, in an open space on a mountainside, a high priest in a green mantle led 20 elderly acolytes in honouring the spirit of the mountain. It deserved respect because this mountain, Iwao, had an eminent pedigree: it was one of three where the ninth-century founder of Buddhism's Tendai sect, Saichō, built temples and trained. A respectful audience of two dozen included five ladies in white, who would later offer light refreshments. There was much single-note, rhythmic chanting, punctuated by the sound of two conch shells being blown like bugles. Once upon a distant time I played the trumpet, so I tried one after the ceremony. It had a simple mouthpiece, and its sound was something between a hunting horn and a very resonant one-note fart, which could be briefly pushed up an octave if you felt ambitious. Everyone was in traditional costume – white shirt, baggy white plus-fours, white bootees moulded to divide the big toe from the other toes, a white cape and a sort of harness with two red bobbles on the back. In the middle of the open area was a pyre of green cedar branches. After more chanting and conch-blowing, a devotee picked up a bow and arrow, and prepared to fire. For a moment I imagined the creak and twang of a longbow, and an arrow zipping away over treetops, but it was a ritual bow and a toy arrow, which flopped to the ground after a couple of metres. Never mind: it did its symbolic job, which was to break the power of evil spirits. A ritual axe and a few ritual chops cleared the holy space of invisible trees.

Then, despite my scepticism, the ceremony began to get to me. The high priest threw some bits of wood and paper with writing on them on the pyre. They were messages to the god, I discovered later, to be burned like a child's Christmas list. 'It's very, very strange,' the priest told me, 'but if you make a wish, it often comes true.' Candles lit long broom-like tapers, which were applied to the pyre. Smoke poured out along the ground, like liquid oxygen in a stage show, before the heat built, and the crackling branches slowly caught, and the smell of fir spread like incense, and smoke billowed round us, turning the participants to ghosts and the cathedral of trees to a faded backdrop, all this happening to the hypnotic, regular beat of a chant. *Ma ka han ya ha la mi ta . . .* It was, I discovered later, a Japanese version of the Sanskrit Heart Sutra.

Afterwards, I asked the high priest to explain. 'We do this twice a year, in autumn and spring, wishing everybody good health and success in business. We are praying to a dragon god. A long time ago, a white snake was found here and someone heard the god saying that one should pay respects to it, because when snakes become old and die, they often become a dragon god. There is also *Fudō-myōō*' – a guardian god – 'which you can see carved into the stone up there, where the shrine is. Have some *sake*.' He gestured to a tray held by one of the white-clad women. 'It is the best *sake*, and now purified because it has been touched by the god, which makes it taste even better.'

The shrine, up a flight of steps, was a wooden side-chapel of this natural cathedral, set on stilts. It shielded a rock face into which was carved a rough bas-relief of a man with a club over his right shoulder, as if he were a bodyguard ready to spring to the defence of the dragon god.

It was, of course, as much theatre as many a Christian

religious service. But I was touched by an element absent from Christianity: the sense of being present at something primeval, stemming from a time when we were awed by nature and were part of it and eager to please its good spirits and defend ourselves from the bad ones. The spirits were once part of life. For these worshippers, they still are. I'm no believer, but I could imagine myself believing that the good wishes and the smoke and the chanting and the shell blasts summon, or create, the very spirits that must be honoured or banished. A Stone Age shaman would have understood. A shadow warrior would surely have been inspired.

All of which is to explain the background to the Forty-eight Waterfalls, which in their foundation narrative reach back to the roots of Shugendō. You can't actually become a modern *yamabushi* or ninja by walking or running through these towering cliffs and looming forests nowadays, because the Forty-eight Waterfalls is a protected area, but it doesn't take much to see the challenges they present from the safety of the paved path.

White waters foamed under little bridges and past massive boulders shaken loose by earthquakes. Falls tumbled into the sudden silence of pools that would have been crystal clear, except for the grey-green cloudiness left by the recent floods. Not far upstream, a sheer cliff and a series of falls, flickering in the dappled sunlight, once blocked the way, which today is carried on upwards by a footbridge. It was entrancing. If I ever seek enlightenment, this is my sort of a place, especially on a still September day, with the heat of the sun reduced by leaves above and cool waters below, and absolutely no chance of defying death on some vertiginous rock face or overarching forest. I glanced down, and saw, where rock gave way to rising undergrowth, the stone statue of a cow with red eyes.

'Yes,' said the guide, Kazuya Yamaguchi, raising his voice

above the roar of rushing water. 'When En was training here, he saw a red-eyed cow, which is how this place got its name – Akame, Red-Eye.'

This, apparently, was as far as ordinary people could go in the old days. But off to the right, clear of trees, was a petrified cascade of boulders. In heavy rain, like the storm that had hit earlier, it turned into a torrent that stripped it of vegetation. Now, after a few days of warmth and sunlight, it was a steep and rocky way leading up into the overhanging forest. That, said Kazuya, was where Shugendō practitioners and their ninja students could climb to get to the upper falls. Remember this place: we shall be returning here to follow the last of the ninjas as they escape the army sent in to eliminate them, some 900 years after En opened it up.

Another tale of ninja-like intrigue takes place during a famous rebellion in the tenth century by the warlord Masakado against his own family, the Taira. This was a time when local lords had all but broken free of the central government and set up what were in effect independent kingdoms with their own armies. Masakado was the most ambitious of these great landowners. He claimed that the sun goddess Amaterasu had actually intended him to be emperor, and set about making this a reality by seizing eight eastern provinces as a prelude to taking the capital Kyoto and ruling the whole country. He had one main obstacle, the opposition of his uncle Yoshikane. In early 940, Yoshikane attacked, devastating his nephew's lands, forcing him into hiding, but inspiring in him a fierce determination for revenge. The main source, *Shōmonki*, describes the two armies skirmishing back and forth, without either gaining an advantage, until Yoshikane found himself a spy, in the form of one of Masakado's young servants. The teenager, a boy named Koharumaru, had been travelling back and forth to a nearby farm to visit relatives. Thinking that the boy might be a useful source of information, Yoshikane summoned him and put the idea to him, bribing him with a bolt of silk and talk of high office and all the food and clothing he could ever want. The young man happily accepted, his only condition being that he wanted an accomplice in the form of one of Yoshikane's farmhands.

So the two spies, ninjas in all but name, went to Masakado's residence as nightwatchmen, each carrying a load of charcoal. Over two nights, Koharumaru took his accomplice around, showing him the armoury, Masakado's sleeping quarters, and the four gates. Yoshikane's man then returned to report to his boss.

All to no purpose. Masakado infiltrated Yoshikane's army, discovered the plot, executed the young servant and was ready when Yoshikane's attack came. Yoshikane's soldiers dropped their shields and ran away, dispersing 'like mice unable to find their holes, while those who gave chase showed the strength of a hawk leaving the hunter's gauntlet'.

In the end, Masakado's victory was in vain. A few months later, he himself was defeated, killed by a stray arrow, and beheaded, his head being exposed in Kyoto as a warning to other rebels.

The stories of Yamato and Masakado do more than show the importance of deception. They also highlight opposing themes in Japanese history: the capital, the emperor and unity, set against the provinces, warlords and diversity. It would take 700 years for that conflict to be resolved in favour of capital, emperor and national unity. Along the way, shadow warriors would play vital roles, though largely obscured by the glitter and drama and public displays of their counterparts, the samurai.

2

HOW TO BE A SHADOW WARRIOR/1: MIND AND SPIRIT

If a ninja steals for his own interests, which is against common morals, how can the gods or Buddha protect him?

Ninja instructional poem

It seems almost magical, this art of night stealth that enables you to make yourself invisible.

From the Foreword of the *Shoninki*

SOME PEOPLE LIKE TO ATTRIBUTE MAGICAL POWERS TO NINJAS. Recent ninja films and manga suggest that with magic all things are possible. If so, then the ninjas are masters of time and space, and my days are numbered. Some 16th-century ninjas will know the contents of this chapter, know I am guilty of betraying secrets that should never be revealed, and be on my trail. One dark night, when I am asleep, a hooded figure will slip open the sash-window, reassure the cats, bypass creaking floorboards and turn my bedroom into a morgue with poison, sword, dagger or noose.

It's true, I'm guilty. Am I worried? Hardly. Not even the most fervid imagination has suggested that ninjas were masters of time travel. Besides, I am not the only guilty one. The first to reveal the secrets of the ninjas were the ninjas themselves, long ago.

Throughout their history, the ninjas were by definition secretive. It would have been against all their training and teaching – indeed, self-destructive – to make public their way of life. But the secrets *were* revealed, not long after Japanese unification made the ninjas an irrelevance. Why? Perhaps it was to help train recruits into the contingent of 200 ninjas taken on by the shogun as secret police; or simply to record a way of life that seemed about to vanish. Whatever the motive, it was done at least three times. The best of these records is the *Shoninki* (*Sho Nin Ki*, 'True Ninja Tradition' or 'Account'), probably written by Natori Masatake, a samurai in the service of the shogun, a century after the ninjas' Iga homeland was destroyed in 1581.

Probably written by Natori Masatake. He does not name himself, but a friend who provides the foreword mentions a name which has enabled scholars to agree on an identification, even though this Natori used several names, as was common in Japanese history. There are three versions of his book in English (see Bibliography). I rely on the one translated and edited by the British ninjutsu scholar Antony Cummins and his Japanese colleague Yoshie Minami, because it best takes into account the difficulties of dealing with 17th-century Japanese. What follows is a combination of indirect and direct quotes, presenting the essence of Natori's teaching.

To modern eyes, the most surprising thing about the *Shoninki* is what it leaves out. Being used to seeing ninjas on film – more on that later in the book – you might expect

a) many weapons and b) a list of martial arts moves. But weapons get short shrift, and there is absolutely nothing about martial arts, raising the possibility that, for all its long life, ninjutsu, the art of the ninja, did not focus on martial arts at all until well after the *Shoninki* was written. Its focus is primarily on attitude, or right-mindedness; deception; and charms, which is surely where the origin of the idea of ninjas as masters of magic lies, an idea rejected by Natori right at the beginning.

First, to explain the essence of a ninjutsu, Natori writes a little dialogue between the Apprentice and the Master. The Apprentice is in awe of the rumoured skills of the ninja. I have vaguely heard, he says, that even if a father, a son, or brothers see each other they would not be able to recognize each other while they are engaged in ninja covert acts. They say a ninja can move instantly from in front of you to behind, that they appear and disappear from moment to moment. 'Surely,' he concludes, 'this art cannot be attained by mere human beings?'

The Master is scathing. True, ninjas are masters of deception, able to talk about a province they have never been to, tell a strange story about a place they don't know, buy things with gold or silver they don't have, eat food nobody gives, get drunk without drinking alcohol. They go out acting covertly all night and sleep out in the wilderness without shelter. There is nowhere they cannot go. Even so, 'What have you seen or heard in order to so misunderstand this path? Nothing is mystical about the true tradition and correct way of ninjutsu.'

You must understand (says Natori) that when we speak of ninjutsu we are speaking of life skills. Nakashima Atsumi, who modernized the *Shoninki*'s 17th-century Japanese for translation into English, writes in a preface: the *Shoninki* 'offers instruction for every aspect of your life and provides help in any circumstance'.

But it will only provide help if you have the right attitude, namely one that derives from the teachings of Confucius, which were back in fashion at the time Natori was writing: 'A ninja can do anything as long as it is in accordance with his own sense of value and the justice of the group he belongs to.' In other words, he must serve an impersonal cause. Sometimes he will be told to undertake assassination, theft or robbery, but even dirty jobs like this are justified if the ninja is 'right-minded', i.e. if he acts for the benefit of his employer. 'If ninjas used ninjutsu for their own interest, it would be mere theft and robbery', and no one would hire them. 'Right-minded', however, is not necessarily 'high-minded'. Obeying orders does not equate to morality.

So serving your master's interests rather than your own is only the most basic requirement. A ninja should aim higher than that, in accordance with the oath sworn by the warriors of the ninja heartland, the old provinces of Iga and Kōga, the great oath known as *Ichi Gun Ichi Mi*, 'one district, one band'. By doing this, it is said, they 'show that their family tradition was extraordinarily exquisite and outstanding, and also show the marvel of their tradition of ninjutsu at its best'.

What does this mean? Firstly it means behaving in the right way. 'You must always appear graceful and calm, just as waterfowl do on a calm lake.' Those who uphold the true way of the ninja 'should stay on the path of perseverance, which makes them righteous, even though others around them disrespect the ways of the ninja; thus can they not be described as saints or even enlightened?'

Above all, your purpose is to survive and return home, for otherwise you cannot do your job, which is to bring back information, as Natori emphasizes. 'What a *shinobi* [ninja] is meant to do is fulfil his mission without losing his life . . .

Those who can succeed on a mission are, in the end, described as good *shinobi*, even if they sometimes get behind schedule or hesitate.'

For success, it is important not to fear death, for fear disturbs the mind. In modern terms, you must live a paradox: to fear death is to court death; to accept death is (perhaps) to gain life. Serenity is all. 'If you enter into a dangerous situation and if the occasion arises, you should not value your life over death. Tradition says that life exists within death and death exists within life. Therefore if your actions risk the losing of your life and you have no fear, you may find a way out of a desperate situation. However, if you try to survive, you may lose your life because you are too stressed to see the way out.

'If you hold on to your ego, you will be unsettled or upset. If you come with a serene mind, you have nothing to fear.'

Natori returns to the same theme several times, sometimes sounding like a modern self-help guru. 'Do not get involved in things. If you get stuck on a problem and entangled within it, it is because you cannot let go of yourself but are pre-occupied with pursuing your self-interest.' And again: Don't indulge your emotions. Develop mental strength. If you neglect to nourish your true mind properly, you will run out of energy, get tired and will end up failing. Generally, when you have inner peace, you can fathom things that other people cannot and outmanoeuvre their thought processes. 'Nothing is as amazing as the human mind!'

In practice, subtlety is the key quality. Perhaps the wisest advice in the *Shoninki* is summarized by a chapter title: 'How to Avoid Defeating Other People'. Do not defeat your enemy? But isn't that the ninja's whole purpose? No. The purpose is that of the true secret agent: to learn and return. For that you must nurture your sources, not dominate. 'If you psychologically defeat others, you will not be able to attain a desired result or get your needed information. If you offend them too much, they will lose their temper and get upset and become competitive, thus your aim will not be achieved.'

So in conversation, be flexible. Those who are too inflexible will be hard when they should be soft, strong when they should be yielding.

Such skills demand great sensitivity, empathy, as we would call it today. You should 'identify with your enemy, which means you should guess with your own mind what he is thinking'. As all things in the universe are common to us all, you can use what is in your mind to second-guess your enemy. 'If you can achieve this desired result, it could be said you have attained the skill of "the taking of the enemy's mind". How clever it is and what a godlike skill to have!'

3

ANTI-NINJA: THE SAMURAI

The way a good ninja works is: to know about people with-out letting them know about him.

Ninja instructional poem

IF REAL SPIES WERE SELDOM MENTIONED IN WESTERN AND Chinese sources, they hardly got a look-in in Japan until recently. Almost from the beginning of Japan's military traditions, all things covert were deeply unfashionable, the agenda in military matters being set by the proud, prickly and extremely overt samurai. Yet, of course, spies and commando-style fighters were necessary. Indeed, sometimes samurai also acted as ninjas; *most* ninjas were samurai, *some* samurai were ninjas. To understand why ninjas were necessary, and why they remained hidden, you have to under-stand the very outward and visible ways of the samurai, which hardened over time as real events and warriors were transformed by tales into an ideology.

The samurai, of course, considered themselves the only true

warriors, inheritors of a tradition that stretched back to the 9th century. It started with bows and arrows shot from horseback, from which evolved a complex set of highly public rituals. Opposing sides would line up, and fire whistling arrows to call upon the gods as witnesses. Then top warriors, boxed into their leather-and-iron armour, would call out challenges to single combat, each boasting of his achievements, virtues and pedigree. They would then discharge arrows at each other, either galloping past each other or at a distance – not a great distance, though, because Japanese bows were much weaker than those used by mainland warriors, like Huns, Mongols or Turks; and their horses, too, were much less sturdy than Central Asian breeds. If there was no winner, there followed a rather unseemly grapple, with each trying to unseat the other, followed by a final bout with daggers. Since both warriors were totally enclosed in armour, the rounds of horseback archery were usually more to do with show than substance, designed to give the individual warrior a chance to display himself and his skills and cover himself in glory, whether he lived or died. Display was the essential element, for the warriors were, in the words of Karl Friday, 'like modern professional basketball players, more apt to think of themselves as highly talented individuals playing for a team, than as the component parts *of* a team'.[1] The best way to showcase their skills was in battle.

In the late 12th century, two clans, the Taira, who had ruled Japan for 200 years, and the upstart Minamoto, vied for dominance, each seeking to sideline the cloistered emperor. After a five-year war, the Taira were swept to oblivion by the Minamoto, under their great general, Minamoto no Yoshitsune, the greatest of Japan's popular heroes, indeed (in the words of one scholar) 'probably the single most famous

[1] *Samurai, Warfare and the State in Early Medieval Japan.*

man in all of pre-modern Japanese history'. Much is legend; but much is accepted as truth, both historical and personal. Cocksure, blunt and impetuous, he had all the traits that came to define the medieval samurai.

Moreover, he lived at a turning point in Japanese history, when the ancient regime – whose super-refined ways are detailed in Japan's first novel, *The Tale of Genji* – had proved hopeless at imposing the sort of tough rule that Japan needed to hold it together, whether as a nation or as a collection of independent provinces sharing the same culture. The only way life worked, it seemed, was by using force to impose what would come to be called feudalism: a peasantry kept in line by a warrior caste that was absolutely loyal to its masters and to its emperor. It was as a general in the forefront of change that Yoshitsune made an enduring name.

There is also a deeply human story here. Yoshitsune was fighting on behalf of his elder half-brother, Yoritomo. After Yoshitsune's victorious campaign in the so-called Gempei War (1180–85), the jealous Yoritomo condemned him, drove him into exile, and then hunted him down, until in despair Yoshitsune committed suicide by slicing open his belly. Yoshitsune quickly became the subject of admiring legends, carried around Japan by blind storytellers. Collected (and translated), they form vivid sources, with much passion, incident and character. He is still with us, in novels, manga, and kabuki and noh plays, as 'the perfect example of heroic failure', in the words of Ivan Morris. 'If he had not actually existed, the Japanese might have been obliged to invent him.' In 2005, there was a 49-part TV series devoted to him.

One of the most famous stories has a ninja dimension to it. Yoshitsune is fleeing with his retainer, Benkei, a man of prodigious strength and resourcefulness (a sort of Little John to Yoshitsune's Robin Hood). They come to the Ataka Gate, one of the barriers set up to catch them. Benkei and the other followers are disguised as *yamabushi*, which was a favoured disguise for ninjas. This is my justification for including the story, one of the most famous incidents in Japanese myth and literature, celebrated in a popular 19th-century kabuki play, *Kanjinchō* ('The Subscription List').[2] Yoshitsune himself, whose heroic nature contrasts with his delicate, girlish build, is dressed as the insignificant bearer. The gate's guardian, Togashi, has been warned of Benkei's ruse and is determined to kill all *yamabushi* on sight. Benkei counters the threat by claiming to be collecting subscriptions for a great temple. Togashi demands to see the list of subscribers (hence the play's title). Of course, there is no such list, but Benkei brilliantly improvises. He thrusts a blank scroll close to Togashi's unfocused gaze and makes up the sort of preamble such a list would have. Togashi is in two minds, torn between admiration for Benkei's daring and the call of duty. He cross-examines Benkei on the rituals and dress of the *yamabushi*. Benkei knows all the answers. Togashi is so awed that he gives permission for the retinue to pass through the gate, which they are doing when a guard points out Yoshitsune. Togashi halts the column. Benkei, in a stroke of genius, pretends to blame his 'bearer' for the delay and beats him. Togashi is aghast: surely no mere servant would act in this unpardonable way towards his master. He sends them all on their way. No sooner is he out of sight than Benkei grovels in tearful apology to his master, who forgives him. Togashi, eager to apologize for his suspicions, reappears with some *sake*, which Benkei consumes in massive quantities and the party proceeds:

> Feeling as though they had trodden on a tiger's tail
> Or escaped from a serpent's mouth.

---

[2] Also in a noh play, *Ataka* (on which *Kanjinchō* is based), and a film by Kurosawa, *The Men Who Tread on the Tiger's Tail* (1945).

It is Benkei who is the hero of this story, a man utterly devoted to his master, brave, resourceful, witty, scholarly and a great drinker, neatly blurring the lines between retainer, *yamabushi* and shadow warrior.

Seven years after his victory in the Gempei War, Yoritomo took a step that would define Japanese administration for the next 700 years. With the approval of the emperor (who was in no position to disapprove), he appointed his own officials in every province and estate so that he could hold power throughout the land. Yoritomo also had himself awarded the highest military rank, *sei i tai shōgun*, 'barbarian-quelling great general'. This title once referred to the general empowered to wage war against the wild indigenous tribes of the north. Its holder, known simply as the shogun, ruled the whole country as top samurai – in effect, military dictator – in the name of the revered but impotent emperor.

In *theory*, at least: though the system broke down in practice for centuries, the principle remained as an ideal towards which all would-be rulers aimed. Basing his military government, the *bakufu* (shogunate), at his HQ in Kamakura, the shogun did his best to rule a patchwork of 60 provinces and 600 estates, all scrapping with their neighbours. To cram four centuries into a sentence, rule from Kamakura lasted just over a century, collapsing in 1333, ushering in a new line of shoguns, the Ashikaga, who, after a 60-year interval of civil war with two rival emperors, re-established rule from Kyoto, where they ruled and misruled for another 200 increasingly anarchic years.

From about 1200 onwards, therefore, the main focus for any local leader was war, war and more war, with all its trappings. No lord or commander could survive without an investment in armour, horses, bows, swords, daggers and fighting men. There arose an elite of land-owning warriors – *bushi* – fighting for their masters, the two being bound by mutual need: the lord providing land, war booty, and protection in exchange for the skills of the specialist warriors, the samurai (originally *saburai*, meaning 'one who serves', in particular, one who provides military service for the nobility).

But there was an inherent instability in this relationship. If a vassal prospered, the status, power and wealth he won was enough for him to claim his freedom. Why, as a boastful, independent, thuggish warrior, would he continue to devote himself to a lord? How could a master ensure his loyalty? How, in brief, could the feudal system be made stable?

The answer was to raise loyalty – to one's lord, not to the far-off emperor – ever higher, turning it into an ideal more loved than life itself, guaranteeing status and glory both in life and death, with a father's position and emotional commitment being inherited by his sons. Loyalty to a lord, or *daimyō* ('great name'), was like a gene, written into a samurai's DNA. Against provincial armies welded together by such bonds, no emperor or shogun had much chance of wielding local influence.

As an elite separate from the aristocrats, intellectuals, peasants and brigands, the samurai were fiercely proud of their skills, status and valour. To survive in this tough world, in which power and life could be snatched away in an instant, image and self-image were vital. Every man had to strut and preen like a cockerel, or seem a loser. In war, a warrior equated his very being with extreme acts of bravery and self-sacrifice, especially in the face of overwhelming odds, for this was the way to gain reputation and rewards. Crucially, his action had to be public – witnessed, remembered, talked about. One early 13th-century warrior determined to be noticed dyed some of his horses purple, crimson, chartreuse and sky blue, and covered others with stripes and spots. Another wrote, 'If I were to advance alone, in midst of the enemy, and die in a place where none could witness my deeds,

then my death would be as pointless as a dog's death.'³
Reputation was all, as another 13th-century commentary
concludes: 'To go forth to the field of battle and miss death
by an inch; to leave behind one's name for a myriad generations; all in all, this is the way.' Honour, or shame, would be
passed down the generations, to be upheld or redeemed by
descendants. So honour was above life itself. The samurais'
whole being was dominated by their extreme sensitivity to
any threat or insult to their honour, and their near-
instantaneous readiness to take violent action in its defence.
Only in this way could 'honour' be asserted, protected or
restored.

For rich samurai, the supreme item of self-advertisement
was his armour, which underwent its own evolution in
response to the growing sophistication of weapons and
tactics, from bows and arrows to swords, from infantry to
cavalry, from warrior gangs to field armies. In Europe,
knightly armour made to be worn by horsemen eventually
turned them into the military equivalent of crabs, so unwieldy
that a fallen knight could hardly stand up without help. In
Japan, the style of combat with bow and sword meant that
armour had to be kept flexible, which was done by using
scores of little plates or scales sewn together to make so-called
lamellar armour (in Latin, a *lamina* is a layer, from which
comes *laminate*, and its diminutive *lamella* is a 'little layer' or
small piece of something, usually metal). Designs evolved.
Lamellar armour could be a misery in extreme heat or cold,
and the bindings became heavy in rain and tended to rot, all
of which forced experimental variations in scales and single-
piece elements. By the 16th century, armour had become so
rich and varied that a battle array looked like a confrontation
between many species of exotic beetle.

³ Both these examples are quoted by Conlan in *State of War*.

A rich samurai's ō-yoroi, or 'great armour', had plates and scales bound into skirts and aprons and shoulder pads and shin pads and ear flaps, all designed to stop arrows and deflect swords, but also to proclaim wealth and status, and at the same time allow the wearer to shoot and swing and ride and walk. His helmet alone was a work of art. Some helmets were made of dozens of semi-circular plates, others of a single piece of metal in a conical shape, like a witch's hat, with a visor and anything up to six side-flaps to protect both ears and neck. Some helmets sported vast horns or wave shapes, or mountains or crabs (to suggest crab-like powers of self-protection) or rabbit's ears (to suggest longevity). The samurai might also have a mask covering the whole lower face, with a detachable nosepiece, a bristling moustache, a little hole in the chin for the sweat to run through and a built-in grimace to terrify the opposition. Since the outfit covered the whole body, it was impossible to recognize who was inside, so – since the whole purpose was to advertise himself – our hero would be a walking, riding flag, gaudy with coloured scales and flapping banners.

The ultimate weapon was, of course, the sword, or rather the two swords, the long *katana* blade and the shorter blade, the *tantō*, used in hand-to-hand fighting. Vast collections and worlds of expertise are devoted to the accoutrements of both: mountings, belts, suspension braids, scabbards, scabbard knobs, hilts, handles, handle covers (rayskin gives a particularly good grip), sword collars, guards – all are subspecialities with their own arcane vocabularies and schools and histories.

The samurai's sword was his greatest treasure, one that occupied – occupies still – a multidimensional world of magic, spirituality, chemistry, artistry and skill, each aspect with its own arcane vocabulary and traditions, and all focused by the mind and body of the swordsman, ideally at least, into one or two or three lightning blows. Armour, however exotic and all-encompassing, was no guarantee of protection – and anyway, it slowed you down. The ultimate samurai swordsman wore nothing but his kimono. There was no shield but the sword itself, which was strong enough to deflect a blade that was its equal in resilience and suppleness. Japanese smiths, many of a renown reserved in the West for the greatest artists, created several major schools or traditions, each with several subgroups, all of which developed their own variations of the basic sword styles. The result, refined over 400 years, was a glorious combination of practicality and beauty. The best blades – sharp as razors, heavy as hand-axes, fast as a whip in the right hands – could sever iron helmets, and cut through skin and bone like a kitchen knife through asparagus.

I once had the good fortune to wield a *katana*, under the eye of master-swordsman Colin Young, one of the few English *senseis*. It was at the end of a lecture, under the gaze of an audience. My task was to cut through a roll of *tatami* matting soaked in water, which has the consistency of human flesh and the thickness of an arm. We played to the crowd, instructor and pupil. The sword, swung from overhead, went through as easily as an axe through sponge-cake – no discernible resistance. I had half expected that result, having seen Colin do it. What I had not expected was the surge of emotion: the elation inspired by an act of power. For a few seconds, I was Rambo, a dealer in death, power incarnate. The feeling came partly from the sword and the blow; but also because I was on display, in public. What would have been the point of performing in private?

Death-defying bravery and an overriding ideal did not guarantee victory. What should the loser do, if he happened to survive? The answer lay in the concept of loyalty unto death. This was first taken to its logical conclusion by

Minamoto no Yorimasa, whose revolt against the ruling Taira clan was crushed in 1180 (briefly: revenge and final victory came five years later). When he saw all was lost, he determined to die while his sons held off the enemy. He ordered an aide to strike off his head, but the aide refused, weeping, saying he could not do it while his master lived. 'I understand,' said Yorimasa, and retired into a temple. In one version of the story, he joined his palms, performed a Buddhist chant and wrote a poem on his war fan:

> Like a fossil tree
> Which has borne not one blossom,
> Sad has been my life.
> Leaving no fruit behind me.

Finally, he released his spirit, which traditionally resided in the abdomen, by thrusting his short sword into his belly. This was the first recorded instance of the painful and messy act usually known to outsiders as *hara-kiri*, which Japanese more commonly call *seppuku* (because that is the higher-status word deriving from the Chinese).

'Cutting the belly' became an established way to avoid the disgrace of defeat. One of the best-known and most dramatic examples occurred in 1333, after rebellion brought the Kamakura shogunate to an end. The rebels – bandits and armed peasants – forced the shogun's troops to flee from Kyoto for 50 kilometres along the shoreline of Lake Biwa to a temple in the little post town of Banba (now part of Maibara). The story is told in the collection of war stories known as the *Taiheiki*, which we shall be returning to later. In this tale, 500 warriors gathered in the courtyard before the single-room temple. The general, Hōjō Nakatoki, saw that the end was near, and addressed his men in a moving speech:

'I have no words to speak of your loyal hearts . . . Profound indeed is my gratitude! How may I reward you, now that adversity overwhelms my house? I shall kill myself for your sakes, requiting in death the favours received in life . . .' He stripped off his armour, laid bare his body to the waist, slashed his belly and fell down dead.

There was no expectation that anyone else would copy him. But at once, one of his vassals responded: 'How bitter it is that you have gone before me! I thought to take my life first, to prepare the way for you in the nether regions . . . Wait a bit! I shall go with you.' Seizing the dead man's dagger from his stomach:

he stabbed his own belly and fell on his face, embracing Nakatoki's knees. And thereafter four hundred and thirty-two men ripped their bellies all at once. As the flowing of the Yellow River was the blood soaking their bodies; as meats in a slaughterhouse were the corpses filling the compound.

The description is, of course, highly poetic, capturing the elements – commitment, failure, intense emotion, formality, public display – thought essential by those who listened to it. But there was no exaggeration in the numbers: a priest recorded the names of 189 of those who killed themselves that day; the same priest had gravestones made for all 432, which still stand, running in five lines up a gentle slope.

Since relationships between lord and vassal varied in strength, vassals were free to make their own decisions. A member of a household might feel his lord's death as his own, and choose death; a mercenary who would be able to offer his services to another lord could well choose life, as would a landowner with a workforce to look after. Either way, living or dying, the samurai was asserting his control over his destiny and pride in his elitism.

All this – the equipment, the actions, the theatricality – were the outward, visible and very public means by which a samurai proclaimed his status. No samurai would for a moment accept the idea of doing anything secretive or underhand. It would be a denial of everything he stood for.

Yet – here's the paradox – everyone knew their Sun Zi, every commander knew that it would have been courting disaster not to have spies acting in secret, gathering intelligence and undertaking other covert operations. Hence the ninja, with an ethos that was the mirror image of the samurai's, and hence also a difficulty for historians, for if operations were not only secret but also considered infra dig, well, no one would record them.

So the formal bravado of the samurai is only a part of the story. Surprise attacks, artifice, betrayal and deception played equally significant roles in warfare. Witness several incidents in medieval sources: a Taira warrior named Sadamichi, ordered to kill another warrior, befriends the man, then rides out of sight, puts on his armour and returns to shoot his unarmoured victim; a samurai revenging his father's murder disguises himself as a servant, sneaks into the man's room while he is sleeping and slits his throat; Minamoto Yoritomo, wishing to execute one of his men, orders him to be entertained at a feast, during which he is beheaded. These incidents hardly rank as honourable, yet there is no suggestion they are actually *dis*honourable or in any way improper. Indeed, a warrior was supposed to be on guard at all times, so who is to blame if he is taken off-guard by an assassin or successfully spied upon? *He* is, of course, all being fair in war. Ends justified means. Warriors and bards alike may have tacitly agreed not to mention it, but deception was as much part of Japanese culture as public glory.

4

HOW TO BE A SHADOW WARRIOR/2: DECEPTION – AND CHARM

Ninjas should not be ashamed of falsifying, for it is their duty to outwit the enemy.

Ninja instructional poem

FOR NATORI, DECEPTION IS THE KEY SKILL, TO BE PRACTISED ON several levels, not least by charming the information you seek out of the opposition. This is how you 'analyse people's minds without letting them know that they have been analysed' – by using flattery to gain knowledge. 'By using this technique, you can steal into the opponent's mind with great ease without drawing his attention in a way to make him wary; meanwhile he bleeds all the information that you need. Truly amazing.'

At the most basic level, however, you had better master the art of disguise. There are seven types of disguise a ninja should master.

1. Zen monk: useful because the big straw hat allows good visibility while hiding the face.
2. Buddhist monk: useful for getting close to people.
3. *Yamabushi* mountain priest: this allows you to carry a sword without being questioned.
4. Merchant: for mixing freely with people.
5. Street entertainer: always travelling, and therefore arouses no suspicion.
6. Actor: ditto.
7. Dress like those around you to blend in.

As a monk of any kind, you may also become a pilgrim, because that gives you a good reason to move around between temples and shrines. In this case, you may choose to join a small group.

You should also master the technique of *dakko*, which is to understand all the local customs and dialects. Originally, this skill involved imitating the dialects of more than 60 provinces with great fluency. Those with this skill 'knew and were aware of all the points of interest, historic spots and places of natural beauty within each area'. However, warned Natori, 'this technique used to be achieved only by ancient masters and seems to be too difficult for people of the present time to master completely. Your efforts could easily be interpreted as tricks that are the tricks of con men and thus could be self-damaging.'

In addition to a disguise, it is useful to change your appearance. To do this, wear a long jacket or rain cape. You could also reshape your eyebrows, blacken your teeth with iron (filings), change the shape of your hairline, wear black ink on your face, tousle your hair, and/or 'put some tresses' (grass or straw?) in your mouth.

You may sometimes need to fake an illness at short notice. Here are some ways to help your performance: don't sleep at night, burn your skin with moxa,[1] fast to the utmost limits to make you emaciated, don't shave or cut your hair, don't clip your toenails or fingernails, and don't wash.

Be careful with whom you consort. Of course, whatever you do, luck plays a large part in whether you give yourself away or not. But remember you put yourself at risk if you talk to low-minded scum and take them into your company.

You can ply someone with booze, sex or gambling for the purpose of taking him in and getting your way. As you will be included in these pleasures, you must keep control of your mind and be sure not to lose yourself or your self-control.

If you think you are about to be revealed, create a diversion of some kind. Leave a tool or some other object that will confuse an investigation. Leaving a fake letter, tricking someone into creating something strange or making up false traces of you, anything that gives misleading information – these are methods that are all commonly used by a ninja to throw people off his scent.

Or you can head off in one direction and then double back unseen. People will give false information about you, and will do so willingly, because it makes them seem important. It is

[1] I had never heard of moxa, but it's common in Oriental medicine, which explains this long footnote. The word comes from the Japanese for 'mugwort'. *Artemisia moxa* or *vulgaris*, a herb with a soft, downy skin, is ground up and compressed into little cones or cigar-shaped cylinders which are burned on the skin, usually as a companion to acupuncture. The treatment is known as moxibustion. The moxa may be removed before it hurts, or left on until it scars the skin. The purpose is to strengthen the blood and stimulate the flow of *qi*. It acts as an emmenagogue – an agent that increases blood circulation to the pelvic area and uterus. For this reason, it has been associated, amazingly, with the correction of breech births. A paper in the *Journal of the American Medical Association* (November 1998) found that up to 75% of women suffering from breech presentations before childbirth had foetuses that rotated to the normal position after receiving moxibustion: 30 minutes a day, with an intensity 'just below the individual tolerability threshold'. The really astonishing thing is that the moxa was placed on a traditional Chinese acupuncture point BL 67 (known as *zhiyin*), which is *beside the outer corner of the fifth toenail*.

vital for you to master this deception above all things. The main point is that you should devise the simplest method possible, without any complications. If you create something difficult or complex, it could arouse suspicion and result in a more intensive investigation.

Intuition plays a major role in ninjutsu. For example, supposing you are on an unfamiliar mountain path in a dark forest. You come to a fork. Which way do you choose? Maybe there are clues: cast around for abandoned sandals, horseshoes, dung, trampled grass, easily startled birds. Such things may tell you which road is better used, which to avoid, which to choose. But if not – simply let fate decide. 'Buckle up and recite an old verse. Then count how many syllables there are in the verse and choose to go right if the number is odd, and left if even, and do not have any doubts about the decision. This is because if you simply use the first thing that flashes through your head without any intention or contemplation, you are consigning yourself to divine intervention and fate. Wonders can happen when you abandon your ego!'

One common task for a ninja was to infiltrate a castle. It is an iconic image – the ninja with hook and rope creeping over a wall at the dead of night. But there is a much easier, safer and more effective way – deception. Talk your way in. For this you need confidence and charm. Stroll past the gate a few times to gain confidence. Then fake an illness in front of the gate, a sudden illness like food poisoning. On no account pretend to be drunk. Take a rest, and have your servant or accomplice ask for medicine or just some hot or cold water. Thank those inside, and go on your way. Later, to show your gratitude, return with a present – no, two presents, one for the owner, one for his wife . . . no, three or more presents. Speak to the owner. 'Don't forget to give his wife her present first.' Praise his children. Give little presents to one or more of the favourite servants. 'The master will be pleased about that, as he sees that his people are happy and this will influence him. In this way you could glean information about what you want while talking to the people of the mansion . . . If you creep into someone's favour with smooth words, you can deduce valuable information even from the smallest of small talk.'

Remember this:

A WELL TRAINED *SHINOBI* (NINJA)
LOOKS LIKE A VERY STUPID MAN.

'It is a core principle to praise others as much as possible to keep them carrying on about a subject at their own leisure.'

Here's a way of recording information about the size of a place or numbers of people. Prepare bags of pebbles or beans, counting them so you know the number in each bag. Then as you count whatever it is you want to record – the length of a wall, the number of houses or people – drop a pebble or bean for each unit. No need to count as you go. At the end, count what you have left in the bag. Subtract that from the original total. That's your number. You've counted without counting.

When infiltrating an army column or a retinue, deal only with the lower ranks or servants. If you ingratiate yourself with those of higher status, you will be hated by the lower-ranking people for the favour you are being shown by those above you.

When spying on a province, by far the best way is to visit shrines and temples. Give priests or other men of the cloth gold and silver coins, sparing no expense. Don't give to ordinary people, because this is not normal and will draw suspicion. But Buddhist and Shinto priests will be delighted to accept an offer to treat you with meals and hospitality. 'Taking advantage of this opportunity, you should probe them for information while getting them drunk.'

Natori has a pretty low opinion of priests, regarding them as naive, garrulous and easily manipulated. You can start them talking by asking if there are any plans to construct a new building to pray for the fulfilment of wishes. If so, you will naturally ask: whose wishes? What wishes? Thus, by hinting at your willingness to help financially, you may get wind of a possible rebellion or a family dispute or unrest in the army. 'They will not be able to stop themselves bragging about their wonderful religious power or divine wonders, and then they will give away everything you need to know at great length. Thus by exploiting their nature, you can gain your goal.'

Or you could go to a 'licensed house of assignation' – that's a high-class brothel – 'where the highest rank of courtesans are appointed to their clients'; or to the public baths; or a gambling den. 'There are no secrets that cannot be revealed at places such as these.'

Deception and charm come way above any technical advice, on which Natori has surprisingly little to offer. He makes just one mention of a sword: 'Whenever you steal up on someone you had better carry a short sword.' Except for a brief reference to using a sword to give you a step up when climbing a wall, that's it for swords. Given the Japanese obsession with swords, this is odd. There are two possible implications. One is that for routine work as a spy or secret agent, a sword was not required. The other is that carrying a sword was so completely part of everyday life that he didn't think to mention it. Perhaps (he might have said, if asked) both were true: take your sword if you want to, but you probably won't need it.

This is the sum total of what he has to say about equipment:

He recommends only six fundamental items, none of which

can really count as a weapon: a straw hat, which allows you to see others but hides your face; a grappling iron and thin rope, for climbing, tying people up, locking sliding doors, and other uses too numerous to mention; a pencil to take notes and make marks on buildings; basic medicine in case you fall ill on the job; a metre-long piece of cloth, used as a headband or an extension to your waistband, to improvise a rope; and a fire starter to make a body-warmer, cooking fire or for arson.

Ninja are often called the original men in black, but Natori says that brown, dark red or dark blue are all fine colours, because they are so common that they don't stand out.

In a perfect world, he says, you should not carry any tools at all. Even a tiny object like a needle might give you away if it falls at the wrong moment. But most covert actions demand tools of some kind. He doesn't give a list, remarking only that they should not be strange, or they will attract attention. By implication, therefore, the choice is up to you – but make sure you carry tools that can also be used in everyday life on the land. You probably have your grappling iron. A simple long stick leant against a wall will allow you to climb or descend. Or you can use a sword leant against it as a footrest (though be sure to tie the cord to your foot so that you can pull the sword up after you).

To break through rammed-earth walls, you can use a tool with a round or oblong blade, which has saw teeth around the edge. For opening inside doors, you can use a smaller saw.

To get through a hedge, cut off the end of a barrel and push it into the hedge to make a hole – but remember to remove it afterwards.

If you think someone might try to break into your bedroom, it's no good staying awake to catch him. What if your enemy decides to delay his break-in until the next night, or the night after? You will be worn out, and fall asleep anyway, so deeply that nothing will wake you. Instead, leave the window slightly ajar to tempt the intruder, tie a string from the window to your topknot, and sleep tight without worry (presumably with your sword to hand), knowing that any movement by the window will wake you.

5

A WORLD OF VIOLENCE AND UNDERCOVER OPS

It is a fundamental lesson for ninjas to think more of the way out than the way in.

Ninja instructional poem

FROM TODAY'S MANGA AND FILMS AND GAMES, YOU MIGHT think that the ninja was the only non-aristocratic, non-samurai force in the land. In fact, they were one of many wild elements that kept medieval Japan in a state of ferment, swirling undercurrents of opposition to the lords and their samurai sidekicks. Near-anarchy started in the early 14th century, and would last for almost 300 years. This was the chaotic context within which the ninja evolved.

Central Japan, though hardly crammed by modern standards, seethed with variety, especially along the single-lane main roads, which were no more than tracks on which two horses could hardly pass. Convoys carrying rents in the form of rice, messengers, pilgrims, slave-traders, horse-dealers and merchants all went by, and all needed rooms at the frequent inns, where they crowded round puppeteers, jugglers, musicians and storytellers. In the words of Yoshihiko Amino, one of the greatest of modern historians (though little known in the West), these people formed 'the wandering world', a counterpoint to the fixed world of rulers, nobles, temples and landowners. Beyond all this lay the other worlds of mountain and forest, occupied in folklore by demons and monsters and in reality by a scattering of esoterics devoted to pilgrimages and the Shugendō training regimes described in Chapter 1. Such was the rich mix that interwove with the violence in what is now central Japan, Honshū and northern Kyūshū (while the northerly island of Hokkaido was so remote from all this that it might have been in a different universe).

It was not all bad. In the right circumstances, violence can stimulate as well as destroy. It happened in China's Warring States period almost 2,000 years earlier, in medieval Japan, and in 15th-century Italy, where bitter rivalries and brutal little wars coincided with the height of the Renaissance. It seems that under the pressure of constant, though less than total warfare, leaders also yearn for peace, creative minds struggle to make sense of life, and an obsession with war can produce equal and opposite obsessions: diplomacy, art, philosophy, poetry, trade. And it is one of the paradoxes of social evolution that peace usually has to be imposed by violence. This was certainly true of medieval Japan, where everyone expected violence and fought for peace, though always on their own terms. From such diversity no unity could come. Every special-interest group – warlords, warrior priests, Buddhist temples, Shinto shrines, bandits, ninja villages – would have to be crushed or won over by any would-be leader aiming to unify Japan.

Anarchy, suspicion and fear do strange things to minds and

behaviour. People took to concealing themselves with disguises and masks. Travellers wore wide-brimmed sunhats that hid their faces. Women veiled themselves. When warrior monks paraded through Kyoto in protest against some act or law of which they disapproved, they disguised their voices, wore masks, or wrapped their faces in shawls, cutting slits to see through (like other men of violence of recent times, in Palestine, or the Basque country, or Northern Ireland). Things came to such a pass that when the Ashikaga seized the shogunate in 1336, they banned outlandish clothing. It didn't make much difference. People responded by adopting the fashions associated with *hinin* – the 'unhuman' pariahs who performed 'unclean' tasks, like dealing with corpses on the riverbanks, tasks that were unclean but also vital, which gave the *hinin* a cachet despite their occupations. Riverbanks were outside the reach of any lord. They were places where gangs staged stone-throwing battles, troops practised manoeuvres, artisans set up informal markets, and performers and artists gathered. From a world of lepers and corpses and sand and pebbles sprang great talent, like the landscape gardener Zen'ami, who created the sand-and-stone Zen gardens that we now see as typically Japanese. The 'people of the river-banks' made a vibrant demi-monde, a sort of medieval Left Bank, a hip, arty, decadent, free-wheeling world, which produced weird mixtures of male and female fashions that were adopted by those who liked to proclaim themselves yet hide their faces.

All this was against a background of anarchic violence, involving every subgroup: classes, families, temples, land-owners, city-dwellers, peasants and many more. Another was formed by bandits known as *akutō*, the 'evil groups', gangs of ruffians of many different sorts – disaffected warriors, pirates, vagabonds, farm-workers eager for pillage, mercenaries, poachers – who sometimes resorted to a sort of uniform, carrying bamboo spears and rusty swords, wearing sleeveless war kimonos and six-sided caps, and covering their faces with yellow scarves to make themselves look 'strange'. They were, perhaps, the equivalent of roving gang-members terrorizing a neighbourhood, taking anything unattached and undefended, and moving on. A monk writing in Harima province (in the southwest of Honshū, part of today's Hyōgo prefecture) about the years around 1300 portrayed an area 'awash in blood and fire and abounding in violence, assaults, piracy, robberies and manhunts'.[1]

Yet another force were the warrior monks, who had their 10th-century origins in the rivalry between two Buddhist factions with temples on Mt Hiei, near Kyoto. The two fought over land and the appointment of abbots, their violent conflicts often spilling over into Kyoto itself and mixing with other wars between warlords. In 1117, an ex-emperor commented, 'There are three things that are beyond my control: the rapids of the Kamo river, the dice at gambling and the monks of the Mountain'[2] (that is, Enryaku-ji, the temple on Mt Hiei). They settled to a more peaceful existence in the 13th century, but would surface again in the 14th, when anarchy again threatened and violence rose to new levels.

So far, the sources make no mention of ninjas, not because there weren't any, but because their equivalents had many different names, depending on where they lived. There were

---

[1] Souyri, *The World Turned Upside Down*, p. 106. Souyri's excellent and well-translated book is the source of much of this chapter.
[2] The emperor was Shirakawa (1053–1129), who entered a monastery in 1096, but remained in control for the rest of his life as a 'cloistered emperor'. These words, though widely quoted, appeared only two centuries after Shirakawa's death. They may well be apocryphal, but most scholars agree they summarize a widely held view about the warrior monks, who in the words of the British historian George Sansom 'failed miserably to provide the moral force the times demanded . . . spreading disorder, corruption and bloodshed'.

several famous ninja-like operations, stories told in the great late-14th-century chronicle, the *Taiheiki* ('Chronicle of the Great Peace', an odd title given that it's all about war). Like other medieval epics, it was rooted in the tales told and sung by blind bards, Japanese Homers who went from castle to castle, entertaining the courts with tales of derring-do. Unlike the two great Homerian epics, it lacked a good editor; two-thirds of it, as Helen Craig McCullough says in the introduction to her translation, is 'dull reading for any but the specialist'. But the narrative was based on real events and real people, and here and there it soars. The problem for historians is that they can seldom separate out truth from exaggeration and invention.

These actions happen in the 1330s, during a would-be revolution started by the emperor Go-Daigo (in Kyoto) in a supposedly secret attempt to destroy the shogunate (in Kamakura) and restore direct imperial rule, something that had not existed for centuries. A man named Hino Suketomo went off to recruit allies, disguised as a wandering monk. The plot was revealed and the shogun sent an army to stop Go-Daigo. He protested his innocence, and Suketomo, left to carry the can, was exiled to Sado, an island off the north coast where dissidents were sent. The military leaders debated. Order had to be restored, dissidents killed. Suketomo was sentenced to death. It happened that Suketomo had a 13-year-old son, Master Kumawaka, who heard of the sentence and decided to do something about it. And so the story with its ninja-like hero, sometimes called the 'first ninja', begins:

The boy says to his mother, 'Why should I prize life? Let me perish together with my father, that I may share his journey to the nether regions.'

His mother cannot bear the thought. Sado is a dreadful island, she says, unfrequented by human beings. If he goes, she will die. In that case, he says, he might as well throw himself into a river and drown. So, unwillingly, she relents, and he goes, walking, in straw sandals and tilted sedge hat. He reaches the coast, takes a ferry and arrives at the castle of Sado's governor, a monk named Homma. He begs to see his father. Homma is moved, bathes the boy's feet, treats him with all consideration, but refuses to allow father and son to meet. It would only increase Kumawaka's anguish, he says. But father and son are so close that the father, imprisoned in a place overgrown with bamboo, hears of his son's presence. How cold was Homma's heart, laments the poet. Since the father was a prisoner and the son but a child, why was it dangerous to place them together?

Men come to Suketomo, inviting him to bathe as a prelude to execution. He takes the news calmly, as a samurai should. They lead him to a river beach, where he writes a farewell poem seated upright on an animal skin, and even as he finishes, 'his noble head fell on to the animal skin while yet his body sat up straight'. He is cremated, and his bones taken to his son.

Kumawaka is grief-stricken and swears revenge. 'If there is a chance,' he says, 'I will stab Homma or his son and rip out my belly.'

So to avoid returning home with his father's remains, he feigns illness for four or five days. Then one night a storm comes. The boy takes his chance, but fails to find either of his intended victims. Instead, in a well-lit room, he comes across the executioner. 'Very well,' thinks Kumawaka, 'he too may be called my father's enemy.' Moreover he has his sword and dagger beside him. But the candle is too bright. Kumawaka notices moths on the outside of the door. He opens the door. The moths swarm in, and put out the candle. He carefully draws the sword, kicks the executioner awake and stabs him twice, ignoring his cries, through the navel and the throat. Then he hides in a bamboo thicket.

Guards come, see the little footprints and at once guess who has committed the crime. The boy must still be on the premises, they say, because the moat is deep. They start searching. Kumawaka wonders whether to kill himself; but no – and this is what marks him as more ninja, less traditional samurai – better to live a useful life than die a useless death: 'If I can preserve my life in some way, may I not assist the emperor as well, and accomplish my father's desire of many years?'

So he climbs a bamboo, which bends until it reaches across the moat, depositing him on the other side. Day dawns. He hides again, this time in a growth of hemp and mugwort, while guards gallop this way and that hunting him. In the evening, he comes out and looks for the harbour, where he intends to take a ferry. Perhaps the spirits were protecting him in reward for his filial resolution (despite the fact that he has not killed his intended victim), for he meets a monk, who carries him on his back to the harbour, summons a boat and climbs aboard, just in time to evade their pursuers. Thus it was with divine protection that Kumawaka 'came forth alive from the crocodile's mouth'.

The story is told with no great narrative technique, for we never learn what happens to Homma or whether Kumawaka ever gets to aid the emperor. But it does reveal something about ninja-style acts, though of somewhat dubious morality: vengeance is a valid motive; any victim will do; opportunities must be seized; escape must be improvised with whatever means are available; better to survive ninja-like to fight again than die a samurai's death; and if the motive is pure – apparently the intention is more vital than the deed – then luck will be with you.

Meanwhile, Go-Daigo had fled south from Kyoto with the imperial regalia to the mountains and forests of Yamato province, where scattered castles – so-called 'hilltop' castles, though few were actually on the very top – guarded remote valleys. He holed up in one of them, on Mt Kasagi, while his greatest general, Kusunoki Masashige, and his son, Prince Morinaga, based themselves in other castles. The shogun's army went in pursuit. The consequences were horribly complicated – castles were taken and Go-Daigo exiled to 'Oki Island', as most sources claim; in fact, Oki is a group of four islands, none of which is called Oki, 50 kilometres off the north coast; never mind the details, because he escaped, hiding under seaweed in a fishing boat; he returned to Kyoto, made a total mess of governing for four years, and fled again to Yamato. The Kamakura *bakufu* (shogunate) fell, leaving power in the hands of the incoming Ashikaga; Go-Daigo set up a rival Southern Court in Yashino, a division that would last, with almost continuous warfare between Northern and Southern Courts, rebel *versus* loyalist, shogun *versus* emperor, for another 60 years.

Fortunately, we do not need to know much about the war as a whole. We are interested in the opening actions against the 'hilltop' castles, because these assaults, sieges and defences demanded new and unconventional tactics from both attackers and defenders. The way Kusunoki, in particular, established his bases and fought held lessons for anyone fighting superior forces in similar landscapes, which is precisely what the ninjas were doing as they developed their communities and their techniques in neighbouring regions.

In this world of steep forests, rocky outcrops and precipitous ravines, set-piece battles were impossible, and cavalry useless. Both sides had to use other means. Kusunoki, later to acquire a reputation as the epitome of loyalty, was a noted guerrilla fighter, so skilled in covert warfare that some wishful thinkers, of which there are many in the world of martial arts, credit him with setting up his own martial arts 'school' (*ryu*). His opponents, the shogun's generals, were faced with the need to take four great mountain castles, the first shielding the emperor, the others his partisan defenders, including the great Kusunoki himself.

It is autumn 1331. The emperor is holed up in a 'mountain-top' castle on Mt Kasagi, a holy place of wooden palisades and towers set about with massive boulders that have images of Buddha carved into them (the *Taiheiki* mentions the boulders but not the Buddha images, which remain to this day). The shogun's forces, 75,000 of them, are preparing an assault. The numbers are arbitrary: they grow with each new chapter, adding a steady crescendo to the drama, for the *Taiheiki* at its best tells a tale in the style of epics from Homer to Hollywood, in which every feature and every action is larger than life, with a wealth of detail, some realistic, some poetic, all designed to make the events appeal to the imaginations of an open-mouthed audience.

The peak is covered in cloud, and mossy crags drop away below for a myriad fathoms. The winding approach path is walled with immense boulders. It is no easy climb, even without a single defender. The attackers yell their battle cries, as loud as a hundred thousand thunderclaps, and fire humming arrows to announce the assault. Yet from the castle – not a sound, not an arrow. Perhaps it has been abandoned. The shogun's forces climb, and see the emperor's banner flapping over the walls. His men are ready, 3,000 archers moistening their bow strings and lining the wooden walls like clouds. The battle that follows is fierce enough to knock the earth off its axis. A giant monk tosses boulders from the walls to smash shields below. Valleys fill with dead, the river below runs red with blood, but the castle holds out. Then news comes of other bases falling to the rebels. It seems the imperial army must withdraw to face them.

No! Two samurai, Suyama and Komiyama, urge a covert

operation. Too many have fallen uselessly, they say, their names forgotten because they died without doing great deeds. 'How much the more glorious if by our strength alone we bring down this castle . . . Our fame will be unequalled for all time; our loyalty will stand above that of a myriad men. Come! Under cover of this night's rain and wind, let us secretly enter the castle precincts.'

So in pitch darkness and foul weather they and 50 volunteers make knots in a rope tied to a grapnel, which they use to clamber over branches and boulders, and then to scale the cliff that leads to the castle's northern rampart, where even a bird could not fly easily. Halfway up, they are stopped by a mossy overhang. Suyama blazes a trail upwards, carrying the rope, which he loops over a branch, allowing the squad to climb safely to the top. After that, the castle wall is no obstacle at all, for the defenders thought the cliffs unclimbable and 'no warriors watched there, but only two or three soldiers of low degree', who had fallen asleep on their straw mats beside their camp fire.

'Then in stealth they spied upon the castle's interior by following a sentry making his rounds', noting the numbers and positions of the defenders. Suyama and Komiyama decide to pinpoint the emperor. A guard accosts them from the shadows, but Suyama has a quick answer: 'We are warriors of Yamato, guarding against attackers slipping in by night, for the wind and rain are violent, and there is much noise.'

'To be sure,' comes the voice from the darkness, and they hear no more. So they proceed, boldly pretending to be guards, shouting, 'All positions be on the alert!' They find the main hall, where candles burn and a bell rings faintly. Three or four retainers, capped and robed, ask where the intruders are from. They come out with convincing answers, 'giving the names of such and such persons and thus and so provinces'.

And finally they and their 50 comrades fulfil their mission, lighting a fire that tells their waiting forces to attack, while they themselves run from place to place yelling war cries and starting fires in offices and towers. It's still dark, and the defenders think a whole army has broken in. They cast off their armour, throw down their weapons and flee, 'falling and tumbling over cliffs and into ditches'. Only one warrior has the courage to fight back, leading his son and thirteen servants, but having shot off all his arrows and broken his sword, he sees death looming and all fifteen commit *seppuku*.

The emperor too flees, barefoot and aimless, along with his princes and nobles, all but two losing their master in the wind, rain and darkness. Thus did the Son of Heaven 'transform his august person into the figure of a rustic and wander forth without an object. How shocking it was!' Hiding behind hillocks by day and by night stumbling through dewdrops on desolate moors, he is eventually captured, along with his entourage and hundreds of courtiers and retainers. Kasagi castle is left burned out and abandoned, while the emperor is sent into exile, from which he will shortly escape.

On goes the shogun's vast army to the next hilltop castle, Akasaka, 40 kilometres to the southwest. (The *Taiheiki* says the army numbered 300,000 riders, and scholars agree it was large, though not *that* large, consisting of three divisions attacking the loyalists from three directions. No one knows the true numbers of the shogun's army, but a likely figure is 100,000.) Akasaka is Kusunoki's base. But it doesn't seem all that formidable. 'The moat was not a proper moat and there was but a single wooden wall, plastered over with mud. Likewise in size the castle was not more than 100 or 200 yards around, with but 20 or 30 towers within, made ready in haste. Of those who saw it, not one but thought: "Ah, what a pitiable spectacle the enemy presents!"' They try a frontal assault. But it isn't so easy. Archers (scholars estimate their numbers at 200) fire devastating volleys, and contingents of horsemen mount raids that throw the attackers into confusion. They try again. This time they scale a wall – which turns out to be a false wall, built to fall when the supporting ropes are released. 'More than a thousand of the attackers became as though crushed by a weight, so that only their eyes moved as the defenders threw down logs and boulders on them.' A third assault is met by cascades of boiling water. So the attackers decide to starve the castle into surrender.

Kusunoki opts for deception in a rousing speech announcing that he will, in effect, become a shadow warrior:

During the past weeks we have overcome the enemy in one engagement after another and killed countless quantities of his soldiers. Yet so great are his numbers that these setbacks mean nothing to him. Meanwhile we have used up all our food, and no one is coming to our rescue. Being the first warrior in the land to enlist himself in His Majesty's great cause, I am not likely to begrudge my life when virtue and honour are at stake. Nevertheless in the face of danger the courageous man chooses to exercise caution and devise stratagems. I therefore intend to abandon this castle for a while and to make the enemy believe I have taken my life. If they are convinced that I have killed myself, those eastern soldiers will no doubt return to their provinces rejoicing. If they leave, I shall return; and if they come back here, I shall withdraw deep into the mountains. After I have harassed them a few times in this way, they are sure to grow weary. Such is my plan for fulfilling my [mission] and destroying the enemy.[3]

[3] This is Ivan Morris's down-to-earth translation, which in this case I prefer to Helen Craig McCullough's more poetic style.

Luckily, a storm, with 'rain violent enough to pierce bamboo', allows the defenders to dig their pit, gather bodies, set them ablaze and then slip away by twos and threes. 'When the flames died away, [the attackers] saw a mighty hole inside the castle, piled with charcoal, wherein lay the burned bodies of many men. And then not a man of them but spoke words of praise, saying: "How pitiful! [Kusunoki] Masashige has ended his life! Though he was an enemy, his was a glorious death."'

Not so, of course. He is more ninja than samurai. Over the next two years, he learned his lesson, regrouped, created a new castle close by – at Chihaya – and also rebuilt Akasaka on higher ground as an outlying defence, his 'front gate', in his own term. It was therefore the rebuilt Akasaka that the shogun's army had to take first when they returned to the attack in 1332. 'Tall cliffs like folding screens fell away below this castle on three sides, while on the south side, which alone was near to flat land, there was a wide and deep ditch with a wall on its bank bearing a line of towers.' A head-on assault fails. The commander guesses that Kusunoki has prepared for a long siege, but is puzzled that there is no obvious source of water, 'yet they extinguish our fire-arrows with water-jets'. So there must be an underground water supply. He orders his men to dig on the only piece of flat land, and 'they uncovered a trough twenty feet below the ground, with stone walls and cypress tiles on top, bringing water from a place more than a thousand yards distant'.

With the water cut, that's the end in sight for Akasaka. For four or five days the defenders lick morning dew from leaves and grass. Fire-arrows set the place ablaze. A monk negotiates surrender, with the assurance that the defenders will be spared because to kill them would be to harden Kusunoki's opposition. So 282 warriors – epic poems are often exact to give the impression of realism – are sent off as prisoners with their arms bent at the elbows and tied, to Kyoto, where the shogun promptly has them beheaded. When they heard of this deception, Kusunoki's men 'ground their teeth like lions, nor did any man think of coming out to surrender'.

This leaves two remaining fortresses, Yoshino under Go-Daigo's son, Prince Morinaga, and Kusunoki's extremely formidable Chihaya.

Yoshino, a fortified monastery named after its 455-metre mountain, is today a town of many hilltops and ridges which is one of Japan's favourite spots for viewing cherry blossoms, because the trees range up the hillsides and come into bloom at successive altitudes, flowing uphill like an incoming tide.[4] In the words of a famous haiku:

> 'Ah!' I said, 'Ah!'
> It was all that I could say –
> The cherry flowers of Mt Yoshino![5]

The mountain no doubt had its springtime charms back then, but this was high summer, 1333, and the blossoms were long gone. This cross between monastery and town is 'a place of steep heights and slippery moss'. For a week the two sides fight, until 'green things were dyed with blood and bodies lay across the paths'. A warrior monk tells the attackers they will lose more men uselessly if they keep on with frontal assaults. What's needed is guile, says the monk. 'I shall choose a hundred and fifty foot-soldiers, men acquainted with the mountain, to steal inside the castle in the darkness, and raise

---

[4] It is also a place of many shrines and pilgrimage routes, now protected as a UNESCO World Heritage site.
[5] By Teishitsu (1610–73), Kyoto paper-merchant and musician.

a battle shout when the light of dawn appears.' In the chaos, the main army will attack. The plan works well. The 150 special ops men – lightly armed *ashigaru*, 'light feet', ninja in all but name – make their entry, raise their shout and set the place alight. 'Powerless to stand against their enemies in front and behind, the monks of Yoshino perished each after his own fashion, cutting open their bellies and running into the blazing fire to die.'

But Prince Morinaga launches a counter-attack, and . . .

A brief interruption about this prince, because he was already a noted loyalist hero, and still is today. His father had made him abbot of the Enryaku-ji monastery, known as the Great Pagoda, at only 18 – it helps, of course, if your father is the emperor – but he trained as a warrior, at which he proved a champion, becoming a master-fencer with an ability to leap over 'seven-foot screens', as the *Taiheiki* says, and a determination to read 'even the shortest of the secret military treatises. Never had there been so strange an abbot.' At twenty-three, when his father started the civil war, he gave up life as a monk to join him. On the prince's way through the old capital of Nara, Kasagi fell and his father was captured, which meant that the shogun's forces would be after him. 'The prince's peril was even as that of one treading on a tiger's tail.' He hid in a monastery, where in due course his enemies came looking for him.

At this the *Taiheiki* tells one of its detailed stories:

There is no way out, and the prince is considering whether to commit *seppuku* when, in the main hall, he sees a monk reading near three Chinese chests which contain Buddhist scriptures. (Why the monk? I have no idea. In terms of the narrative, he's not necessary, and creates a problem, for modern readers anyway, because he does nothing except read.) Two of the chests are full, but the monk has removed some manuscripts from the third, which stands open. The prince climbs in – apparently without disturbing the scholarly monk – covers himself with books, and begins muttering prayers, but holding a dagger against his stomach in case discovery should force him to commit *seppuku*. Just in time: the searchers enter, hunt high and low, then become suspicious of the boxes, and turn the two full ones over, scattering the books. Wonderful to relate, they do not look in the open box, and leave, for no reason (narrative technique today would demand one – a shout from outside, perhaps). Again, no reaction from the scholarly monk. The prince thinks: perhaps they will be back. So he gets out, and hides again, in one of the other two chests.

Yes, the warriors return, having decided to check the remaining chest. Nothing of course, except books. They all leave. Prince Morinaga thanks his lucky stars. It's all due to the protection of the scriptures, he says, and of Marishiten, the multi-faced Indian goddess, also known as Marici ('light' or 'mirage'), the deification of mirages who could make warriors difficult to see or even invisible. This is a story recalling the myth that ninja – for this is a very ninja-like act – could make themselves invisible. So he was able to escape and continue his journey in the guise of a wandering monk, ending up after many adventures in Yoshino.

Now here he is, driving the enemy back briefly, allowing him time – despite seven arrows sticking out of his armour and blood pouring from his wounded arm – to organize a drinking party to celebrate their coming death. With the battle still in progress outside, a warrior named Murakami Yoshiteru appears 'with sixteen arrows drooping in his armour like lingering winter grasses'. He offers to don the prince's armour and stand in his place while the prince escapes. After demurring briefly, the prince agrees. While the prince flees, weeping – accompanied by Yoshiteru's son – Yoshiteru takes his place on a tower and addresses the enemy, announcing that he is the prince, and will now commit *seppuku*. 'Mark me well,' he yells, 'that you may know how to rip open your bellies when fortune fails.' Stripping off his armour, and 'clad only in brocade trousers, he pierced his fair white skin with a dagger. He cut in a straight line from left to right, flung out his bowels onto the board of the tower, thrust his sword into his mouth, and fell forward on to his face.' The prince, though, is not yet safe. An enemy force surrounds him. Yoshiteru's son stages a rearguard action on a narrow path, holding off 500 men until wounds and imminent death force him to rip open his belly. The prince once again escapes.

Now the story reaches its climax, with a million riders – a million! – approaching Chihaya. 'Thicker than plumes of pampas grass on an autumnal moor were their plumes; as morning dew on withered herbs were their weapons, glittering and shining in the sunlight.' Chihaya is small – probably defended by some 2,000 men – but in a fine position, with deep chasms to the east and west, and a high mountain protecting it to north and south. (I can't quite imagine this, but today's ruins lie three kilometres below the peak of Mt Kongō, 1,125 metres, a great shoulder of rock that is Osaka prefecture's highest mountain, and a popular destination for mountain walkers; there is also a cable car that takes you almost to the top.) Frontal assaults fail – Kusunoki had prepared boulders and tree trunks, which flattened 'thousands', so many that 'twelve scribes recorded their names day and night for three days'. The attackers wonder about the water supply, and stake out a possible source; but Kusunoki has water enough inside, stored in two or three hundred troughs made from tree trunks. More frontal attacks, repelled by more falling tree trunks, 'by which four or five hundred attackers were smitten, who fell over dead like chessmen'. So the attackers start a siege. Time passes. They turn to poetry writing, checkers and backgammon. Inside, Kusunoki's defenders are bored out of their minds.

So Kusunoki makes a plan to raise their spirits with a ninja-like trick. He orders them to gather rubbish and make 20 or 30 life-size figures, which are placed at the foot of the castle by night. In the morning the besiegers draw close, not quite daring to attack the figures, at which the defenders drop boulders on them, mocking them for their cowardice. The attackers pull back again, demoralized, and entertain themselves with prostitutes and games. Some quarrel. Orders come from headquarters, demanding they do something positive. The commanders decide to build a bridge, an immense structure 65 yards long, which they haul into place across the chasm and rush across. But the defenders throw down torches and spray oil, setting the bridge and its crowds of warriors alight and consigning thousand to a fiery death in the chasm.

What can break the deadlock?

The answer is Prince Morinaga, who we left escaping into the backwoods from Yoshino. He and his warriors attack the shogun's troops from the rear, cut off all paths of retreat, seize their armour, and leave them to run wild in tattered straw coats and plant leaves. So thanks to Kusunoki's brilliant defence, he and the Southern Court survive to continue their resistance to Kyoto and the Northern Court, helping to restore Go-Daigo as emperor.

Can the unconventional, night-time attacks in these campaigns really count as ninja operations? Not quite. There were too many warriors. But there are many of the right elements there for the emergence of the fully fledged ninja: lightly armed soldiers, opportunities taken to fight in stormy weather, night operations, wild landscapes, secrecy, deception, hilltop fortresses and fortified villages, the impossibility of using cavalry and traditional samurai methods. It was the early campaigns in the Southern–Northern Wars – focusing on Go-Daigo's courtly 'mountain-top' redoubt of Yoshino – that showed the way forward for those who would create a ninja homeland.

Go-Daigo did not remain emperor for long. In late 1334, a year after the successful defence of Chihaya, the shogun, Takauji, made false charges that Morinaga was planning to overthrow his father, and forced Go-Daigo to hand him over. Morinaga was then sent to Takauji's brother Tadayoshi in Kamakura and imprisoned in a cave for eight months. In July 1335, when a rebellion forced Tadayoshi to retreat from Kamakura, Tadayoshi had Morinaga beheaded.

The following year, a rebellion against Go-Daigo threatened Kyoto. Go-Daigo wanted to confront them in battle. Kusunoki, certain of defeat, advised evacuation to prepare for battle later in the summer, when the rebel soldiers would have been keen to get home for the harvest. Go-Daigo would not hear of it. Kusunoki accepted the decision, a perfect example of a samurai accepting death on behalf of his lord, who was in this case also his emperor. He did this willingly, he told his 10-year-old son, because he knew that one day the boy would take up the cause.

The two sides met on the site of present-day Kobe, beside a small, dried-up river, the Minato, after which the battle is named. It was high summer, 5 July. Kusunoki was vastly outnumbered on land, and threatened also by a naval force. Attacked on all sides, he fought for six hours until he could fight no longer. Finally, severely wounded, with 700 of his men dead and the day lost, he committed *seppuku*, in the proper samurai fashion, winning himself an almost unparalleled reputation as the ideal of gallantry and loyalty.

So ended the attempt by the emperor to restore ancient powers to imperial rule. Go-Daigo fled again, back to his Southern Court capital of Yoshino, now restored, and the war between the courts continued for half a century after Go-Daigo's death in 1339, his heir (another son) and grandson still vainly trying to reassert imperial power as of old, with the real power being exercised by the new shogunal family, the Ashikaga, from Kyoto. In the end, in 1392, the not-so-old pattern was restored: the shogun claiming executive authority in the name of the semi-divine, pampered but impotent emperor.

But this merely papered over the cracks in a society that was divided against itself in many ways, even at the top: the shogun's supporters themselves quarrelled, so even those who claimed to rule were divided three ways, while everyone else was divided many ways if you take into account the bandits, the 'light-feet' soldiery, the increasingly independent war-lords, and the warrior monks in their fortified monasteries, among others. In the words of Pierre Souyri, 'the most dangerous enemy was the neighbour who had his eye on one's land or the cousin who rejected the superiority of the leader'. As one war-loving Ashikaga vassal put it, 'If you want to build yourself a fief, take the neighbouring estate!' He might have added, 'If you want to feed your army, loot the country-side!' That's what happened, frequently. In 1336, the peasants of Mino province in central Honshū complained to their landlord, the local monastery: 'During the war the armies of both Kyoto and Kamakura invaded the estate and took every-thing from the houses. We do not know how to express our misfortune. The war started last winter, but this year the violence was such that nothing remains on the estate. Everything has been taken . . . Our distress is so great that no complaint can do it justice.'

What could a poor man, or village, or collection of villages do? The only thing possible was self-help, which was exactly what the provincials of Iga and next-door Kōga set about doing.

6

HOW TO BE A SHADOW
WARRIOR/3: MAGIC

*If there is an unlucky aspect to the direction or date of your
mission, you should back out and choose another day or time
for departure.*

Ninja instructional poem

NOW WE TURN TO AN ASPECT OF LIFE THAT SURVIVES ONLY IN
vestigial form in the West: the world of superstition and
magic. If I see a ladder, I walk under it, just to prove I am not
so superstitious as to believe it will bring me bad luck. So far,
so good, touch wood. Millions take their horoscopes
seriously. I don't, because I'm a Taurus, which means I'm a
sceptic. But this is nothing compared to times when astrology
and astronomy were flip sides of the same subject, and when
so-called medical treatments were based on unproven beliefs
about 'humours'. Mumbo jumbo ruled supreme because there
was nothing else to go on. So it was in 17th-century Japan,
and a ninja was supposed to have an intimate knowledge of

those physical signs that provided insight into character and destiny, most of which now seem as ludicrous as phrenology. For example:

- If you are a leader with a large head, you will not be poor, but also you will not live long.
- These traits give life-long bad luck: small and elongated head, knees shake when sitting, small waist like a bee, and down-turned corners of the mouth.
- A short torso means an early death or an evil nature.
- If the torso is shorter than the legs, you are poor and mean, or sickly, or will move to another province.
- If a woman laughs at others while covering her mouth with her hand, and scratching her eyebrows, and looking at them sideways – she is a prostitute.
- Women with tiny bodies are servants.
- People with flared nostrils are mean and shabby.
- The signs of a long, prosperous life include: a fully fleshed top of the head, a mouth like a halo, to look like a mountain when sitting, and smelling like orchids.
- If a woman has shaking knees and rubs her face while bowing, she is adulterous.

Natori proceeds with a detailed list of the signs indicating good and bad luck, wealth and poverty, long and short lives, wisdom and stupidity, and many other qualities as revealed in the main parts of the body: head, eyebrows (thin and flat are good, long linear ones a sign of wisdom), eyes (a bad downward slant indicates a quick divorce), nose (a mole on the top means you will have many sons, horizontal wrinkles indicate an accident with a horse and carriage), ears, mouth, teeth, tongue (if you can touch your nose with your tongue you will ascend the throne or become a lord), and hands. He ends by listing twenty-three signs of negativity on the palms and analysing the meanings of moles according to colour and position.

This is all vital knowledge for ninjas, but Natori has the sense to warn against being too rigorous. Reading character in this way is difficult, he says, and not always accurate. (Indeed! If you apply his information on teeth, royalty (which rates 38 teeth), nobility (36) and wisdom (34) must be non-existent, given that humans have 32 teeth at most.) Besides, if you try too hard to read an opponent's character and devise his intention, you may end up staring to the point of discourtesy. Only with great care will you be able to use the information for your ninja activities.

It's fine to help yourself with esoteric knowledge, if you can. But you can do so actively, with – and this is his chapter title – 'Charms and Secret Rituals that Protect You from Being Targeted by the Enemy's Agents'. It's easy to sneer. But remember that at this time in the West (the late 17th century), women were still being burned for witchcraft, and few dared assert that belief in witches was one vast, murderous delusion. Almost everyone, everywhere believed in the spirit world, and believed that with the right acts and incantations you could persuade spirits to act on your behalf, freeing yourself of disease, or casting spells on others. The belief is still alive today: that's why religious people say their prayers, that's why adherents of Shugendō send requests to heaven in the smoke of their fires.

Natori reveals five powerful spells, the number five having special significance deriving from Chinese beliefs and practices: there are five elements (wood, fire, earth, metal, water), five emotions, five senses, five stages of life, five seasons, and many other sets of five, which passed into Buddhism, and thus to Japan and ninja teaching.

The five spells: The *Shoninki* advises: **1)** For protection, hang this in the corner of your bedroom. **2)** Write your name and that of an acquaintance alongside this charm. If you fold the names together, you will get along; if apart, you will fall out. **3, 4 and 5)** These charms freeze people's blood and cause them to make mistakes. If used correctly, they will enable you to walk on blades and all arrows will miss their mark.

Of the first, which provides protection, he says: cut some heavy paper into a 21cm square, write the spell on it, and paste it in the corner where you sleep. You should also carry a copy with you and perform cold-water ablutions. The second makes people stick together or split up, depending on how you write the spell. You can cement friendships or cause a falling out. The third, fourth and fifth protect you from wounds. Write them in vermilion ink mixed with your blood on a silk cloth embroidered with gold and wear it on your chest. 'Then even if you fight against a mountain of swords, you will not be hurt. Fear not!'

Well, perhaps. Natori adds a note of scepticism. 'Some people say that those who rely on charms and spells and use this kind of sorcery are no different from women and children.' So don't rely on spells alone. They are like good armour: useful but not infallible.

7

BUILDING THE NINJA
HEARTLAND

Even if a ninja does not have impressive physical abilities,
remember the most vital thing is to have acute observation.
Ninja instructional poem

THE CAMPAIGNS OF THE SOUTHERN–NORTHERN WARS HAPPENED
close to what would become the ninja homeland, and they
introduced many of the elements that would make up the ninja
ethos. One of these elements was the growth of lower-class,
peasant violence. When this started in the late 13th century, it
was a novelty. Traditionally, while warriors fought, peasants
were supposed to remain humble tillers of the soil. Since time
immemorial peasants had been as compliant as sheep, concerned only to avoid disease, bad weather and the taxman,
leaving samurai armies to march across farmland and extort
taxes without fear of reprisal. But peasants are not infinitely
patient. Those who lived near main roads, for example,
objected to the way campaigning armies flattened crops, stole

food and destroyed houses. Villagers took to confronting generals, negotiating to supply food and horses in exchange for considerate treatment.

It worked. Villages turned themselves into communes, known as *sō*. The oldest known *sō* dates from 1262, when the people of a village called Okitsushima on Lake Biwa got into a dispute with their lord over fishing rights. Under the aegis of the village council, which controlled the worship of the Shinto spirits, they drew up a secret document by which they agreed to oppose their lord, and 'those who break this agreement will be expelled from their land'. In 1298, villagers threatened to direct the anger of the gods on to the lord, in forms both known (such as illnesses and accidents) and unknown (monsters and ghosts). Apparently resistance worked. At the same village in 1342, a similar protest forced the lord to apologize and make amends.

Landowners also looked after their own interests. Some time in the 1330s, 67 small landholders who doubled as warriors formed themselves into a self-help group, or league, known as an *ikki*. Under the terms of their constitution, a majority had to agree that service was necessary before they joined up as a group, and all swore to look after the families of those killed. This was nothing more than a straw or rice husk in the wind, but the *ikki* and similar groups planted the seed of an idea that low-ranking warriors-cum-landowners need not always remain sheep, but could take control of their own lives if they acted collectively.[1]

As the country descended into near anarchy – trade guilds

---

[1] Japanese peasants were far readier to stand up for themselves than their Chinese counterparts. Pierre Souyri suggests this was in part because they were healthier, with better cultivation producing higher yields; and partly because their holdings were not on plains watered by huge, erratic rivers, but in valleys with streams, which did not require large-scale irrigation projects, based on forced labour and oppression.

turning to violence, tenants ousting landlords, provincial warriors seizing power from the shogun's officials, families destroying themselves in disputes over succession, not to mention the pirates terrorizing the coasts – peasants fought for their own interests. One way was to run away from a lord and become an *ashigaru* ('light-foot'), so called because they habitually joined up, fought, deserted, looted and rejoined when it suited them. These low-class characters, usually armed with just a single sword or spear or halberd, were the equivalent of cannon fodder, but they also had a use as ninjas in all but name and expertise, sneaking into enemy camps, taking prisoners, or setting fire to watchtowers under cover of darkness. In wartime, they performed all the subservient but vital roles needed in the ranks – making up squads specializing in bows, guns, spears and swords, or working as grooms, cooks, signallers and standard-bearers. Between wars, if they had not returned to a farming life, they formed armed gangs. By the mid-15th century, they were a well-established military essential and equally well-established menace. 'Proper' soldiers and upper-class types looked upon the rise of the *ashigaru* as the end of civilization as they knew it. 'These men, who have recently been used by the armies, are excessively dangerous rascals.' So wrote the aristocratic scholar and statesman Ichijō Kanera in the late 15th century. 'They tear down or set fire to any place in or out of the city where they know they will not be caught by their enemies. They do not spare either private dwelling or monastic buildings. They search only for loot, and they are nothing but daylight robbers. They are a new evil and should be done away with. They are a disgrace to our country.'

Another way for ordinary men to look after themselves was to join an *ikki*, a term that came to apply to both landowners and peasants. This was an attractive alternative because as a fighting unit the members all knew each other and trained together. They were very effective, controlling the abuses of lords, mounting protests and demanding rent rebates. In 1428 peasants objecting to tax increases ran riot in Kyoto. In 1441, when the shogun was assassinated and there was no central government to speak of, tens of thousands converged on Kyoto, and several thousand made camps within its walls, burning buildings and setting up road blocks that isolated the capital. The rulers bought peace by promising 'virtuous government', returning land sold over the previous 20 years and cancelling debts. Peasant uprisings followed every one or two years for the next 15 years, including one ending in an all-out battle in which the *ikki* forces thrashed a samurai army of 800.

The peasants had a point. At the other end of the social scale, lords and samurai could, it seemed, do nothing but fight battle after battle, with results well displayed by a decade of extremely bloody unrest (1467–77) known as the Ōnin War, after the year it started.[2] Amidst a welter of causes, a major one was the rivalry of two families fighting to succeed the ineffective shogun, Yoshimasa, who had been childless, adopted an heir, then promptly produced a son. Adopted son and new baby acquired their own factions, who started to tear the country apart. One side was led by a priest so famous for his paroxysms of red-faced fury that he was known as the Red Monk; on the other side was his son-in-law, equally famous for his restraint. In just one year, their conflict turned Kyoto's palaces, temples and great houses into burned-out ruins. After one action, eight carts were filled with heads, the rest – uncounted – being tossed into ditches. The streets were barricaded, the gardens trenched. 'The flowery capital which we thought would last forever,' lamented one official, 'is to

---

[2] The Japanese divide their history into 'reign eras'. 1467 was the first year of the short Ōnin Era (1467–9).

become the lair of foxes and wolves.' Kyoto became a miniature Western Front, with the two sides glaring at each other across a no-man's-land of weeds and blackened timbers, divided by a trench seven metres wide. It was a war of negatives – no war aims, no heroes, no leadership, a total waste of lives and resources. Finally, the death of the leaders ushered in war-weariness. One night at the end of 1477, one side burned their positions and fled into the darkness. Looters moved in to complete the city's ruin, and all to no purpose. The historian George Sansom calls the unheroic leaders 'unfortunate creatures demented by their own ambitions'.

An uneasy peace came to ruined Kyoto, but the surrounding countryside remained at war, with armies and bandits prowling for loot. To the south, in Yamato and Yamashiro, villagers intent on self-defence and self-government built their houses behind earth levees, and surrounded themselves with ditches, ponds and moats. They had good reason, because Yamashiro was still at war with its neighbour, Kawachi, a focus for the fighting being the main road between Kyoto and Nara (a mere 15 kilometres from Kasagi, where Emperor Go-Daigo had based himself at the beginning of the civil war a century and a half before; even in a chaotic world, some things never change). On the frontline, armies from both sides pillaged, plundered, looted, stole, raped and burned, until the locals had had enough. In 1485, lower-order warriors and *ashigaru*, appalled by the loss of crops and farmland, deserted from both sides, and marched to a local shrine. Peasants joined them. The decision was made to turn the whole southern part of Yamashiro into an *ikki*. They sent an ultimatum to both armies, demanding withdrawal or else, forcing mass desertions. The following year, warrior chiefs proclaimed virtual independence as a 'provincial commune'. This was not a peasant or a village commune, but rather a new government, which quickly alienated its peasant constituents, with the result that after eight years and the appointment of a new governor by Kyoto it collapsed.

Two hundred and fifty kilometres east, in what was then Kaga and is now Shizuoka, there was another sort of rebellion from below, this one driven by warrior monks belonging to the Buddhist True Pure Land (Jōdo Shinshū) sect. This sect, which appealed to ordinary people because it was rooted in village life without the usual trappings of monasticism, had been in existence for 200 years, without making much impression on those beyond its communities, referred to as Ikkō (meaning 'single-minded, devoted', or as we might put it today, 'fundamentalist'. Not to be confused with *ikki*). The True Pure Landers believed that to escape the tribulations of this life you only had to have faith in a form of Buddha known as Amida, a symbol for the transcendent reality and mystery, which is unborn, uncreated and formless. No, I don't know what that means either, but anyone desiring rebirth into this mystical realm could do so by calling on Amida's name ten times or more. Its founder was said to have repeated Amida's name 60,000 times a day, which must have qualified him for many instant rebirths.

The history of religions suggests two universal laws: 1) that all religions spawn sects; and 2) that extremist sects, drunk with self-righteous certainty, often turn to violence. Such was the case here. After a century and a half of ineffective non-violence, True Pure Land changed. In 1457 a charismatic monk named Rennyō set up shop in Kaga, preaching salvation by faith in Amida, rejecting the established Buddhist church and appealing directly to ordinary people. Like Martin Luther, he taught that anyone could arrange their own salvation without recourse to priests, and as Luther promoted German over Latin, so Rennyō taught in direct, simple language, avoiding Chinese, so that 'even women and the most miserable peasants' could understand, political

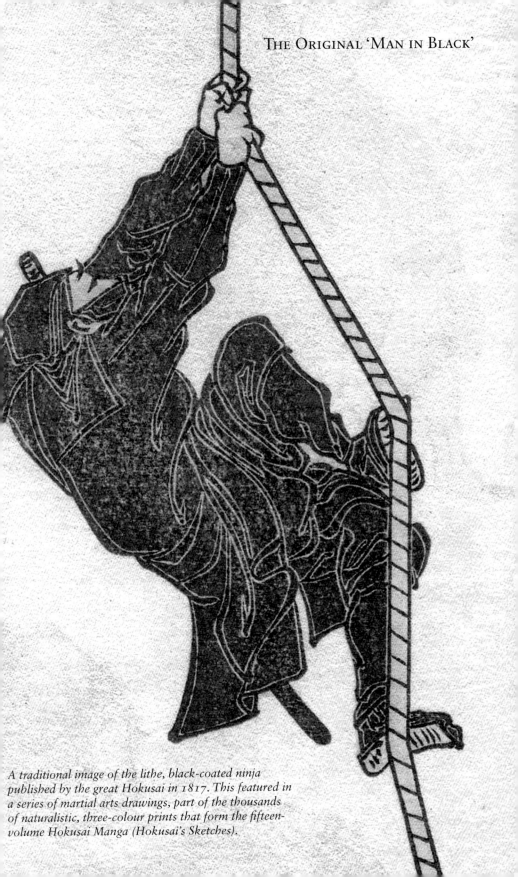

A traditional image of the lithe, black-coated ninja published by the great Hokusai in 1817. This featured in a series of martial arts drawings, part of the thousands of naturalistic, three-colour prints that form the fifteen-volume Hokusai Manga (Hokusai's Sketches).

SHUGENDŌ: TRAINING FOR PURITY

The ninja often undertook training to hone minds as well as bodies. They shared the training with the adepts of Shugendō (yamabushi, mountain ascetics), who isolated themselves in mountains to follow tough regimes of purification. Today's Shugendō rituals, combining elements of Shintōism, shamanism and Buddhism, recall the ancient beliefs to which ninjas were exposed.

Above: *In this Shugendō fire-ceremony on Mt Iwao, the leading priest wears ancient regalia – little back hat, ribband and staff.*

Left: *The conch, used to summon good deities and banish bad ones, is the shell of a giant sea-snail. When the end is cut off, it can be blown like a bugle, either with or without a mouthpiece.*

Right: *The bonfire of cedar branches is to honour the local dragon-god and burn prayers for health and good luck.*

Left: *Kōzō Yamada, amazingly young-looking at seventy-six, is both a Shugendō adept and a yamabushi. He displays a small snake to show one of the hazards of training – as ninjas once did – in the forests of Mt Hando in present-day Kōka.*

Main: *To conquer fear, trainee yamabushis were dangled over a precipice until their fear died.*

Above: *The routes of mountain pilgrimages, like this one on Mt Koshin, are marked by carved stones.*

IGA AND KŌGA: LAND OF HILLS AND FORESTS

The ninja heartlands of Iga and Kōga (centred on today's Iga-Ueno in Mie prefecture and Kōka in Shiga prefecture) are set apart by forested mountains, yet well positioned close to Japan's old capital Kyoto and right on the Tōkaidō, the main coastal road to Tokyo. Ninja skills derived from a sturdy independence, which kept both regions free of warlords

Above: *This ancient lantern marked a pass on the Tōkaidō where it breasted the Suzuka Hills between old Kōga and Iga.*

Above: *Looking north over what used to be Kōga, from the hills dividing Iga and Kōga.*

Below: *Iga-Ueno castle, built after the destruction of the ninjas, offers fine views of the hills that for centuries guaranteed Iga's independence (right).*

Left: *In the open space below the castle, schoolchildren practise traditional archery with asymmetrical bows, the upper sections being bigger than the lower ones.*

IN SEARCH OF NINJA FORTS

One little-known feature of the ninja heartlands is that their samurai and farmer landholders built simple earth-work forts into which they would flee for a few days until danger passed. There were dozens, perhaps hundreds of them – no one knows, because so many of them have eroded back into the earth. A few sites are now known to archaeologists, but most are tree-covered.

Above: *From afar, this double fort (Murasame-Jizen), five kilometres south of Kōka, seems to be no more than a copse on a hillock.*

Above: *Toshinobu Watanabe enacts a defence, standing on a worn and overgrown wall.*

Left: *A detailed plan shows how the two forts were built – but no one yet knows how the different areas were used.*

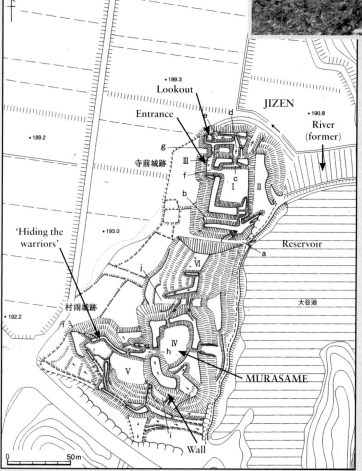

One fort, Hijayama, was the site of one of the final battles in which the ninja were defeated by Oda Nobunaga. It's hard to find. A monk pointed the way (above left), but the site itself is covered by a temple (above), which is approached by steps (right).

In a late nineteenth-century print, a would-be assassin of Oda Nobunaga (standing calmly in the doorway) is caught by Nobunaga's aides. The year was 1573, and the assassin Manabe Rokurō, chief steward of a samurai whose lord, Hatano Hideharu, had been destroyed by Nobunaga. Having failed, Manabe committed suicide. The print, by Toyonobu Utagawa, shows Manabe in typical ninja costume, but has no claim to authenticity.

correctness not being much in evidence at the time. One of his articles of faith was that death in battle was rewarded by eternal bliss. 'Advance and be reborn in Paradise,' read his banner. 'Retreat and go instantly to Hell.' Official Buddhism insisted on celibacy and hard work, like copying religious tracts and paying for religious services. Rennyō dispensed with all the rules, proclaiming that only his followers went to Paradise and everyone else didn't, a simplistic creed that appealed particularly to those who had been barred from salvation by their occupation as killers, whether of people or vermin. He had many wives and fathered 28 children, the last when he was 84, just before his death. When he retired, he built himself a hermitage, Ishiyama Hongan-ji, which became the heart of a city. It lay on a well-forested plateau on the coast downstream from Kyoto at a place called the 'Long Slope' – Ōsaka, the core of today's city. He was hugely successful. His church was thronged with believers of peasant stock, eager for women, war, death and paradise. Ishiyama Hongan-ji grew from a hermitage into an immense temple-fortress with 10,000 monks and a score of major and minor outlying temples.

Soon, other Ikkō leagues sprang up. In Kaga itself, a local lord recruited battalions of warrior monks under the command of his samurai. In 1488 they revolted, threw out the samurai and seized a dominant role, so that Kaga became 'a province held by commoners', in a much-quoted phrase – the first time a province was ruled by a non-aristocratic, non-samurai group. This was people power, Japanese-style, and just the beginning. Ikkō bands would seize temples and land, and rule and fight for a century, escaping from their peasant roots to build commercial and military strongpoints defended by walls and ditches.

Everyone had an idea of Japan as a unified nation, for all shared the same literature, religions and culture. Unfortunately, they didn't share the same idea of political unity beneath the umbrella authority of the emperor and shogun, for war had reduced both to impotence, even penury. When one emperor died in 1501, there was no money to bury him. Another sold autographs to passers-by. Without a universal victory, there could be no political unity, and thus no lasting peace.

Everywhere war continued, family against family, warriors against Ikkōs, province against province, shogun against emperor, and the *ashigaru* against everyone else. It was a world turned upside down, and thus became known as *gekokujō*, translated as 'the low oppress the high', or 'the lower commanding the upper'. To compound this chaos, around 1500, there were some two dozen major warlords and 300 minor ones, all acting as gods in their own domains, all eager to expand their little empires. To track them would be like following particles in a cloud-chamber. In Shinano – today's Nagano, a landlocked province in the middle of Honshū – two rival lords fought in the same place every year for five years, as if determined to do no more than provide their samurai with chances to display themselves. Every leader struggled to find some advantage, and for over a century – the long century (1480–1600) known as the Age of the Warring States – none achieved lasting success.

These chaotic times inspired the evolution of the ninja proper. Several sources refer to ninja and its Japanese-language counterpart *shinobi*, while others mention soldiers who acted in a ninja-like fashion as spies, scouts, surprise attackers and agitators. But the ninja training and activities were mainly focused in the areas still most closely associated with them, the regions then known as Iga and Kōga (now parts of Mie and Shiga prefectures, Iga being a province and Kōga a town and its surrounding area).

Together, the two offered unique advantages to their

villagers. Both straddled the 80-kilometre-wide neck of land between Lake Biwa and the coast, neatly bisecting the main island and placing them in a potentially dominant position. To the north was the ancient capital Kyoto, and the road that would one day become the great east–west coastal highway linking Kyoto and Edo, the Tokaido (Western Sea Road), which ran through a pass on the borders of Kōga. Yet both were isolated by their mountainous landscapes. Iga is a basin about 40 kilometres across surrounded by hills ranging from 500 to 1,000 metres, through which the Nabari river cuts a dramatic gorge. Kōga lies over the hills to the north, where high ground falls away to the shores of Lake Biwa.

These areas were only two or three days' walk from Kyoto, but were never natural centres that would have made cities from which lords could build miniature empires. Instead, they had networks of villages and fortified manors, several hundred of them, which were proud of their independence and self-reliance. Iga, in particular, had no military governor for many centuries, being under the loose control of a temple in the ancient capital of Nara, and so never paid a land-tax either to the shogun or to the emperor. Both relied on a main river, and both had managed to control floods and distribute water cooperatively. And both were sturdily independent, with families known as 'warriors of the soil', who would not tolerate empire-building landowners and towering castles, such as dominated the rest of the country.

These days both are easy to cross by road. But in the Middle Ages, the going was tough; still is, actually, when you get off the roads. The pine-covered slopes are divided by streams that turn to torrents in rain, carving deep gorges. The one-horse paths linking the villages were narrow and steep – 'tiger's mouths', as they were called by the locals, who knew all the passes intimately, and could block them with just a few men. This was a happy balance between accessibility and remoteness, between density and diffuseness. They had something worth defending, and moved from near-anarchy to communality in order to do so.

Several other elements made these remote-yet-accessible areas just right for the development of ninja self-defence forces.

Firstly, both areas were a natural base for bandits – the *akutō* – attracted to the rich pickings available on the high-way from Kyoto, the future Tokaido, which in the early Middle Ages was mainly used to get to the great Shinto shrine at Ise, dedicated to the sun goddess from whom all emperors descend. You can understand the attraction for bandits even now, if you follow what is still the Tokaido from Minakuchi, the 50th of the 53 post-stations that marked the way from Edo (as Tokyo once was) and Kyoto. Go eastwards, towards Kyoto, for 10 kilometres or so, a day and a half's journey on foot.

I did, with my host Yoshihisa Yoshinori, who was keen to show it to me because he lived right on the Tokaido. Along the way, now neatly paved and suburbanized by single-storey grey-tiled houses, the old track is the same width it always was, still hardly wide enough for two palanquins, or cars, to pass. 'That's where I was born,' said Yoshihisa, pointing out a house as plain and simple as most others, its front right on the road. I wondered if this was a choice made by his parents, a way of buying into a privileged community, perhaps? No, nothing like that. 'My great-grandparents wanted the rice field behind it, that's all. Better a rice field than a house.' But he was proud of living on such a historic way, like his neighbours, as the houses themselves showed. There are no formal planning regulations, but – this being Japan, with a strong sense of community – residents conform with tradition when they build.

The low grey houses marshalled us out into flat, open

lands, which gave way to one of the two ranges on the whole route, the Suzuka hills. The track rose steeply. It was up here that travellers faced danger from lurking highwaymen. We were far beyond houses. Back then, it was hard to find your way at night, especially in winter when the slope was slick with mud, and you had to dismount to climb, if you were rich enough to have a horse, and if not, then your straw sandals, bought from some wayside stall only a few hours before, were already falling apart. So the locals had made a huge stone lantern, still in place after 500 years (well, almost in place; a motorway runs in a tunnel underneath, and the builders had to move the lantern 50 metres). It's a monstrous thing, 38 tonnes and over 5 metres high, consisting of a bulbous base, a pillar supporting the hollowed out lantern, and a roughly carved, monolithic roof to keep the rain away from the flickering oil-lamp. The 'road' may have been nothing but a muddy, three-metre-wide track, but this lantern proclaimed its importance.

Besides the bandits, several other groups contributed to the radical nature of Iga and Kōga:

- Since they were only two or three days' walk from the old capitals of Kyoto and Nara, if there was a sudden need for additional troops they could quickly be summoned. We are talking individuals, not armies. The result was that in both areas, fighting was in the blood.
- Though largely peasant communities, they contained a strand of sophisticates (relatively speaking), which derived from the Chinese and Korean immigrants to Yamato, centuries before: monks, military families, potters, merchants, craftsmen. Their intellectual and artistic abilities had worked their way into the villages and temples.
- The forested ranges, with their fast-flowing streams and steep valleys, were favourite haunts of the *yamabushi*, who

needed to know about living in the wilderness and surviving on nuts, berries, fish and game, and treating themselves with medicines made from plants.

- The same landscapes were ideal for anyone wishing to escape being swept up by civil war – high-ranking families who had lost their positions and property, ordinary folk who had seen their land ruined by rampaging soldiers, others wishing to escape being drafted into the ramshackle army of some upstart lord, or the survivors of yet another inconclusive skirmish.
- Lacking a centralized authority, both Iga and Kōga were open to those who loved the open road, the monks, entertainers and craftsmen. And the inhabitants were, of course, farmers, with easy access to dozens of tools which were easily adapted to become weapons.

It was (at a guess, because there are no sources from the earliest days) all the challenges and threats from outside combined with their own advantages that inspired the people of Iga and Kōga to build on their centuries of independence, to continue to look after their own interests, and to defend themselves by turning themselves into ninja.

While much of the country was at war with itself, Kōga and Iga had kept themselves relatively isolated behind their mountain bulwarks. Traditionally, both consisted of families that were forever feuding. Kōga had a mere 53, and Iga, being a much larger place, some 300–500, at a rough estimate ('I heard there were five hundred and thirty,' a monk in one of Iga's temples told me). Neither had any powerful, ambitious lords, so the fighting was small-scale, low-level, more like the jousting between rival stags than the all-out destruction suffered elsewhere at the hands of predatory armies. The skills they developed were as much life skills as military ones, evolving to preserve not destroy, to conserve secrets rather than proclaim status.

The first mention of the ninjas by that name came in 1488, in the official government annals.[3] A local governor, Rokkaku Takayori, appointed by the shogun, had started taking over the estates of local landowners, clearly aiming to make himself a lord, a *daimyō*. The landowners protested to the shogun, Yoshihisa. It was Yoshihisa's unexpected birth in 1465 that had snatched the shogunate from his father's adopted heir, thus starting the Ōnin War. In 1488, after eleven years of peace, he was still only 23, and keen to prove himself by slapping down his upstart governor. He laid siege to Rokkaku's castle, with an Iga family, the Kawai, 'earning considerable merit as *shinobi* (ninja) . . . Since then successive generations of Iga men have been admired. This is the origin of the fame of the men of Iga.' Unluckily for Yoshihisa, he fell ill and died. It was his successor who managed to take the castle, using ninja in some unspecified way. Recording the campaign, the annals say: 'Concerning ninja, they were said to be from Iga and Kōga and went freely into enemy castles in secret. They observed hidden things, and were taken as being friends.'

By then the villagers of Iga and Kōga had decided that cooperation offered a better way of life than constant low-level feuding. No one knows exactly when this was first formalized, but it seems there was a precedent nearby, from an estate named Oyamato, marked today by a small temple 13 kilometres south of Nara. In the summer of 1494, right at the beginning of the time of the Warring States, the men of Oyamato recorded two contracts – sworn, legally binding declarations – witnessed by a monk named Shinsei. The first,

---

[3] This incident is from the Muromachi *bakufu*'s *Nochi Kagami*, retold by both Zoughari and Turnbull.

signed by 350 land-workers, was a sort of local constitution or code of conduct, made up of five articles, designed to preserve the peace. According to one of the articles: 'The common people shall not fight over paddy fields, mountains or forests. They shall not seize cultivation rights or steal.' In the second contract, dated a month later, 46 wealthy locals – *jizamurai*, 'samurai of the soil', as they were known – promised not to fight over taxes on peasants, and to control both troublesome subordinates and themselves: 'If anyone acts badly, inside or outside Oyamato, he will be judged and sentenced.' Since both contracts were witnessed by the same monk, it seems clear that the two groups, landowners and farm-workers, were cooperating to impose peace. On whom, we may ask? There was no war, no centre of warrior monks. Nor were the signatories being told what to do by a local princeling, baron or warlord. This was a community, a network of otherwise unremarkable people, united in their determination to sort out their problems – mostly administering land and water rights – peacefully, eradicate bandits, use taxes locally and build a strong community on their own terms.

There is a subtext to this little piece of evidence. It suggests a sort of idyll: cheerful and friendly villagers trooping off from their fields to link up for mutual support. But almost certainly the pre-contract life of these farm-workers, and of those who lay outside the contract, was very un-idyllic: a life made nasty, brutish and short by inter-village feuding and by immigrants fleeing the effects of the Ōnin War.

Not that communes were all that charming. They worked because they were tough, even barbaric in the way they imposed justice, with zero tolerance of any deviation from their own laws and no appeal to any other court. An imperial dignitary, Kujō Masamoto, described an incident that occurred when he visited his estate around 1500.

He invited peasants from one of the local villages for a New

Year's Day banquet in honour of the village chiefs. During the banquet, a villager announced that his dagger had been stolen. To catch the thief, Masamoto told the chiefs to meet at the local shrine, where they would hold a trial by the ordeal of boiling water. Trials by ordeal were for much of history a common, indeed virtually universal, way of finding criminals, the idea being that if a person was innocent they would show no ill effects, or simply survive – the grounds for judgment varied – but in any event the trial would reveal the guilty because God or the spirits would look after the innocent. (In Europe, language itself preserves a memory of this process: the German for 'judgment' is *Urteil*, which has the same root as the English *ordeal*.) In this form of ordeal, everyone was required to retrieve a stone from a kettle of boiling water. The scalded hands would be bound and examined after a few days to see whether they were healing (innocent) or festering (guilty). In this case, the mere threat of an ordeal worked, and the guilty man stepped forward. Masamoto deprived the man of his rights, but that was not good enough for the villagers. The theft had, after all, occurred on a special occasion when they were their lord's guests. They felt humiliated, and applied their own form of justice. A few days later they went to the thief's house, killed him, his wife and his three sons, and burned his house down.

Oyamato's peasant commune worked, and the neighbours took note. Next door, in Iga, the villagers adopted a similar if somewhat more ambitious scheme, the 'Iga Commune', as scholars call it. The written evidence for when it started has not survived, but it seems to have begun around 1500. Iga called itself an *ikki*, a 'league', though it was a good deal bigger than other *ikkis*, perhaps following the example of the Yamashiro 'provincial commune' as it might have been if it had had more peasants and fewer warriors. Iga's *ikki* was a province-sized confederation of villages under the control of

66 warrior families, who had their own fortresses and came together as a council in the Buddhist temple that once stood on the site of today's castle in the local capital, Iga-Ueno. So the council was prepared to fight against more than just a few bandits.

Despite the lack of a foundation document, a constitution – probably a refined version of something that had been in effect for decades – was written some time around 1560, which included the following (but see box on pp. 98–9 for the full text):

- All foreign troops to be repelled.
- Upon receiving alerts from watchmen at the fortified passes, villagers to spread the alarm and provide food, arms and reinforcements along all defended routes.
- All men between 17 and 50 to be mobilized; captains to be designated; monks to pray.
- Peasants giving exceptional service in action to be raised to samurai status.
- Traitors to be beheaded and their heads to be displayed.

But this is a document with rather vague provenance. It has no year-date. It lacks signatures, which suggests it is a draft. And it was preserved by a family living in Kōga, not Iga. Ishida Yoshihito, a specialist in medieval Japan at Okayama University until his death in 1996, suggested it was written in Iga because it refers to a 'self-governing league' (*Sokoku ikki*), which was what Iga called itself. He also concluded that it was written in the 16-year period between 1552 and 1568, because a) the document mentions a clan, the Miyoshi, who seized power in central Japan in 1549, but only after 1552 were they powerful enough to rate a mention; and b) only before 1568 was Oda Nobunaga, the great unifier of Japan, *not* powerful enough to rate a mention.

Kōga, too, followed the examples of Oyamato and Iga, forming a commune of villages. Iga and Kōga warrior families had agreed to recognize each other as allies. Indeed Iga's constitution contained a clause stating that 'we now see fit to unite our forces with Kōga' and hold common assemblies at the border, so-called 'field meetings'.

So by the second half of the 16th century, this whole area was a collection of communes, each overseeing irrigation, land clearance, and the collection of cash to fund self-defence against warlords and their forces from outside. At the entrance to one village stood a notice: 'It is forbidden for local warlords to enter this place, which is under autonomous judicial administration.' Other places demanded that warlords could only enter if they signed a contract restricting their authority to named vassals.

(It is no coincidence that at the same time similar conditions in Europe – lack of central authority and a drive to assert it in the teeth of local resentment – produced similar results. As towns started to grow after the year 1000, townspeople sought protection from nobles, bandits and churchmen hungry for loot and taxes. To establish and preserve their liberties, they formed self-governing communes, promising mutual defence and vengeance for assaults on their members, and winning charters guaranteed by a local lord, or king, or emperor. The commune movement grew in the 11th century in northern Italy, then spread across most of Western Europe in the early 12th century. In northern and central Italy, dozens of communes – Milan, Genoa, Padua, Ferrara and many more – were able to create stable city-states. Some German communes – Frankfurt, Nuremberg, Hamburg – survived for centuries. Rural communes formed, notably in France and England, and other groups fulfilled similar and more specialized roles: parishes, craftsmen's and merchants' guilds, monasteries. The Swiss were particularly successful: in

The Ninjas' Foundation Document:
The Constitution of Iga's 'Self-Governing League'[4]

1. When any other domain's army intrudes on our province, the collective of the *Sokoku* [self-governing village] should fight to defend against them together, with each other, as one.
2. Upon the alert sent from the gateway when the enemy are spotted, all the bells in every village should be struck and everyone should take up a position immediately. Everyone should prepare himself with food, weapons and shields and set up an encampment so as not to allow the enemy to enter the gateways of our realm.
3. All people of the ages 17 to 50 should be stationed for war. If a battle is a prolonged one, and they have to be stationed for a long period, they should rotate on a system. In every village and every area commanders should be appointed so all the men in the *Sokoku* can follow the orders of those said commanders. As for the temples in the *Sokoku*, the elders should carry out a devotional service for the prosperity of our province, while the young should take part in the camp.
4. All the *hikan* [lower-order people] of the *Sokoku* should write a solemn oath, stating that they will follow their lord whatever be the situation of our land.
5. The *ashigaru* ['light-feet' or common soldiers] of our land may even capture a castle of another domain. Therefore, those who serve as *ashigaru* during a siege and go beyond the borders and attack a castle in another land and succeed in capturing it should be rewarded liberally for their loyalty and promoted to samurai.
6. If anyone intentionally lets an army of another domain in, the combined *Sokoku* will subjugate him and his clan and

---

[4] Thanks to Antony Cummins and Yoshie Minami for this translation.

annihilate them without leaving any trace, and the land will be given over to a temple or shrine. Similarly, anyone who communicates with the enemy secretly and gives them any inside information about our land will be treated just the same as those who let the enemy army in. If someone brings information of anyone's treason in the above manner, he will be highly valued.

7. No samurai or *ashigaru* foot soldiers of our land should serve the Miyoshi clan.

8. If someone refuses to pay the *Yumiya Hanjo* tax [a 'bow-and-arrow signed document' tax, presumably a war fund], he, his father, sons or brothers will not be eligible to benefit from the fund for 10 years. Neither should they be allowed to use the *Yado Okuri* or *Mukae* transportation system [a system of relay stations].

9. When positioned in a village or camp, any disorderly behaviour or violence should be prohibited within the borders of our alliance.

10. As the Yamato province has unjustly attacked our province over a prolonged period of time, we should not employ any *ronin* [samurai unattached to a lord] who once served in the Yamato military.

11. As we have controlled our province without any problems, it is of utmost importance for us to obtain cooperation from Kōga. Thus, we should have a meeting with Kōga at the border between Iga and Kōga at an early date.

The above commandment should be in effect with the signatures [of all who are concerned].

16th day of November [year unknown, probably *c.* 1560]

1291, three cantons signed an 'Everlasting League' in order to break free of their local rulers, the Habsburgs; one of them was Schwyz, which would go on to give its name to the whole nation; and together, like Iga, they produced warriors whose skills were valued far beyond their own borders. All well and good for the communes themselves; not so good from the point of view of a central administration ambitious to enforce peace nationwide.)

As in Europe, so in Japan, and in particular in Iga, where the commune showed much greater resilience than the one next door in Yamashiro, probably because it was both more remote from major trade routes and better rooted in the peasant community.

In any event, the strength of the bond remained fixed in the memory of the people of Iga and Kōga. Over a century later, well after the destruction of the ninja homelands, the *Shoninki* records how Kōga and Iga swore the friendship oath of *Ichi Gun Ichi Mi*, 'one district and one band', joining the people together. They went out expansively to various provinces to utilize their skills. Thus, being universally recognized as the premier *shinobi*, they exchanged a firm written form of oath, which says, 'If I come to where you are, you should show me everything of your province, and if you come to where I am, I will show you everything about my province'.

Kōga, too, was an incipient democracy, a 'parliament without a prime minister', as Toshinobu, one of the local historians, put it. Iga's 'parliament' seems to have met in several different places, but Kōga's 53 top families had one particular shrine as its focal point. Toshinobu explained: 'Everyone had to make promises with their lives in a god's hands. That was why the meetings were held in one of three shrines, in succession. Often the contract was written on a special paper which had the god's name on the back. Everybody signed.'

One of the shrines is still there today, or rather its re-constructed successor. On the outskirts of today's Koka, a strange semi-circular structure, like an impractical bridge, straddled a stream. A grand Shinto gate of thatch and many-jointed beams gave on to the gravel courtyard of a shrine, Yagawa. On this hot September afternoon, Yagawa was a place of peace and silence. Springwater flowed through the mouth of a metal dragon into a stone tank, with ladles lying alongside for dusty pilgrims. Halfway across the yard was what Noriko called a dance hall. This was not for social occa-sions, but for priests and sumo wrestlers to perform for the god. Beyond that again was the shrine itself, guarded by four Chinese-style stone lions. It was locked.

'There's a balcony,' I said. 'Maybe I can get a look inside.'

'No!' Noriko was shocked at the idea. 'This is the house of the god! No ordinary humans! Only the priest can allow you in, perhaps when you wish to introduce a new baby to the god.'

To one side was a house, which in the old days would have been a storehouse or stable, and was now a place for the priest to live. A woman spotted us, and vanished. I was ready to leave, eager to catch a train back to Kyoto, when the priest, Somanosho by name, appeared, looking bleary, in his vest. We had woken him from his afternoon nap, but he was happy to talk, because the shrine, and he himself, had interesting histories.

In Edo times, the place had been a Buddhist temple run by the Tendai sect, though as usual with a Shinto element. Then when Shinto was banned after the Meiji Restoration in 1868, it had become totally Tendai. Tendai priests were not allowed to marry – yet the last Tendai priest had been Somanosho's father. How could that be? Because after the war, Shinto-ism was allowed again, 'and my father stopped being a Tendai priest and became a Shinto priest, so he was allowed to marry, and he had a child, and the child inherited his father's role, and that's me!'

I had almost forgotten the reason for being there. What about before all that, before unification in 1600?

'Well, this is an ancient place of worship. There is one sentence in the sources which confirms that this was the place where the Kōga families met, when it was both Tendai and Shinto.'

That was what I had hoped to hear. I was standing on the spot where Japan had experimented with a form of democracy which sounded like something the Athenians developed in the 5th century BC: each village represented by a top family, so that only property owners participated; each family represented by its most important male, whose position would have been inherited by his son. Of course, there was no voting system, and no way that every qualifying adult male could have a direct say. But still, since this was being made up from scratch, it was not a bad start.

Unfortunately it came to a bad end before anyone could refine it.

8

THE RISE OF THE CONQUEROR

*Though there are so many principles a ninja should learn, the
first thing of all is to get close to the enemy.*
Ninja instructional poem

BEYOND THE HILLS OF IGA AND KŌGA, NEW THINGS WERE AFOOT
that would aid the rise of the man who would, over three
decades, lay the foundations for the unification of Japan: Oda
Nobunaga. His rise would bring the world of the ninjas to its
peak, and then to a violent end.

In his background, as in his rise, Nobunaga almost
matched Genghis Khan, starting from nothing much and,
over 20 years, fighting his way up towards nationwide rule,
though not quite achieving it before his death (unity took
another 18 years of warfare). He did it, in the words of his
biographer Jeroen Lamers, by using 'rational cruelty in the
service of government'. The story interweaves two themes –
Nobunaga's brilliant, ruthless leadership, and new technology

in the form of handguns. We must follow them both to understand why and how the ninja fell.

The story of how firearms came to Japan is usually told in simple terms: the Portuguese arrive with guns, the Japanese see how effective they are, and hey presto, the world changes. In fact, it's not that simple. Guns had been made in China from the late 13th century. They were primitive, but leaders recognized their potential. Guns took longer to load than bows, and they were not as accurate, but they had one supreme advantage: to use a bow, you had to train for years and then keep in training to build and preserve shoulder, arm and finger muscles; but any weakling could use a gun. A century later, Korea was making handguns. Yet the technology did not instantly spread to Japan. In 1510, a priest in Odawara (halfway along Honshū's southern coast) acquired a Chinese matchlock and showed it to his lord, who apparently was not impressed, because he did absolutely nothing with it. Others were more ambitious. Chinese guns were used in a battle in 1548, but only as a stopgap alternative to bows and swords. Why? No one knows, because no examples or designs have survived. Possibly, the barrels were not cast in one piece, but as two bits welded together, which made them liable to explode.

It took a slightly more advanced design to convince the Japanese. In the early 1540s Portuguese merchant adventurers approached northward from Okinawa, hopping along the Ryūkyū islands as if they were stepping stones across a river. Among their weapons were some hand-held, muzzle-loading matchlock guns known as arquebuses. Two Portuguese adventurers, both armed with arquebuses, joined the 100-strong crew of a Chinese junk, which was bringing merchandise to Japan, aiming to dock on Tanegashima, the island off the south coast where all trading vessels had to register (and which is now famous for Japan's space centre).

Damaged by a storm, the junk limped to shelter in a bay on the southern coast of the island.[1]

It was 23 September 1543, as we know from a local monk, who 63 years later wrote a meticulous account, because no one had seen a ship of this size or such strange-looking, long-nosed, bearded foreigners; and by then it had become clear that the incident had changed the course of Japanese history. The chief of the nearby village, Nishimura, could read *kanji* – Chinese script used to write Japanese. Since he knew only the Japanese pronunciation of the signs, he could not talk to the crew. But he 'spoke' with them by drawing characters in the sand with a stick, asking where the foreigners came from. 'They are traders from among the southwest barbarians,' came the sandy reply.

Nishimura then galloped the 50 kilometres to the capital with the astounding news. The island's lord, Tokitaka, a curious 15-year-old, demanded to see the ship and the foreigners. Back went Nishimura to organize a dozen rowing boats, which towed the damaged junk around the coast to the main harbour. An astonished crowd gathered, among them young Tokitaka, who invited the two foreigners to his house. There he asked about the long stick that each carried, 'an object which could not be compared with anything known. Its use was both strange and wondrous.' They gave him a demonstration, hitting a target 100 metres away, and he, of course, bought the two muskets on the spot, eager to get them copied. He had reason to think this would not be hard. His island was iron-rich, with a tradition of sword-making.

In four months, his blacksmith, Yaita, made Japan's first effective musket, receiving instruction from a Portuguese, in exchange – according to tradition – for his 16-year-old daughter, Wakasa. Folklore claims that she had a miserable

---

[1] The main source for this account is Olof Lidin.

time in this, the first Japanese–European marriage. Yaita, however, prospered. His creation was instantly used to help retake the neighbouring island. After a few lessons in how to make gunpowder (local sulphur, saltpetre from China), word spread. That same year, 1544, home-made muskets were taken to the main island of Honshū, and leaders soon saw the potential: five years later, Portuguese-style arquebuses were first used in battle, though not with the discipline that would make them truly revolutionary.

Soon Oda Nobunaga, warlord and future shogun, heard of the new weapon, and ordered 500 of them. When he finally realized how to make the best use of them, he would change the course of Japanese history, tackling other warlords, communes, warrior monks, ninjas – all of Japan's divisive, vested interests. But right then the guns were of less importance than the most powerful weapon of all – Nobunaga himself, the cause of much destruction and much novelty, and the survivor of several ninja-style assassination attempts.

Nobunaga, one of the greatest – as well as the most ruthless – leaders in Japanese history, was not marked out for leadership. The Oda family, rising from obscure origins, had become the shogun's deputies in their home province, Owari, which was Iga's next-door-neighbour-but-one to the northeast, a small province centred on today's Nagoya and edging Ise Bay. Nobunaga inherited his father's rank as an assistant deputy to the shogun's representative, not a great start for the future unifier of the nation. But he was ambitious and merciless. At 20, he had enough loyal followers to crush opposition from his own family, which included killing one of his brothers (as Genghis did). At 25, he chased out the shogun's representative and ruled the province, with the shogun's support.

The following year (1560), a neighbouring provincial ruler, Imagawa Yoshimoto, led 25,000 men into Owari on his way to Kyoto. One of Imagawa's generals seized a fort, and sent seven heads to his boss. Nobunaga ordered a counter-attack, despite being outnumbered four to one. Luckily, the invaders were camped on the coast, near a little village called Okehazama, in a wooded defile (a *hazama*) that Nobunaga knew well. Leaving a few men with many banners to give the impression of a large force, he took most of his little army, some 3,000 strong, through forest behind Imagawa's position. Suddenly, around midday, stifling summer heat gave way to a violent thunderstorm. Nobunaga attacked and Imagawa's army fled, mired in mud, their guns soaked and useless. Imagawa's tent was left unprotected, and he lost his head, literally, to one of Nobunaga's men. It was all over in minutes. By chance, one of Imagawa's allies, a man who would later name himself Tokugawa Ieyasu, was away from HQ at the time, and survived. Soon, he would switch his allegiance to Nobunaga and complete his new master's revolution. The battle of Okehazama made history: if Imagawa had been less arrogant and more circumspect; if Nobunaga had been less bold; if there had been no rainstorm; if Ieyasu had been near Imagawa – why, then, Nobunaga would be a mere footnote and Ieyasu even less, rather than the founders of post-medieval Japan.

Meanwhile, Ieyasu had a problem. His family was held as hostages in the castle of the son of Imagawa, who had just lost his head to Nobunaga. How to remain true to his former master's family, thus ensuring his family's survival, while coming to some accommodation with Nobunaga, thus ensuring his own survival? As it happened, the gods were with him. His plan was to declare himself for Nobunaga, then, to prove his loyalty, seize one of Imagawa's castles, and take hostages of his own which he would then exchange for his family. This was a high-risk strategy, which would work only if he could take the castle fast enough to forestall the execution of his family. Failure would undoubtedly result in the death of his wife and children, an end to his ambitions, and probably his own death.

The castle he had in mind that spring of 1562 was Kamino, southeast of Nagoya in Mikawa (today's Aichi prefecture), near his birthplace of Okazaki. Kamino was a tough nut, 'built upon a formidable precipice', according to the main source,[2] so 'we will be condemning many of our allies to suffer great losses'. There was only one way to guarantee a quick victory – by using ninjas. 'By chance, there are [among our allies] men having relations with Kōga' – i.e. ninja – so 'let us convene Kōga's leaders through their compatriots and then they can sneak into the castle.' Clearly, then, Kōga's ninjas had a reputation that reached far beyond Kōga's border, and were available for hire as mercenaries. Some 80 (or more: another source says 200) responded to the call. In mid-March, this group, having dressed up so that they would be mistaken for defenders, 'were ordered to lie down and hide in several places, and . . . sneaked inside the castle'. Once inside, they made their way around in silence, killing as they went, communicating with each other by using a password. The defenders were totally bemused by what was happening, thinking that the shadowy figures were traitors from within their own ranks. 'Before long they were setting fire to towers inside . . . the garrison was utterly defeated, and fled.' The commander hid beside the Hall of Prayers, where the ninjas' leader found him, speared him and took his head. Some 200 defenders perished in the flames, and many others were taken hostage, among them the two sons of the slain commander, exactly as Ieyasu had planned.

He followed his stunning victory with an offer to exchange his hostages for his family. The deal was done, his family

[2] The story is told by both Turnbull and Zoughari, quoting the original Japanese sources.

restored, his loyalty to Nobunaga established, his new career well launched.

With one glitch. As part of the deal, Kamino's burned-out wreck was returned to the Imagawa clan. It was soon repaired, and handed over to the two sons whose father had been killed in its defence. Rather foolishly, they sought revenge, reopening the feud with Ieyasu, who once again sent a force of Kōga ninjas to repeat their previous success. This they did 'taking advantage of an unguarded point', and this time making sure of their victory by killing the two brothers, 'who thus', as Turnbull says, 'earned their place in history by being probably the only samurai to have been defeated by the same ninja twice!'

Ieyasu was grateful, though it took him a while to express his thanks for the victory. In a letter to the leader of the Kōga ninjas, a certain Tomo Sukesada, he wrote, 'Since that time, I have been occupied with one thing and another and have neglected to write for some years. [I wish you] good health, and have the honour to congratulate you.'

In 1568, Nobunaga set out for the capital, Kyoto, marching via southern Omi – right past Kōga – and defeating its local lord as he went (with interesting consequences that we'll get to shortly). In Kyoto, Nobunaga appointed his own compliant shogun, with the obvious intention of unifying the country.

No one was better qualified for the task. The following year, a leading Jesuit missionary, Luís Fróis, from Portugal, became the first European to meet Nobunaga, and left a pen-portrait of this ambitious, ruthless, brilliant and extremely scary leader:

This King of Owari, who would be about 37 years old, is tall of stature, lean, sparsely bearded, with an extremely sonorous voice, given to military exercises, indefatigable, inclined to works of justice and compassion, arrogant, a great lover of honour, very secretive in his decisions, a master of stratagems, hardly or not at all mindful of the reprimands or advice of his subordinates, and is feared and venerated by all to the highest degree. He does not drink wine, is brusque in his manner, looks down on all the other kings and princes of Japan and speaks to them with disdain as if to his inferiors, is totally obeyed by all as the absolute lord, has good understanding and sharp judgment, despises the gods, the Buddhas and all other kinds of idolatry and pagan superstition.

In his actions, Nobunaga followed Chinese emperors who had established or re-established unity: the First Emperor who crushed rival states and intellectuals; the Tang emperor Wuzong (reigned 840–46), who destroyed thousands of Buddhist monasteries and had some 250,000 priests defrocked. Utter ruthlessness in politics and war, moderated only by pragmatism, those were his guiding principles. 'Rule the Empire by Force' was his motto; but first he had to conquer it. Among the challenges Nobunaga faced were not only the many independent warlords but also those from the three main groups of non-samurais: the warrior monks of Mt Hiei, the Ikkō *ikki* and the ninjas of Kōga and Iga, all of whom he dealt with in a series of overlapping actions that lasted 12 years, from 1570 to his death in 1582.

He was lucky to live to start his campaigns, because he at once became a target for ninja assassins. One incident took place shortly after Nobunaga had marched through Omi. His arrival and victory were much resented by one of Omi's principal clan leaders, Rokkaku Yoshisuke, whose family had been dominant there for 300 years, but was now rather less so, thanks in part to Nobunaga. Yoshisuke also had considerable experience with ninjas, who outside their own territories were happy to work for whoever paid them. So it was natural for Yoshisuke to seek revenge on Nobunaga by sending a ninja to kill him. Nobunaga, being by now the most powerful commander around, was too well protected for a ninja with a knife to get near him. So Yoshisuke (so one version of this story goes) hired a sharpshooter called Sugitani Zenjūbō, who lay in wait for Nobunaga and got off two shots, both of which were absorbed by Nobunaga's armour and padded costume. Two shots – how? Even if Sugitani had two guns, it is hard to imagine Nobunaga waiting around long enough to receive the second bullet. I asked the owner of a hotel where I was staying in Koka. By chance, he was a member of a historical study group and had written on this very incident. It happened on 19 May 1570, near the Yokkaichi area, over 30 kilometres east, the other side of the Suzuka hills. No, no, he said, not two shots. It was a single shot, and it just missed, passing through Nobunaga's right sleeve.

First on Nobunaga's list were the warrior monks, principally those of the temple-fortresses of Ishiyama Hongan-ji in Ōsaka, Enryaku-ji on Mt Hiei and Nagashima. Not only were they fiercely independent; they were also potential allies for any rival warlord, and all extremely tough nuts. An attempt to crush Ishiyama Hongan-ji in 1570 was thrown back by volleys of arquebus fire, which taught Nobunaga two important lessons. The first was that the way to use muskets was for the matchlockmen to form ranks and fire in controlled volleys, one rank after another, giving time for each rank to reload. The second was that to follow convention by giving pride of place to samurais with swords and spears would not do; ordinary foot soldiers with muskets could add a new dimension to battle, if they fired in volleys.

Volley-fire a new idea? Not really. It was an old one in China, used by archers, in particular crossbowmen, for centuries. China's First Emperor, ruler of Qin and the nation's unifier in a series of campaigns ending in 221BC, commanded crossbowmen who were legendary, both for their powerful weapons and their discipline, as portrayed in the formal lines of the Terracotta Army guarding the emperor's tomb. Possibly they operated, as an 11th-century source described,[3] 'so that the men within the formation are loading while the men in the frontline of the formation are shooting . . . each in their turn draw their crossbows and come up; then as soon as they have shot bolts they return again into the formation. Thus the sound of the crossbows is incessant and the enemy can hardly even flee. Therefore we have the following drill: shooting rank – advancing rank – loading rank.' It seems that Qin crossbowmen fought rather like early 19th-century European riflemen, advancing rank by rank, each kneeling, firing and reloading in sequence, except that crossbowmen withdrew after firing, allowing the next rank its turn, instead of advancing before firing. There was nothing new in this, even then, for Qin crossbows, with their finely engineered copper triggers, already had a long ancestry, as presumably did the tactical techniques. It was the whole coordinated package – the food supply, the recruitment, the vision of conquest and unity, centralized control, communication, training, discipline, weaponry – that set the Qin army apart, and put it on the road to conquest and their commander on course as China's unifier.

The First Emperor lived the best part of two millennia earlier. But for Japanese scholars, especially Buddhist ones, China had been the ultimate fount of knowledge for almost 1,000 years. There is no direct evidence, but it is more than possible that the warrior monks of Ishiyama Hongan-ji realized how to use matchlocks efficiently from hearing stories about the First Emperor and his crossbowmen.

---

[3] Zeng Gongliang, quoted in Joseph Needham, *Science and Civilisation in China*, Vol. 5, section 30, p. 122.

In the autumn of 1571, Nobunaga turned on Mt Hiei. He deployed his 30,000 men in a ring round the mountain, then had them move uphill, burning and killing as they went. By nightfall the main temple was ablaze. In the words of a chronicle, many of the monks and their retainers 'threw themselves into the raging flames, and not a few were thus consumed by the fire. The roar of the burning monastery, magnified by the cries and countless numbers of the old and the young, sounded and resounded to the ends of heaven and earth.' The Portuguese Jesuit missionary Luís Frόis rejoiced in the slaughter: '[Nobunaga] put his men into every hole or cave, as if he had been in chase of some wild beasts, and there butchered these miserable wretches.' Possibly 20,000 or more perished (though all such big, round numbers are guesstimates).

Nobunaga was then free to turn on the Ikkō *ikki* of Nagashima, whose monks had five strongholds on a long, thin spit of land in the swampy lower reaches of three rivers running in parallel into Ise Bay, near today's Nagoya. For Nobunaga, this was personal, twice over: Nagashima was part of his home province, Owari, and the *ikki*, holed up in their castle and a fortified monastery, had killed his brother (or rather 'forced' him to commit suicide by defeating him) in a previous skirmish. The first attack on this 'water world' in May 1571 had been a disaster, with Nobunaga's samurai trapped in muddy reedbeds, falling easy victims of the *ikki*'s muskets and arrows, then being swamped when the *ikki* opened a dyke.

In 1573, he tried again, and succeeded in taking only some outlying villages. A rainstorm soaked his muskets, while the defenders of the castle and fortified monastery were able to keep their powder dry and return withering fire. That might have been the end of all campaigning, because that same year he also crushed a family named Hatano, who decided to seek revenge by commissioning the steward of one of their vassals to undertake a ninja-style assassination. The killer, Manabe Rokurō, intended to enter Azuchi castle and stab Nobunaga while he slept. He was caught, committed suicide, and his body displayed in the marketplace – a failure hardly worth a mention except that, 300 years later, the incident was portrayed in a print, with Manabe in the role of the archetypal ninja.

The following year, having recruited a former pirate, Nobunaga mounted a third assault on Nagashima, using ships to isolate the two strongholds, then battering them with cannonballs and burning them with fire-arrows. Inside, the 20,000 inhabitants – more big, round and doubtful numbers – were beginning to starve. They offered to surrender. But Nobunaga wanted revenge for his brother's death and for previous humiliations. 'As I want to exterminate them root and branch this time,' he said, 'I shall not forgive their crimes.' Dismissing the monks and their dependants as 'worthless beings' who did not deserve to live, he planned an annihilation as thorough as the one unleashed on Mt Hiei. He built a palisade around both positions, piled brushwood behind it, then, with the approach of a typhoon, set the brushwood ablaze so that the gale carried fire across the flat land into the castle and monastery. All 20,000 inhabitants died, with another 20,000 dying in battle: 40,000 dead, and still no end was in sight.

The Ikkō *ikki* had several other complexes owing allegiance to the formidable Ishiyama Hongan-ji, whose inmates were, in effect, kamikaze fighters, quite ready to die for their faith, because they were utterly convinced of the truth of their banner: 'Advance, and be reborn in paradise.' The struggle dragged on for six more years, with Nobunaga using every means possible to gain power: inspiring rivalry between religious factions, disarming rural populations, blockade, outright assault on temples.

Meanwhile, in June 1575, one of the most momentous battles in Japanese history occurred. It was a showdown with Nobunaga's notorious rivals, the Takeda clan of Kai province. The background was this: one of Ieyasu's top ministers was a man called Oga. A genius at finance, he turned traitor and plotted a campaign with the Takeda clan's current head Katsuyori to take the great castle of Nagashino. Unhappily for the traitor Oga, he was himself betrayed. Ieyasu seized Oga's wife and four children, and had them crucified. When Oga heard the news he is supposed to have remarked, 'You have gone on first. You are lucky. I must follow after you.' Which he did, in gruesome fashion. He was buried up to the neck, and a saw placed beside him so that passers-by could take turns cutting his head off, very slowly. It took him seven days to die.

Katsuyori, meanwhile, was on his way, leading 15,000 men. Despite the loss of Oga, he set about attacking Nagashino. Not an easy target, because it lay in the fork of two high-banked rivers and its 500 defenders were led by a spirited 24-year-old, Okudaira Sadamasa. Several assaults with mines, river rafts and assault towers all failed, with the death of 800 attackers. But Katsuyori was clearly not going to give up, so Sadamasa sent messages asking both Ieyasu and Nobunaga for help. Katsuyori settled down to starve the castle into surrender, building palisades and throwing a network of ropes across the rivers 'so that not even an ant could get out'. Remember how new the alliance was between Nobunaga and Ieyasu. Both foresaw disaster, both prevaricated. Perhaps, if young Katsuyori was going to prevail, Ieyasu would serve his own interest best by breaking with Nobunaga and allying with Katsuyori. Nobunaga gambled: better keep the alliance intact than let Nagashino fall without a struggle. He and his 30,000 men joined with Ieyasu and his 8,000, and the two approached Nagashino together.

Nagashino had two days' supply of food left. Who knew if and when relief might come? Someone had to get a message out to Ieyasu, the closest of the approaching allies. One of Sadamasa's retainers, Torii Sune'emon, volunteered. His bravery and his fate made him part of history, and also part of folklore, so the tale of what he did and how he died is now a tangle of fact and fiction:

Already famous for his ninja-like skills, he says that if all goes well he will light beacon-fires to signal that he is clear of the besieging forces and that help is on its way. The first problem is to escape the castle unseen. A powerful swimmer, he leaves by night perhaps simply through a gate, or perhaps (in another version) through the castle sewer, falling into the nearest river. He swims downstream, cutting through the netting as he goes, and the following morning lights a beacon, as planned, to show that he is safe. What he does not know is that the cut cables and the beacon have been spotted by Katsuyori's men, who are on the lookout from this moment on, spreading sand on riverbanks to disclose telltale footprints and restringing the network of ropes, with bells attached this time. Meanwhile, Torii makes contact with Ieyasu and Nobunaga, tells them of the castle's dire situation, receives a promise of relief the following day, signals the good news to the castle with beacon-fires, and heads back – right into Katsuyori's arms. Katsuyori is full of praise for Torii's bravery and skill, and offers him a job. Torii accepts – but with duplicity in mind, because at heart he remains loyal to his lord – at which Katsuyori gives him new orders: go to the walls and shout that there is no hope of succour, and that surrender is the only option. He agrees. He is strapped to a cross, perhaps to attract attention, perhaps also to warn him of what dreadful fate lies in store for him if he does not do as he is told. In another version of the story, soldiers surround him, their spears pointed at him. Yet instead of calling for surrender, he yells for the besieged force to hang on, because relief is on its way. He is, of course, either crucified or speared, either way achieving legendary status.

That left Katsuyori, with his 15,000 men, between a stubborn citadel and the approaching army of 38,000. Outnumbered, he might have decided to surrender or flee, but of course neither was acceptable to a samurai. Moreover his troops were experienced, his cavalry formidable, while Nobunaga's were not. He would fight.

Nobunaga, too, knew the odds, and decided to increase them in his own favour with a brilliant tactic using arquebuses, the antique muskets copied from those introduced by the Portuguese in Tanegashima 30 years before. By now every warlord and armed temple had guns; Nobunaga, though, had a vast number. Almost a quarter of his army, 10,000 of the 38,000, had arquebuses. They were as rudimentary as ever – it took a good 20 seconds, perhaps a minute in battle, to reload them through the muzzle, and they were effective up to only about 70 metres, so guns alone did not offer an overwhelming advantage, especially in the face of charging cavalry. Nobunaga knew the answer. In many accounts, the idea seems to spring out of the blue; in fact, he had learned the hard way fighting the warrior monks of Hongan-ji five years before. He ordered 3,000 of his best shots to form a unit, divided them into three ranks, 1,000 each, and told them to fire in sequence, in volleys as one rank succeeded another, producing a volley every 20 seconds.

First, Nobunaga saw that the musketeers needed protection against the cavalry. So, on the afternoon before the battle, he had them build a palisade of stakes some 400 metres long, in sections too high for horses to jump. Hills at one end and a river at the other would prevent cavalry outflanking the guns. He gave orders that the troops should fire only when they could be sure of a hit, which meant at less than 50 metres. By now it was dark, and the musketeers settled for the night behind their stockade.

During the night, it rained. Katsuyori, camped in woods in front of the castle and a few hundred metres from the stockade, assumed that the enemy's muskets would be too wet to use. Also his cavalry would cover the ground from woods to stockade in a minute or two, which meant – in theory – that the horses would be upon the matchlockmen before most had a chance to reload. So, soon after a midsummer dawn, while troops to left and right engaged in hand-to-hand combat, he did exactly as expected, sending his cavalry into the attack, a magnificent display of bravery and impetuosity. Out of the trees they came, across a shallow stream, up the bank, and on, laboriously, over rough, wet ground.

Seconds later, within 50 metres of Nobunaga's line, the first rank of Nobunaga's muskets spoke, and the first of Katsuyori's horses and riders fell. At that speed, the survivors would cover those 50 metres in just five seconds. But now the second rank fired, then the third, reducing the charge to a melee of fallen men and horses. Those that survived were impaled by the vast, five-metre spears of the foot soldiers defending the ends of the stockades. Other charges followed, and more slaughter. Seeing what was happening, many in the castle came out to join in the fighting. The musketeers advanced from their stockade, the battleground became a chaos of men fighting hand to hand, and by mid-afternoon Katsuyori's troops saw they were beaten. They broke and fled, many – some 3,000, according to the most widely accepted estimates – to their deaths. Not, however, Katsuyori himself, who lived to fight another day.

This is the strange tale of how Uesugi Kenshin died. All ninja-philes know it, so let's retell it, and then see if there could be any truth in it.

First, a little background. Uesugi was one of the greatest of 16th-century *daimyōs*. He owed his name to a former lord who, in defeat, came to him begging for refuge. He agreed, on the understanding that the lord would adopt him, give him his own name, Uesugi, and make him heir as provincial ruler with immediate effect. The following year, in 1552, he also took the Buddhist name Kenshin. With his new name, he fought many battles in a series of confusing campaigns, attacking some rivals, allying with others, then turning on his allies and allying himself with former enemies. His main enemy, Takeda Shingen, felled by a sniper's bullet in 1573, was succeeded by his less brilliant son, Katsuyori, the one defeated by the fast-rising Oda Nobunaga at Nagashino in 1575. It was Nobunaga, therefore, who emerged as Uesugi's greatest threat, and Nobunaga who in 1578 engineered Uesugi's nasty death – so it is said, because it was he who benefited from it.

The story appears in its most developed form in *Asian Fighting Arts* by Donn Draeger[4] and Robert Smith. It opens with an attack on Kenshin by four of Oda's ninjas, headed by a certain Ukifune Kenpachi. They are spotted by Kenshin's ninja guards, but hide in a ceiling, kill the guards with darts from blowguns, then head for Kenshin's quarters. But the guards' commander has faked death, and intercepts the assassins and kills them.

Then comes the sequel, which involves the brother of Ukifune Kenpachi, a ninja dwarf named Ukifune Jinnai, a sort of Japanese version of Gimli in *Lord of the Rings*. Here is the Draeger and Smith version of the story:

The clever Oda, taking no chances, had dispatched a dwarf ninja, Ukifune Jinnai, weeks in advance to study and make

---

[4] Donn F. Draeger was martial arts coordinator in the James Bond film *You Only Live Twice*.

special preparations to assassinate his rival Kenshin. Ukifune, who stood no more than three feet tall, concealed himself in the lower recesses of the Kenshin private lavatory on the day of the entry of the other Oda ninja. He clung perilously and at great personal discomfort for hours to the unsanitary under-structure by a technique perfected by him known as *tsuchigumo*.[5] Ukifune was accustomed to cramped living: it is said that in training camp he resided in a huge earthenware jar to prepare himself for such a situation. As Kenshin squatted in observance of his daily habit, Ukifune stabbed him with a spear that entered Kenshin's anus and continued through his body until it protruded from his mouth. The screams of agony brought Kenshin's ninja to the scene. But when Danjō [Kenshin's ninja chief] and the others arrived, Kenshin was dead, and his assassin was nowhere to be seen. Ukifune had dived under the reservoir of fecal matter where he remained motionless, breathing through a tube, until Danjō and his ninja left with the lifeless body of their master. Then he quietly slipped out of the lavatory and the castle to report the deed to Oda.

This tale has been repeated in many books and is all over ninja sites on the Internet, as if it were established historical truth. It's no such thing. The source on which Draeger and Smith relied was published four years previously, in 1965; that source's source was an undated manuscript.

Other sources (well reviewed by Turnbull) suggest that Kenshin had not been well for some time. A sickness several years earlier had left him with one leg shorter than another, after which he walked with a stick. He also drank heavily: 'this chaste and vegetarian Galahad of Japan liked wine as he

---

[5] 'Ground spider', with other senses, including (in folktales) a spider-limbed monster and a race of underground dwarves.

disliked women', in the words of Tokugawa Ieyasu's biographer, A. L. Sadler. In the months before his death, an aide noted that he seemed to be getting worse by the day. A diarist recorded that he was very thin, with a pain in his chest 'like an iron ball'; and that he often threw up after eating and had to drink cold water. The symptoms suggest cancer of the stomach. In the days before his death, according to Kenshin's heir, 'an unforeseen bowel complaint took hold, and he could not recover'. The account continues: 'On the ninth day of the third month, he had a stomachache in his toilet. This unfortunately persisted until the thirteenth day when he died.' Another source says his death at the age of 49 was due to 'a great worm'. The most likely cause of death was a stroke brought on by straining to defecate, or in the words of A. L. Sadler, who had an eye for a colourful story, 'he was struck down in his lavatory with an attack of apoplexy', with absolutely nothing to back talk of a ninja assassin. In a poem found after his death, Kenshin seemed to think his life was nearing its end:

> Forty-nine years;
> One night's dream.
> A lifetime of glory;
> A cup of *sake*.

(Or in less condensed terms: 'My forty-nine years have passed like a single night's dream. The glories of my life are no more than a cup of *sake*.') No mention of an assassin in any of this.

What seems likely is that folklore filled the gap left by the death of a great man, myth replacing fact – an old Japanese equivalent of the conspiracy theories which became attached to the murder of Kennedy and the death of Princess Diana. On the question of how the elements of the myth came together, there is no definitive answer; but there are a couple of pointers. Firstly, ninjas did indeed hide in toilets, simply because toilets were among the outhouses that provided cover at night, though not *down* them. Secondly, Kenshin did suffer an 'attack' in his toilet. Linking these two facts to make a fiction seems to have occurred at least by the 18th century, because the story, minus the dwarf, is mentioned in an undated book (*Kashiwazaki Monogatari*), which was probably written in the 18th century because it is referred to in an early 19th-century record of the Tokugawa shogunate (*Tokugawa Jikki*).[6] Some time after that, folklore added in the dwarf, presumably to 'explain' how a ninja managed to hide *down*, rather than in, a toilet. But it leaves some practical problems: how does a dwarf cling to the underside of planks 'for a long time'? How could he be certain that Uesugi would come to the toilet within an hour, or however long he could remain suspended? If he dived under the shit, breathing through his scabbard, he did so to hide from curious eyes – but surely, inevitably, his scabbard would be exposed? How do Uesugi's retainers not realize where the assassin is, given that a) he was not to be seen; and b) there are no shitty footprints? Finally, how does a shit-covered dwarf sneak through a castle unnoticed?

Anyway, this was the version that Donn Draeger (now dead) and Robert Smith repeated, with embellishments, in their 1969 book, from where it escaped into the electronic ether.

Other campaigns followed Nagashino, driven by Nobunaga's need to crush rival warlords and cut the great temple of Ishiyama Hongan-ji from its network of provincial monasteries. That done, he could close in on the temple itself.

[6] Thanks to Yoshie Minami for this information.

It took 10 years, on and off. In 1580, Hongan-ji surrendered, being burned by its defenders to stop it falling into Nobunaga's hands undamaged. In today's Osaka, hardly a trace remains of the temple that once ruled here. This success ensured that the state triumphed over religious institutions, becoming an expression of Nobunaga's own conviction: as Luís Fróis had said, he 'despises the gods, the Buddhas and all other kinds of idolatry and pagan superstition'. From now on, religion would operate only with the consent of the state, rather as Russian Orthodoxy survived under Communism in the Soviet Union, or Buddhism survived in Mongolia over the same period.

There remained one enemy who had to be crushed before all Japan became one: the Takeda leader who had survived Nagashino, Takeda Katsuyori. And that campaign also involved ending the independence of Iga and Kōga and their ninja villages.

9

THE CALM BEFORE THE STORM

Always draw what you have learned while scouting, and then report it to the strategist directly in person.

Ninja instructional poem

BY THE TIME THE SURVIVING WRITTEN EVIDENCE WAS RECORDED, the ninja of Iga and Kōga had been in operation for decades, perhaps a century or more. Doing what exactly, we may ask, in the absence of contemporary documents? The answer is a great deal, because although many were no doubt land-owning samurai administering their estates, many others were ordinary, hard-working farmers. Besides doing their military training and field work, they built up medical expertise, prepared their houses for possible attack, fought far afield as ninja mercenaries, and went off on the equivalent of commando courses.

Training demanded a combination of physical and mental preparation, aims that the ninjas shared with the adepts of Shugendō, working out in the forested mountains. So, to research ninja commando training, it was to a mountain and a Shugendō adept that I turned.

I had seen Kōzō Yamada the day before, when he was taking part in the dragon god fire ceremony. Then he looked the image of the traditional adept, in white cloak, shoulder harness and little monk's hat. Now he was the image of a modern one, though prepared more for hiking than commando training: conical sunhat, dark glasses, white sweat-scarf, multi-pocketed waistcoat, backpack, heavy-duty gloves, a long machete-like knife on his belt, thick trousers, extremely serious walking boots. At 76, he looked 20 years younger, while his light voice was that of a teenager. *Shugenja*, as the Shugendō students were called, *yamabushi* and ninja – the groups all overlap – claim that Shugendō practices have magical effects. In Kōzō's case, it seemed to be true.

The knife was for what exactly?

'This is a *nata*. I use it to cut branches, and sometimes to fight bears.' He saw I believed him, and set me straight. 'We have deer and boars, which can be dangerous. Lots of snakes, particularly at this time of year. No bears.'

With host Yoshihisa driving me and Noriko, Kōzō guided us up a winding track deep into autumnal forest, where he was going to lead the way along a 'training path', a re-creation of the sort of course used by ninjas. As if on cue, a small snake writhed away through the fallen leaves. He picked it up and held it out to me. 'It's harmless. The only one you have to look out for is the *mamushi*. If you get bitten, you have to get an injection, or you may die.' Snakes, in the words of Indiana Jones, why did it have to be snakes? I looked at my track shoes, compared them to his calf-length boots, and wondered how long it would take to get me injected. Luckily, until I checked up later on Wikipedia, I didn't know that every year some 2,000 to 3,000 people get bitten by *mamushi*, a sort of pit viper, of whom 10 die. Nor did I know that the *mamushi* is the same species I had taken care to avoid a couple of years before in the little island of Amami Oshima, where they call it a *habu*. So, in happy ignorance, I fell in behind Kōzō, and – Jesus! There was another one, a metre long, and this one had a frog in its mouth. 'Harmless,' he said again, but it did leave me wondering about the significance of snakes in Shugendō-ninja training regimes.

This, he said, was where Kōga's ninja training started, here on Hando mountain. There were two others nearby, Iwao (where they had held the fire ceremony) and Koshin, but this was his choice, because this was where the founder of Shugendō, En no, came to train in the early eighth century (though the same claim is made for the Forty-eight Waterfalls; adepts say he jumped from that one to this, among others).

Though all around was greenery and silence, this had once been open and crowded. The undergrowth blanketed the shapes of ancient walls, the remains of a Buddhist temple, Hando-ji, a place of dozens, perhaps as many as 50 buildings, with several hundred priests. Kōzō told its story, leading the way to a platform with a view out over the valley below. With the mountain opened up by En no and his trainees, the temple was built in 740, just before the emperor decided to create a new capital down there, in Shigaraki. He pointed out a small town, now famous for its ceramics. I had come that way into Kōga, driving past ranks of the Japanese equivalents of garden gnomes – owls, frogs, and super-cute opossum-like *tanukis*.

'So when work started on the new palace, the officials were pleased to discover that this temple was already here, stopping evil spirits coming into the new capital from the northwest.' Shigaraki was a capital for only two or three years, when a fire (as some say) or disease convinced the court that the gods disapproved of the move, and they went back to Nara. The temple, which like most also included a Shinto shrine, stood for over 1,000 years, until the Meiji Restoration (1868), when the new government decreed that Buddhism and Shintoism should be separated. 'So the Buddhist buildings were knocked down, leaving only the Shinto shrine. You will see. Would like to wear these gloves?'

'Why? Is this a Shinto tradition?'

'No,' he laughed, 'it's a difficult climb. You may need them to protect your hands.'

He led the way down a leaf-coated path, which got steeper and steeper until we had to abseil a few metres, using a chain hanging from a tree. We came to a crag, slung about with two chains. 'There's a cliff the other side,' said Kōzō. 'Very dangerous.' Well, perhaps it would have been in the old days, because the crag marked the edge of a precipice. Here ninjas and *shugenja*, their feet held by fellow-trainees, lowered themselves backwards over the abyss and 'stayed there until the fear went', as Kōzō said. Once they had built up their courage, they were supposed to climb free-style across the face of the cliff ('I did it myself when I was a boy'). Today there is a metal bar set into the rock, and the traverse is only three or four metres, but back then barefoot trainees risked death, especially as they would surely be doing this in winter, just to make sure they suffered. And at speed, as Noriko reminded me. And chanting as they went.

Ahead was another crag, this one with a hole it, through which the fitter, faster and nimbler would have dashed. Kōzō led the way up a near-vertical climb, clinging on to roots, leaving Noriko and me floundering in leaf mould in his wake. I hadn't bothered with the gloves, so my hands were sticky with pine sap and coated with soil. We emerged on the summit – more rocks sticking out of the soft ground, and another terrific view over rolling forest to distant mountains. 'That's Hiei-san,' said Kōzō. I was unfamiliar then with the use of the honorific *san* attached to a mountain, as in

Fuji-san. 'Mt Hiei,' he pressed on as he saw my blank gaze. 'You know – the mountain with the monastery Enryaku-ji, near Kyoto. The one destroyed by Nobunaga.'

I remembered: the one where 20,000 perished in the flames.

'All children are told about it in school. We call it the Enryaku-ji Incident,' said Noriko. 'This temple belonged to the same sect, the Tendai.'

'So did he come on here and destroy this as well?'

Kōzō replied, 'No, because he only destroyed those temples that opposed him.'

We stood for a while admiring the view, content in the soft autumn sun, then moved down to a nearby building, which turned out to be a Shinto shrine, the predecessor of which had been part of the old Hando temple complex. It displayed various unlikely creatures – a yellow-eyed tiger and a *kirin*, a sort of winged lion, after which the beer is named.

Kōzō, meanwhile, explained his interest in the mountain. Actually, he had been doing this on and off during our climb. This is a collated version:

Until the time of my grandfather, my ancestors were *yamabushi* – mountain ascetics – and rice-farmers, living close to this mountain, which belonged to three small communities. When my grandfather was a boy, the temple was destroyed and the mountain became overgrown. Then about 60 years ago, the mayor decided to restore the mountain and suggested that the descendants of the *yamabushi* families look after it. I started as a banker, then I worked for medical companies, before turning to farming rice, but when I retired I thought I should do some sort of community work. The founder of the Tendai sect, Saichō, said, 'Kill yourself for others', which he did not mean literally, but as 'Do your utmost to serve others before yourself.' So I decided to help with the mountain. That was when I started taking part in Shugendō ceremonies, like the one you saw yesterday, and training my body and mind on the mountain. My greatest ambition [he ended with a smile] is to achieve world peace, and my smallest is to be a good person.

It was impossible to know from his words how to separate out the slurry of religious affiliations – different Buddhist sects, Shugendō, *yamabushi*, ninja. One thing seemed clear to me. The ninjas' reputation as sinister men in black who were happy doing the dirty work for their bosses should go. They were as committed to self-improvement and doing good as their priestly fellow trainees, with the proviso that this was part of their preparation for their main military purpose, which was spying.

I went to a tree-covered hill in Iga-Ueno. On a flat space near the top is the Ninja Museum. The place is the architectural equivalent of a ninja, because it is much more than it seems at first glance. Its thatched roof and timbered rooms hide many tricks and devices and hidey-holes and hidden stairways that householders included to ensure they could vanish or fight back in case of attack: a door that pivots on a central hinge, a window that can be opened with a sliver of paper, a trapdoor and hinged floorboard that (if you know how) open to reveal swords. A model ninja, dressed rather incongruously in pink, stands on a dangling ladder, for ever about to climb into the loft. But what the house really has to offer is underground, down twilit steps made mysterious by the sounds of a howling wolf and the call of an owl. Dug into the basement is a museum devoted to ninja life.

Here are all the tools and weapons used by the shadow warriors, far more than are mentioned in the *Shoninki*: grapples and ropes and folding ladders for climbing walls, knives, picks, borers and saws for forcing ways through doors and fences, a fearsome iron claw for climbing trees and warding off swords, a knuckleduster, a sickle and chain for snaring and slicing an opponent, four-pointed caltrops that could be scattered to pierce the feet of pursuers. Swords have broad handguards that could be used to make a first step when climbing, plus a cord to pull the sword up behind you. There is even a little tube, which was supposedly used as a blowpipe to fire a poisoned dart as a means of assassination.

Most of the equipment is safely locked away in cabinets, but one item was hands-on, or rather feet-on: the *mizugumo*, a pair of wooden discs which (so they say) acted as the agricultural equivalent of snowshoes, used to cross bogs, or castle moats if they happened to be drying out. These 'mud shoes' or 'water spider' looked suspiciously new. With me was Hiromitsu Kuroi, the closest you can come to a ninja these days. Having been practising ninjutsu and teaching for 30 years, he is the inspiration behind the museum and adviser to publishers on ninja themes. One illustrated book in English, *Secrets of the Ninja*, has him on the cover and in scores of pictures inside, slaying opponents in freeze-frame.

'I have seen pictures of ninja using these to walk on water,' I said, nodding at the *mizugumo*.

'That's nonsense. You would fall over, or sink.'

'Has anyone tried them?'

'I have. They work on mud, not water.'

I can believe it, sort of. But, like much information about ninjas, it is more than possible that this 'fact' became a fact only later. There is an illustration of the 'water spider' in one of the prime sources on ninja matters, a multi-volume manuscript known as the *Bansenshūkai*, about which I would be learning much more. The drawing shows a single 'shoe', which when doubled makes a water spider like the one displayed in the museum. But take a closer look. There is no strap to hold it on the foot. How on earth are you supposed to lift it in order to walk on mud? You could of course add your own strap. But if the 'spider' was meant for walking, the artist would surely have recorded a strap. If not for walking, how might it have been used? Here's a clue: historically, 'lifebelts' were called 'water shoes'. Another clue is that the *Bansenshūkai* shows a single 'water spider'. The conclusion should be that a 'water spider' was a simple float to get across water, not mud. You either sat on the central section and used a paddle, or sat astride the central section and paddled with your feet. Now that makes sense. Water is a more common hazard than mud, and it would be much easier to carry one of the spiders rather than two.

Almost all of the tools were originally no more weapons than a kitchen knife is. Like the 'mud shoes', they were bits of farm equipment that were adapted for fighting. Perhaps this is why the *Shoninki* makes no mention of them – there's really nothing very special about them. Even the ninja 'uniform', which in popular imagination turns them into the original 'men in black' – loose jacket, loose trousers bound just below the knee, a slipper-and-sock combination with soft cotton soles, leg wraps, mask and hood – was modified peasant clothing, such as would be worn in summer, when a field-worker wished to keep mosquitoes from exposed flesh. Black seems to be a post-ninja imposition. As Hiromitsu puts it in his book: 'In fact dark blue was the colour of choice. In the bright moonlight, black stands out like a sore thumb.'

One type of weapon, the *shuriken* or throwing-star, is both well known and problematical. Made in all sorts of shapes, from simple crosses to many-pointed stars, they are undoubtedly fun to use, because almost any throw at a wooden target gets them to stick in with a satisfying smack. And they would undoubtedly cause a nasty cut in exposed flesh. But they are puzzling things. You cannot sheath them, except by putting them in a bag. But imagine reaching into the bag, especially in the dark, while fighting – wouldn't you risk cutting your fingers? Was it worth the trouble, for a weapon that, as Hiromitsu admitted, 'did not have the power to kill, or even do much harm'? Some claim that they were smeared with poison; but that surely would make them even more dangerous to the user?

Frankly, when delving into the historical realities of the ninja, there is a problem with authenticity. Purists may be surprised to discover that there is not a single authentic tool or weapon in the museum. All were made recently. Should this bother us? The arguments for and against have many buts. Some of the designs were recorded, but only after the heyday of the ninjas; but not *that* long after.

One other example to 'but' at: the ninja museum (and countless books) insist that one of the ninjas' secrets was to tell the time of day by checking the eyes of a cat, because the pupils dilate and contract with the changing light: narrow at midday, wide at dusk. For a moment, the 'cat's-eye clock' sounds resourceful. But give the matter a moment's thought. Firstly, of *course* a cat's eyes dilate and contract with the changing light. *All* eyes do. You might as well tell the time by staring into a mirror. Secondly, do you really need a cat to tell you the time of day? Thirdly, the amount of light and thus the size of the cat's pupil depends not only on the time of day but also on the season and the weather. And once you spot your cat, how on earth do you get close enough to get a good look at its eyes? The more you think about it, the sillier it gets.

Noriko also planted doubts about the significance of the so-called anti-ninja 'nightingale' floors, made of teak boards that squeak when you walk on them. Just south of Kyoto's Nijo castle are the remains of the older Imperial Palace, a house known as Nijo-jinya, which (in the words of the *Rough Guide*) offers 'a thrilling glimpse into a treacherous world – the seemingly ordinary house riddled with trap doors, false walls and ceilings, "nightingale" floors, escape hatches, disguised staircases and confusing dead ends to trap intruders'. Elsewhere, too, 'nightingale' floors are part of the standard tour-guide spiel. Wikipedia says that 'these floors were designed so that the flooring nails rubbed against a jacket or clamp, causing chirping noises. The squeaking floors were used as a security device, assuring that none could sneak through the corridors undetected.'

Not so fast. The *Shoninki* makes no mention of them. When I was in the Tofuku-ji temple in Kyoto with Noriko, we walked over 'nightingale' floors by the acre. 'They say the squeaking wood is to deter assassins, but it's not true,' said Noriko. 'All corridors made of this certain wood over 30 years old squeak like this. My house corridor makes the same noise.' That set me wondering: Why 'nightingale'? The sound is nothing like nightingales, more like armies of mice being squashed beneath one's feet. In fact, the Japanese bird (*uguisu*) is not a nightingale but a bush warbler, traditionally the herald of spring. The translation was coined by the English in the 19th century, simply because both birds sing. So let us consider spoiling a good story by inverting it: the floors squeak naturally, but when the rich started to build ninja-proof houses, ordinary folk, impressed by their ingenuity, granted them even more of it, by giving them credit for an entirely natural effect. Teak floors sang before ninjas walked.

In the 16th century, while the rest of Japan fought itself to exhaustion, the two neighbours, Iga and Kōga, shared similar social systems, family connections and ways of cooperation. With their councils and contracts, they were remarkable little semi-democracies (sort of: as in ancient Athens, only the top men counted; women and servants didn't). They were also capable of operating outside their own borders, designating

10 top men from Iga and 12 from Kōga to meet up on the frontier to sort out the problems between them.

That's the positive view of the two provinces: peace-loving communities inching towards democracy. But there is reason to think that this was an uncertain process, because both communities were also riven by petty feuds. Iga's 300–500 little estates and the 53 families of Kōga squabbled endlessly, and it was in these petty struggles that both sides developed the skills that would make them famous.

Everyone, for instance, built for defence. You can see the results today in the ninja houses that are tourist attractions in both Iga and Kōga. We have seen Iga's with its museum, but of the two, Kōga's claims to be the more authentic.

Kōga's ninja house, which according to its PR material claims to be the 'only genuine historical building of its kind', is a fine old place of dark wood, thatch and undulating grey tiles, full of shadowy corners and steep stairways and secretive nooks and cabinets of curiosities, all evoking the vanished world of the ninjas.

For visitors, first comes a sort of a stage show, in which Hukui Minogu, a gnome-ish old man with flyaway hair and astonishing energy, explains the devices used by houseowners to trick their way out of danger, some similar to Iga's, some unique. 'Here is a steel door, sealing off a *kura*, a storage area, which has an iron ceiling so no one can cut their way in from above, with clay walls to keep it cool and make sure it cannot burn. Lots of houses had *kura*. When Tokyo was firebombed in the war, it was the *kura* that survived. Try this door. It's really heavy. You would think it was locked, wouldn't you? So would an attacker. He would just give up. But the family know that they can move it, if they really try. Go on, *push*. You see? This window – it's got a secret catch, which you can open by sliding a piece of paper or a leaf into the frame. You slam the window, like this, and the catch falls into place.

Look at this doorway. You can escape through it, and inside there's a ladder leading up, but also a false floor, so the owner can vanish. If someone follows, they see nothing but the ladder, so he will climb. See this pit? It's got water in now, because people stopped using the wells and the watertable has risen, but down there is a tunnel that leads to next door. The wire net? Oh, that's not to catch visitors. It's there because a cat fell in there once.'

But there's something odd about this house, with its array of tricks and devices. I would never have known without the guidance of Toshinobu Watanabe, the lean, fit professorial type who was chairman of the Koka History Study Group. There is something about ninja blood and ninja studies that keeps their ageing followers in terrific health and full of youthful enthusiasm. Toshinobu pointed out that the house dates from the Edo period, the late 17th century, after the heyday of the ninja. The owner of the house, Mochizuki Izumonkami, had another reason for building these defences. His family had been in the area for centuries, and had become experts as medical practitioners. The eldest son of an eldest son, and the leader of Kōga's 53 top families, Mochizuki had inherited the business, and built the house as a place to make medicines, founding what would become the Omi Medical Company. In fact, until 50 years ago, the house was not called a ninja house at all, but 'the medical company's house'. Hence some of its major features: the *kura*, the roofless kitchen, which allowed the smoke to rise into the loft, where plants were hung for curing. All his information was top secret. In modern terms, he was nervous of industrial espionage, and for that reason adapted old ninja devices for his own purposes. And, though surely no single ninja house had so many tricks, each of them was indeed authentic.

The ninja house in Iga is similar, if you remember – a revolving door and pits here, retractable ladders and hidden weapons there. But this house was an amalgam, built in the early 19th century and then rebuilt on its present site, on a wooded hill near the centre of town, in the 1990s, with several of the secret devices being added even later. So, to the quiet satisfaction of today's Kōga Study Group, the Iga designers came to Kōga to get ideas for their ninja house.

So both in their different ways lack authenticity. It doesn't really matter. The display cases and the houses themselves distil the reality of pre-1581 ninja life, which was mostly that of farmers anywhere. The peasants who learned to fight back against bandits in *The Seven Samurai*, and its Western version *The Magnificent Seven*, were ninjas in the making.

There was more to the ninjas than farmers who fought. Each was linked into his local community, and each community to its neighbour, making a network of self-defence forces determined to preserve themselves against each other, and then against a world of ambitious lords and marauding armies. What use were ninja skills and secret home defences if your house was burned and your family captured, scattered or killed? You needed somewhere to gather as a group for protection, where food and weapons could be assembled in safety. What you needed was a fort, or two, or three.

We're not talking castles, like the restored ones that stand today all over Japan, with bases of dressed stone and intricate wooden towers and tiled roofs. The local forts of Iga and Kōga were mostly banks of earth around yards, with an entrance, but nothing in the way of towers or stockades. Toshinobu Watanabe was my guide to this little-known subject, which reveals some intriguing details about the nature of ninja society. There are some 500 valleys in Kōga, he said as we arrived at a reservoir flanked by a clump of trees. 'In those days each valley had a village or two. We think there were two to three hundred samurai families, no one knows for sure, but we do know that there were fifty-three strong families. All these top families had at least one fort, and so did many of the other families. This is a typical one, under the trees over there.'

He led the way into the trees, and up a slope kept clear of undergrowth to allow access to archaeologists and local schoolchildren. There, like the body of a giant under a blanket, were the contoured limbs of something the shape of which was impossible to make out. Mounds, ridges, dips and flat areas made a complex of storage places and passageways and walls, all sprouting trees and disguised by a blanket of fallen leaves. Toshinobu tried to make sense of it for me.

Murasame, as the fort was called, had been a natural mound, rising above a valley, where a stream had run, now all drowned by the reservoir. Then, up the slope, the mound had been reshaped, with courtyards a few metres across being excavated and the soil being thrown up to make walls – 'only earth walls, no roof, not even any wooden defences on top of the walls. This was a place for the *bushi* – the warriors – to gather in case of attack. The women and children would have run away to hide.' Here was an entrance, with a steep curving approach; here a narrow passageway, like a large ditch – 'we think this was where warriors could hide'; here what might have been a storage area for weapons and food.

Then, as we walked northwards along the outer wall, the one that rose out of the reservoir, the ground dropped to what could have been a moat, except that we were well above the valley floor. 'No, this was a division between this fort and the next.' Two forts, right next door to each other? Yes, 'and they were both used at the same time'. The second, Jizen, had probably been a secondary defence, so defenders could retreat from one to the other. This one was smaller, 60 metres across, with its own maze of entrance, courtyards and enigmatic dips and bumps.

Later, from a high point over a motorway, the whole valley lay open. Toshinobu pointed to a clump of trees a kilometre away, then another. In fact, within this one small area there were no less than seven 'castle mounds', none of them more than a few hundred metres from its neighbour. The same pattern holds true for the whole of Kōga. Archaeologists have recorded 180 forts; and many more must have vanished, washed away, or been reclaimed by farmers.

'These places were not for long-term occupation,' said Toshinobu. 'One or two had wells, some had a little pond for water, but on the whole, they seem to have been built to be used for only a few days.'

I wondered what this told us about Kōga's society. How many people were involved? How many ninjas per village? It matters, because on this basis it should be possible to calculate the numbers the province could muster to repel the great invasions that were to come in 1579–81. 'It's very difficult to know. Before the unification of Japan in 1600, there was no clear ranking system separating samurai, farmers, craftsmen and businessmen. A farmer was a part-time soldier, and in the evening he would become a craftsman, and sometimes he would travel to sell his produce.'

But wait. Surely you could do a time-and-motion study, based on the size of the forts, and the weight of the soil? What would it have taken to make forts like this? Not all that much. An archaeological plan records some 750 metres of walls. Say the average height was three metres, the average width two metres. That makes about 6,750 tonnes of earth. A man can shift 4.5 tonnes a day,[1] working flat out. So these two forts could have been made in a month by 50 men, in two weeks with 100. I imagined farming communities of 500 or

---

[1] Quantity surveyors assume that the average man can move 1 cubic metre of earth (1.5 tonnes) in 2.7 hours, or about 4.5 tonnes in 8 hours.

so cooperating to make and maintain two or three forts each, where the men, and perhaps their families, could take refuge in the event of an attack; which would come from no formidable army, but small-scale forces of some warlord looking for easy pickings. I started to do sums: 300 villages, 500 people each, total population 150,000, of which say 100 *bushi* per village: 30,000 warriors . . .

Well, perhaps. Toshinobu was sceptical. 'What we do not know, and there is no way of knowing, is the proportion of *bushi* per village. All the men could have been part-time fighters, or they could have had a lot of servants. We are just now starting this sort of research.'

Farmers with growing skills as ninjas needed more than fighting skills. As important was the acquisition of information by travelling widely without being noticed. To do this the ninjas would join the 'the wandering world', those who could travel without automatically raising the suspicion of officials. But to do so, the ninja had to fit in seamlessly as puppeteer, juggler, musician, storyteller, peddler – or, most commonly, as a pilgrim *yamabushi*. Nobody had a better reason to travel or was more sure of a good reception, because, as a pilgrim, he was always on the move from temple to temple.

Just outside the Forty-eight Waterfalls is a temple, the only one to be rebuilt of the eight that were burned when the ninjas were destroyed. It was in remarkably good shape: tilted eaves, intricately carved roof joists and beamed walls standing on a wooden platform, with several small buildings and a little shrine from which En no, the founder of Shugendō and thus the temple's founding father, glared out of the shadows, the whites of his eyes and teeth startling against remarkably black skin. A square arch with its upturned cross-piece married this Buddhist temple to its predecessor, Shintoism. The priest appeared, clothed not in an elegant loose robe but in a

Mickey Mouse T-shirt and shorts. He was in a hurry, couldn't speak for more than a minute or two, but then spoke for 20, the gist of which was that all the eight temples were part of a Pilgrims' Way of 88 temples, centres not only for pilgrims, but also travellers, monks, entertainers, vagabonds, all the chaotic elements that made up medieval life, everyone bringing news and rumours from foreign parts, all therefore part of the wild elements that Oda Nobunaga was keen to control. That was why he hated the Tendai sect. That was why he burned all the temples. Which, as I was to discover later, was a somewhat simplified version of the truth. What better way for a ninja to discover what was happening in the wide world than by pretending to be or actually becoming a travelling *yamabushi*?

Or perhaps even a painter or a poet? Such men were free to travel where they wanted. They even say that one of Iga's most famous sons, the master Bashō, was a ninja. Matsuo Bashō, as every Japanese child knows, was a master of the haiku, with its three-line, approximately 5-7-5-syllable structure, its subtle references to a season and its enigmatic nature. (As Bashō put it: 'Is there any good in saying everything?') He was born in what is now Iga-Ueno, where there is a museum devoted to him, but he was always wandering, making his way mysteriously without any obvious means of support. 'Who was paying him to travel round on his own in the guise of a simple peasant?' Noriko wondered. 'How come he had so many connections? How come he could stay in nice places? He would stare and stare, then always wrote about something really obscure. People were suspicious. They said he must be hiding something. Perhaps he was paid by some lord to report everything he saw. That was why he was so well off without ever earning any money. That's why they say he must have been a ninja.'

But he lived and died in the 17th century, when no one needed ninjas any more, so I think it's fair to ask –

Bashō the master
of enigmatic haikus
– a ninja or not?

By the mid-16th century, the ninjas of Iga and Kōga found their services in demand right across Japan. Thirty-seven areas are known to have employed ninjas from Iga and Kōga (as well as training their own). The following are typical examples of many incidents and raids employing mercenary ninjas from the heartland, untypical only in that they were well recorded, providing proof that the ninjas were working for hire, with no inherited loyalty to the lords involved.

In two raids[2] which took place in 1559 and 1561, roughly when Iga's leaders were updating their contract, ninjas operated both for and then against the same commander, scion of that famous family the Rokkaku, whose castle had been seized by the shogun, with ninja help, a century before (see p. 93).

In the first episode, the Rokkaku clan have been betrayed by a retainer with the name of Dodo, who had seized a castle about 40 kilometres north of Kōga on the shore of Lake Biwa. Rokkaku Yoshikata, the head of the family, determined to seize it back, but after several days without success he sent for an Iga ninja, Tateoka Dōshun. Tateoka, much impressed by a diviner who predicted imminent success, arrived with a team of 44 other ninjas from Iga and four from Kōga. Tateoka tricked an entry by stealing a lantern with Dodo's crest on it, copied it several times, and simply led his team through the gate pretending to be Dodo's men. Inside, his men set the castle on fire, Rokkaku attacked, and won the day.

[2] Both summarized by Zoughari and Turnbull, based on Japanese sources.

It happened that the Rokkaku clan were great rivals with their neighbour, Asai Nagamasa. The two families had feuded for three generations. Rokkaku Yoshikata had seized a castle, Futō, also on Lake Biwa, just 10 kilometres north of the one retaken from Dodo. In 1561, Asai resolved to take it back. He hired two generals, who in their turn contracted three Iga ninjas to plan a night attack. According to the plan, when the castle was ablaze, the two conventional assaults would follow. It all went horribly wrong, as the senior general, Imai Kenroku, saw with dismay from his hilltop HQ. There was no night attack from the ninjas, no blazing castle. But Imai ordered – or allowed – his troops to advance anyway. When he complained about the delay to the ninja commander, Wakasa no Kami, Wakasa sent a scathing reply: why hadn't Imai waited for the signal, which was the castle on fire? OK, it wasn't on fire yet. The ninjas couldn't be expected to explain their every move. They were a law unto themselves and 'a samurai from north of Lake Biwa could not understand ninja tactics'. All was not lost. The thing to do now was for Imai to tell his troops to withdraw for an hour, and allow time for the ninjas to attack, and set the castle ablaze, and then Imai could order the conventional assault; and if he didn't like it, the ninjas would pack up and go home. Imai agreed – but failed to brief his fellow general, Isono Tamba no Kami. As Imai's men withdrew, they came up against Isono's men, who assumed they were under attack. The result was a classic 'friendly fire' incident. One of Isono's samurais, eager to be first into battle, charged Imai, who was facing his own men, presumably trying to restore order, and speared him in the back. Imai's force retaliated. Twenty men died before order was restored. Meanwhile, the ninjas had done their job (though no one recorded how). The castle was at last on fire. Isono, having regained control, refocused his men, followed through on the assault and retook the castle, snatching victory from the jaws of what might have been a total disaster.

So it was that the Rokkakus regained a castle, thanks to the Iga and Kōga ninjas, then lost another, also thanks to ninjas from the same areas.

10

THE END OF THE OLD NINJAS

If the camp is the subject of a night attack or an infiltration by an enemy ninja, you should judge that it is the fault of your own men.

Ninja instructional poem

IN THE MID-16TH CENTURY, WHILE MUCH OF THE REST OF JAPAN fought, the ninjas of Iga and Kōga were doing very well for themselves. But the longer they proved successful, the greater the challenge for any leader aiming to build a nation. What of the authority of the emperor and of his deputy the shogun if local ninja communes kept on asserting their independence? Nobunaga, fighting his way to national unity, could never tolerate them. One day, the storm would break.

The first hint of trouble came from Iga's neighbour to the east, from the province of Ise, the site of Japan's holiest shrines. So far, this part of Japan – Kōga, Iga, Ise – had escaped the violence unleashed by Oda Nobunaga's rise. In the words of Ueda Masaru, the old man who kept a dozen ninja suits of armour in his attic: Iga, with its 300 or so strong communities, 'was like the eye of a typhoon, with winds raging all around the outside, and a still point in the centre'. That was about to change, because Ise was controlled by a certain Kitabatake Tomonori, a former governor who had built himself up as a warlord.

Ambitious to extend his mini-empire by taking Iga, he had commissioned a castle in the middle of Iga, on a hill called Maruyama. Such ambitions brought him to the attention of Oda Nobunaga. As part of his campaign to unify Japan, Oda seized two castles in Ise and sent his second son, Nobuo, to become the adopted son of Kitabatake. This was not an offer Kitabatake could refuse, but it was also in effect a takeover. When in 1576, Kitabatake died – murdered, so it was said – Oda Nobuo inherited Ise. Understandably, other Kitabatake family members objected, and revolted. Nobuo crushed the uprising, but the rebels fled into Iga, and appealed for help to one of Oda's greatest opponents, Mōri Motonari. To forestall him, Nobuo had to take Iga, so in early 1579 he ordered his troops into the castle at Maruyama, the one left empty and unfinished by his adoptive father. The local Iga commanders saw the danger, and took pre-emptive action. They knew exactly what to do, because their ninja spies were acting as labourers in the castle. They 'forced their way into Maruyama, and the keep, the towers, the palace and so on all went up in smoke. They demolished the gates and the walls until nothing remained in any direction' (today a memorial stands on the spot).[1]

When the survivors reported what had happened, Oda Nobuo was so appalled he wanted to attack immediately.

---

[1] This, like all the quotes in this chapter, is from Momochi Orinosuke, *Kōsei Iran-ki* (Ueno, 1897), translated by Turnbull, in his *Ninja*, with thanks.

Some of his officials advised restraint, reminding him that 'from ancient times the honour of the Iga warriors has delighted in a strong army. Because they are not imbued with ordinary motives, they take no notice of death, and are dare-devils when they confront enemies. They neither experience failure, nor allow for it, which would be an eternal disgrace.' But the survivors included Nobuo's humiliated commander, Takigawa Saburōhei, much to the dismay of the Iga men: 'a mortifying situation,' they said, 'and a very sad affair.' Takigawa insisted on instant action, and Nobuo backed him, with disastrous consequences.

Nobuo's three-pronged invasion, with some 12,000 troops, came in mid-September through the three main passes of Iga's eastern mountains. Oda Nobuo led one column along the main east–west road between Iga-Ueno and the coast. 'Ten thousand banners fluttered in the autumn breeze, and the sun's rays were reflected off the colours of armour and *sashimono* [the banners attached to the soldiers' backs].' Having camped overnight, Nobuo's troops woke in fog, and pushed on through 'the steep and gloomy valley' towards the village of Iseji, right into the arms of the waiting Iga warriors:

> They had established strong-points, and fired bows and guns, and taking swords and spears fought shoulder to shoulder. They cornered the enemy and cut them down at the entrance to the rocky valleys. The army of Nobuo were so preoccupied with the attack that they lost direction, and the Iga men, hidden in the western shadows on the mountain, overwhelmed them easily. Then it began to rain, and they could not see the road. The Iga warriors took the opportunity, and aware of the others lurking in the mountain, raised their war-cry. The band of provincial samurai, hearing the signal, quickly gathered from all sides and attacked. The Ise samurai were confused in the gloom and dispersed in all directions. They

ran and were cut down in the secluded valley or on the steep rocks. They chased them into the muddy rice fields and surrounded them . . . The enemy army collapsed. Some killed each other by mistake. Others committed suicide. It is not known how many thousands were killed.

Nobuo's second column, coming through a pass to the south, met the same fate, with one special prize. Riding with the column was the general who had supposedly murdered Kitabatake Tomonori. In the late afternoon, he was surrounded by several hundred soldiers and stabbed to death, the victorious Iga men withdrawing into a misty, moonlit night. The third column, too, was ambushed, cut off and destroyed – in Turnbull's words, 'the end of one of the most dramatic triumphs of unconventional warfare over traditional samurai tactics in the whole of Japanese history'.

An end; but also the beginning of something far more destructive for Iga, Kōga and their ninja fighters.

Twice bitten, twice humiliated: two years later, Oda Nobuo was humiliated a third time, by his own father. 'It was a mistake to go to the boundaries of Iga, and an extreme one,' he said, as terrible as it would be if the sun and moon were to fall to earth. It was unpardonable that Nobuo should have allowed a general to be killed. Obviously, wrote Nobunaga, as if trying to find some mitigating circumstance, Nobuo's 'youthful vigour' had led him astray. His error had been not to use ninjas, he went on, urging his son to go back to basics. Remember Sun Zi! 'To break into an enemy's province which is skilfully defended inside and out a strategy should be devised in a secret meeting place. It is essential to get to know the weak points in the enemy's rear. When war is established, get *shinobi* [ninjas] or treacherous samurai prepared. This one action alone will gain you a victory.'

He knew what he was talking about. Two 'treacherous samurai' from northeast Iga had just presented themselves to him, offering to act as guides should Nobunaga decide on a revenge attack. They suggested a main assault through Kōga, because the mountains there were less formidable than elsewhere. Nobunaga's HQ would be his own castle, Azuchi, on the eastern side of Lake Biwa – a glorious seven-storey structure with the top two floors inside a unique octagonal tower (nothing remains of it now except a stone base; it was burned in 1582). It lay just 30 kilometres from Iga's border. He did not intend to repeat his son's mistakes: he would lead the assault from the north, but there would be five other columns driving into Iga from the north, east and west, avoiding only the impenetrable southern mountains – impenetrable to him, but not so to the ninjas of Iga. And his invasion would muster not 12,000 men but 44,300, almost four times the force led so disastrously by his son. As it happened, when the campaign opened in August 1581, he was struck by some sickness. Sweaty and dizzy, he pulled back to Azuchi to recover.

A month later, he was fit enough to rail against Iga's democratic ways, in words that sum up precisely why Iga's culture had been so successful, and (it seems now, with the advantage of hindsight) so charming:

> The Iga rebels grow daily more extravagant and presumptuous, exhausting our patience. They make no distinction between high and low, rich and poor, all of whom are part of carrying out this outrageous business. Such behaviour is a mystery to me, for they go so far as to make light of rank, and have no respect for high ranking officials. They practise disobedience, and dishonour both my name and ancient Court and military practices. Because they have rebelled against the government, we find them guilty, and will

punish the various families. So let us hurriedly depart for Iga, and bring the punishment to bear.

Iga. This is all to do with Iga. It was Iga that was the focus of Nobuo's ire, Iga that he attacked, Iga that became Oda Nobunaga's target. Why not Kōga, which was equally egalitarian, equally without respect for high-ranking officials, and one would think equally targeted by Nobunaga? Lacking any documentary answer to the question, I put it to the half-dozen local historians who formed the Koka Study Group.

It was clear from Oda's words that there was more to his ruthlessness than a mere desire to avenge the humiliation dealt to his son and the death of a general. Iga's whole way of life was an affront and a challenge. As a future unifier of his nation, he would never tolerate people who refused to allow for large-scale landowners and insisted on the right to govern themselves. That's what they believe in Iga, as I understood it: it was because they were a democracy that he didn't like them. On top of that, they were followers of Tendai Buddhism, and Oda was pro-Christian, so he hated them.

'It's a big lie!' That was the gently spoken Toshinobu, in surprisingly forceful English. He had a rich but long-dormant academic knowledge of the language, which ventured out of hibernation when he wanted to make a point. He hesitated, opted for speed, and went on in Japanese: 'There are more Tendai shrines in Kōga than in Iga, so it was nothing to do with being Tendai. And actually, Oda didn't hate democracy. The reason he attacked Iga and did not attack Kōga was that Kōga decided to work with him.'

What happened was this. The head of the Saji family, one of Kōga's 53 top families, contacted Oda and said he didn't know about the others, but he for one was willing to work with him. That planted the idea of cooperation. So when the others came to discuss it, there was a precedent.

'But why did he do that in the first place?' I asked.

'Because when Nobuo attacked Iga in 1579, Iga unfortunately won, so they thought they would win again. They did not see the real power of Oda's troops. Nobuo also attacked Kōga, and Kōga lost. Saji could see the future, he could see how powerful the enemy was. So when Oda asked if we would cooperate, we said yes. We also had the idea of not wasting our lives in the face of overwhelming odds.'

Which was, of course, an idea fundamental to ninjas: survival, rather than samurai-style self-sacrifice.

'So you were better ninjas than Iga!' I said, to guffaws of laughter. Iga and Kōga may have shared similar systems, and collaborated to solve mutual problems, and intermarried, but here was a hint of friendly rivalry.

It wasn't quite as clear-cut as that, because the two groups had been so close in the past. There were some who refused to collaborate with Nobunaga and joined Iga instead:

An inhabitant of Kōga, Mochizuki Chotarō, was a soldier big and strong, and a hot-blooded warrior. He had a large *tachi* [a long, curved sword], which he brandished crosswise as he fought. One person . . . advanced to meet Chotarō to cross swords with him. Chotarō accepted the challenge, and advanced to kill him. He [Chotarō] parried the swordstroke, and then suddenly struck at him and broke both his legs. He [Chotarō] killed him without hesitation. He was a splendid master of the Way of the Sword, the model and example of all the samurai in the province.

But one or two Kōga men fighting for Iga does not undermine the main point, on which Toshinobu and his fellow historians agreed. Oda Nobunaga's attitude towards Iga 'was completely different than towards Kōga' – with consequences that almost stopped Oda's revolution in its tracks, as we shall see in due course.

Meanwhile, Iga bore the brunt of Nobunaga's anger. This time, there would be no mistakes, and no mercy. Nobuo, given a chance to avenge the disaster of two years before, commanded a 10,000-strong column that entered Iga along the same route as before, down the Aoyama (Blue or Green[2] Mountain) river, except now his force was three times the size. He reached the village of Iseji unmolested, and 'burned people's houses to the ground'. A few kilometres to the north, where Nobuo's army had been slaughtered two years before, they burned a monastery, a 'sad and sacred place . . . when the smoke died down, inside and outside were dyed with blood. The corpses of priests and laymen were piled high in the courtyard or lay scattered like strange autumn leaves lying deep of a morning.' Further on down the valley, three warriors 'put to the sword their ten children and their wives, and set off with light hearts to be killed in action, knowing that their wives and children would have been captured alive and carried off'.

The Iga defenders, meanwhile, saw they had no chance of repeating their success of two years before. They had gathered their forces in the middle of Ueno village (what is now Iga-Ueno) and eight kilometres to the south, near Maruyama. Unable to oppose such overwhelming odds, they scattered into the earthen forts that served as defences in every village.

The campaign was all over very fast, in either two weeks or

[2] Oddly for English-speakers, both Chinese and Japanese *kanji* use the same sign 青 for 'blue' and 'green' (Chinese: *qīng*, Japanese: *sei* in Sino-Japanese, *ao* in Japanese). In the Inner Mongolian capital, Huhot (from Kökh-Khot, Mongolian for 'Blue City'), Chinese sometimes insist that it means 'Green City'.

a month – sources vary. The end came in two places. The first was a castle on Hijayama, a hill that was part of a long tree-covered ridge a few kilometres west of today's Iga-Ueno, beyond the rice fields that once formed the floodplain of the Nabari river. Noriko and I took a cab there one morning to check if there was anything worth seeing. The place is not well known nowadays. The cab driver had never heard of it. But a priest in long-sleeved white shirt and grey trousers pointed us towards a temple named Sai-ren, 'West Lotus', the lotus being of great significance in Buddhism. Nearby, two grim Buddhist statues guarded a flight of steps against demons. At the top was an imposing, well-kept building, with an astonishingly large cemetery – a dozen platforms, making several hectares, with thousands of graves. But why here? Another priest, almost catatonic with age and deafness, responded at last to Noriko's shouted questions: yes, the hill behind the cemetery was Hijayama, and this was where the fort had been. A pillar confirmed it, commemorating the 400th anniversary of the campaign known as Iga no Ran, 'the Iga Revolt'.

The Iga defenders put up a terrific fight, some defending the fort, others setting up an ambush below it, allowing Nobunaga's forces to advance uphill, then attacking from behind earthworks with swords and guns, and throwing rocks and branches. For a while, it worked. As the garrison recorded,[3] 'today the reputation of our army binds us all together in joy when we consider the bravery of our soldiers'. The bravest of the brave were nominated as the Seven Spears of Hijayama, and a decision was made for a night attack that would end in the taking of the general's head, 'which will be amazing to the eyes of the enemy and will add to the glory of the province'.

[3] The quotes are from Turnbull, translated from *Iran-ki*.

Early on 1 October, as the attack opened, Nobunaga's forces 'raised an uproar like a kettle coming to the boil, and, as might be expected, in the army many otherwise experienced and brave soldiers had no time to put their armour on and tied it round their waists. They grabbed swords and spears, went down in haste and stood there to fight desperately.' Then, all became chaos, because 'an intense mountain wind quickly extinguished many of the pine torches, and friend and foe alike went astray in the dark paths. They could not distinguish between friend and foe in the direction of their arrows, so the samurai of the province [i.e. the Iga warriors] made their way by using passwords, while the enemy furiously killed each other by mistake.'

It was no use. With 30,000 ranged against them, the Iga men retreated into Hijayama. 'On top of the mountain there was silence. They did not give a war-cry. More and more their colour faded. The tide of war was moving to the enemy samurai. They took great rocks and large trees carefully, and waited for an attack . . . Each man who remained had the appearance of a wooden Buddha.' In the end, the weather was against them. It was dry, with a strong wind which favoured fire. Nobunaga's men set fire to local temples, which spread to the whole complex. 'The flames blazed and were seen in the sky like an omen. The inferno eventually died out, but it was many months before the black ashes disappeared.'

The last stand came in the south, where the ninjas had their backs to the wall of mountains from which flowed the old Shugendō training ground of the Forty-eight Waterfalls. A few kilometres north of here stood Kashihara[4] castle, which today is, like so many old forts, a tree-covered mound. Once, it was the centre of a little community: castle, lord's house,

---

[4] Also spelled Kashiwara, even Kashiwahara. Confusingly there is another Kashihara 15 kilometres to the west.

Shinto shrine. There's still an active shrine, built and rebuilt over centuries to honour the souls of those who lived and died here. Today's version, with its simple grey-tiled roof with no turned-up eaves and a porch, looks more like a house than a temple.

'A *shrine*.' Noriko corrected me. 'A Shinto *shrine*. Buddhism has *temples*.'

'OK. What's Shinto about it?'

'The stone columns.'

On the porch were two little towers of flat stones, half a dozen stone memorials, two stone lanterns and two vases of fresh flowers: this was a well-kept working shrine. Working in more ways than one. Inside was a room of historical memorabilia, where I knelt shoeless and with painful knee-joints while the mayor, Tomimori Kazuya, explained Kashihara's significance as the place where the Iga Revolt was finally crushed.

The local hero is the lord at the time of the revolt, Takino Jurobei. Tomimori led the way out of the shrine, uphill towards the castle mound, along a path edged by an electric fence between two rice fields. In one, a man wearing remarkably thick clothing – boots, jacket, hat with ear flaps – was cutting rice flattened by the recent typhoon. 'Be careful of the fence,' said Tomimori. 'It's live, to keep the animals out.'

We reached the edge of the castle mound and its thick covering of trees. Behind the mound was a proper hill, the Dragon God Mountain. Why not build up there, I wondered. No, that was too far and too high. The mound in front of us was perfect: raised above the valley floor, with a good view, and protected on the other side by the mountain. But of the castle there was nothing visible beneath the covering of trees. Could we explore further? Well, as long as we remembered it was the time for the *mamushi*, the pit viper, to lay their eggs. Tomimori led the way over a ditch along a path at the base of a steep bank, while to our left the ground fell away. A wall, no doubt, and perhaps the remains of a moat. It was all earth now, rich with spiders and for all I knew *mamushi*. Was it earth back then? Yes, all earth, said Tomimori, no stones, no solid foundations, no roofs.

That made sense of the story Tomimori told about Lord Takino and the castle beside which we were now wandering, brushing away spiders' webs, scuffing through fallen leaves, wary of *mamushi*. Surrounded by Nobunaga's forces, Takino was besieged, along with his three top officers, Momochi Sandayu, Hattori Hanzō and Nagato no Kami. (Of Nagato, little is known, but the other two are famous. Momochi had a house nearby, which still exists, along with his descendants; and Hattori Hanzō, whose house and castle were a few kilometres west of Iga, was soon to become the staunchest ally of Nobunaga's heir.)

After a few days, Takino used a tactic first tried by the great 14th-century general Kusunoki Masashige. One dark night, when clouds hid the moon and stars, he ordered women and children to join the men in lighting two or three torches each. 'It gave the impression there were more than a thousand in here, but the cloud disappeared, and the moon came out, and Nobunaga's troops could clearly see just how many were holding the torches. Then, as conditions got worse and food low, he had his people use grinding stones to give the impression they had more than enough food.'

Meanwhile, Takino found other ways to fight back, as a contemporary source describes:

From the skilled men of Iga, twenty men who had mastered *shinobi no jutsu* [the art of being a *shinobi*, or ninja] set fire to various places outside the castle and reconnoitred among the smouldering camp fires. Night after night they made frequent excursions in secret, and made night raids on the camps of all the generals and set fire to them using various tactics . . . Over a hundred men were killed, and because of this the enemy were placed in fear and trembling. Their alertness decreased because they could not rest at all.

It was no use. There was no way to win. Takino surrendered the fort, and fled with his officers and half those in the castle. Then came the destruction. There was nothing much to destroy in the fort. Its earthen ramparts were abandoned and soon overgrown. Many were killed. How many? Some sources say 300–500, which would indeed be half of the original 1,000. 'We cannot tell,' said Tomimori. 'But there's a story that in this area of the village, people here used to make a particular sort of sweet using bamboo leaves, which are very sharp and often cut your fingers when you work with them. After Takino fled, the people stopped making the sweet, because they had seen so much blood. That's what they say. So from this story, I guess there was some sort of a massacre, even though the castle was surrendered peacefully.' One thing is certain. There used to be eight temples around here, and all were burned, because the temples – with their tide of monks, and travellers, and entertainers – were centres for the flow of information from all over the country and so were at the heart of the opposition to Nobunaga's rule.

Now, of course, archaeologists were interested. But – Tomimori explained – the hill was owned by several families, and no one could agree on cutting the trees and opening it up for research. But surely it would be worth it for the tourists? There were no tourists, he said. That was a surprise, for did not everyone agree that this was where the ninjas made their last stand? Wasn't that why the local authority had placed a monument here, commemorating the 400th anniversary of the Iga Revolt? One day, perhaps. And then, surely, there would be a big change: Takino's fort stripped of its trees, its walls and gateway revealed, the escape path made clear, a signposted walk in place directing curious crowds to the route taken by Takino, Hattori Hanzō and their surviving ninjas.

Their escape route led south, following today's narrow road above the fast-flowing Taki Gawa, 'Waterfall River', the steep valley of the Forty-eight Waterfalls where for centuries Shugendō students and ninjas had put themselves through their arduous physical and mental courses. So they knew exactly what to do. Pursued by Nobunaga's troops, they followed the river up to the fourth waterfall. Here, where the water from above falls into a cliff-lined pool, the old trail ended. In fine weather, it is a gorgeous spot, with the 30-metre cliffs topped by trees, and the white water roaring into a pool, which, when I was there, was not translucent but a soft emerald green, the colour of minerals and algae stripped from the mountain by the recent typhoon. No way up the river, then. But up the other side of the ravine, cutting through the trees, rose a near-vertical wall of boulders, which in downpours turned into a torrent of water and loosened rocks. It still does today. This was the unstable route *shugenja* and ninjas used to take to reach the upper falls, where they could find themselves yet greater challenges. So this was the route up which the fugitives vanished.

And also the route that the pursuers either did not know or would not take. Anyway, it was getting dark. The light, almost blocked by the overarching canopy, faded into a sunset glow. Perhaps they had also heard of the local species of salamander, which haunts the pools and backwaters, and can grow up to 2 metres long. So they invented, or were given, a good reason to retreat. Perhaps it was the red sky and the name of the falls – Akame, Red Eye, after the red-eyed cow seen by En when he first came – that suggested a nightmare vision. Suddenly – you can almost hear them heightening the fear in their voices as they report back to their senior officer – everything got really red and a huge snake appeared, and that was why they could not continue the chase. And that is why today the recently built path upwards, with steps and a wooden bridge climbing over the cliffs and tumbling water, is called Holy Snake Pass.

The fugitives got away safely and ended up in Ieyasu's territory the other side of Nagoya, 130 kilometres to the east. There, perhaps because they were no longer a threat, they were well received, and allowed to return home – a generous gesture by Ieyasu that would have interesting consequences.

Defeat brought a sudden end to the old ways of Iga, and also an end to the commune system. Iga city was given to a lord named Tōdō Takatora, who had rendered good service during the invasion. He built a fine castle on top of the hill, which still dominates the town today. On a tidal wave of well-shaped stone, a place of overlapping grey roofs and glorious beams overlooks a large open space where, on festivals, schoolchildren practise their archery. It is, as Ieyasu himself said, a treasure. It is a focal point, a symbol of power, where there had been neither before, and a clear statement that the old days were over for good.

But the memories live on, and so do many of the families. By chance, I came across descendants of two of the families, Takino and Momochi.

Takino survived, not to fight another day, but to negotiate a truce, and settle back into farming, and marry and produce many children. So, said Tomimori as we left the woods that covered Takino's earthworks, that's why many people living in the village today are called Takino. 'You see the man who is cutting the rice over there? He's a Takino.' He looked up and called, 'Takino! This man has come from England to see your ancestor's fort!'

It was in the little village of Akame, where tourists enter the path leading up the Forty-eight Waterfalls, that the cheerful old restaurant-owner, Ueda Masaru, led me into his attic and showed me the suits of ninja armour inherited from his grandmother. And his grandmother, remember, had been a Momochi, a descendant of the Momochi Sandayu who had escaped from Takino's fort when it was surrendered to Oda Nobunaga.

Names, shrines, temples, memorials: all recalled what happened here in the autumn of 1581. There is at least one enclave where life seems remarkably unchanged. A winding road led uphill through woodland, and down into a secluded valley, where, among a patchwork of terraced rice fields and up a driveway, stood the house of my dreams, should I ever dream of living in Japan. A curly-tiled porch with heavy wooden doors led to a Zen-style courtyard: a little pond, fringed with sun-dappled, autumnal bushes, gravel, and rocks, on one of which lay a contemplative black cat. The house with its two wings held the garden as a clasp holds a jewel. It was a jewel itself – all dark wood and blue-grey tiles, perfect in its plainness.

Like other works of art, the simple beauty was maintained by hard work, at the hands of the man who now appeared from a garage beside the driveway, dressed in dusty T-shirt, jeans and muddy boots. He had one of the most strikingly beautiful – there's no other word – faces I had seen in any man, let alone one in his fifties. This was Momochi Mikyo, another descendant of Momochi Sandayu.[5] The Momochi family had owned this house then, and still own it now. One

---

[5] Zoughari says that the name 'Sandayu' does not appear in the Momochi genealogies, 'which leads one to suppose he is a fictitious character'. Momochi Mikyo's account leads one to suppose the opposite. Zoughari suggests that, if he was not fictitious, Sandayu was so good at the art of invisibility that he managed to hide evidence of his existence.

of the larger stones in the garden recorded the link, and added: 'This was put up in memory of the 350th anniversary of the Iga Revolt', in 1931. Momochi had the self-contained dignity that you often find in long-established families. They know who they are, they know where they belong, and they work to preserve their house, their family, their inheritance. Momochi was a gardener by profession. His garage was crammed with bits of machinery, the driveway littered with tyres, boxes, bins, a barrow, an old bath. It was lucky he happened to be in, and lucky that Noriko had called ahead to explain my interest. He stopped work, and talked.

'Yes, the house was built before the Iga Revolt. Well, the tiles and the outer walls have been replaced, but the inside is as it was.' Its survival was remarkable, considering this is an earthquake-prone area, but the structure clearly helped. 'It was built in the old-fashioned way, without nails,' he said, which allowed it to flex. Tiles may fall, but the heart remains firm.

I asked: 'Did your family tell you many stories of the Iga Revolt?'

'Oh, many.'

'So what happened when the castle surrendered?'

'We don't know exactly. There is no documentary evidence. But Momochi Sandayu was definitely in there with Lord Takino when they negotiated an end to the siege with Oda Nobunaga. They say he killed three hundred people a day.' (Or was it perhaps just one day, which would fit the numbers better?) 'Sandayu must have got away, because I'm here, the nineteenth generation from him. They both survived, even though the two of them had been part of the force that had defeated his son seven years earlier.'

The two families remained close. Indeed, as Momochi said, all the old families married together. 'My mother,' he nodded at an ancient, stooped figure walking with some difficulty across the courtyard, 'she is a Takino.'

The ninja past is not just present in the tree-covered mounds of the old forts, the shrines and temples, and the names. It's in the genes.

11

NOBUNAGA'S END,
IEYASU'S RISE

*If lightning is behind you, it is auspicious; if it is ahead of you,
be careful.*

Ninja instructional poem

NOBUNAGA WAS GOING FROM STRENGTH TO STRENGTH. IN APRIL
1582, with imperial backing, he mounted a great victory
cavalcade in Kyoto: 130,000 men in full dress marching and
riding past an imperial grandstand for hours, with Nobunaga
taking care to 'show off and enhance his status' in mid-parade
– as the Jesuit priest Fróis wrote – by getting off his horse and
climbing into a crimson velvet sedan ornamented with gold, a
gift from the Jesuits. 'Never had there been an event where all
were such excellent horsemen and were dressed so
splendidly,' wrote a Japanese eyewitness. 'The crowd of
onlookers, whether high or low, would remember in what
glorious times they had been born for the rest of their lives.'
The emperor was delighted. A month later, he decided to offer

Nobunaga the position of shogun. But Nobunaga was focusing on yet another campaign in western Honshū. The shogunate could wait.

At this moment, one of his generals, Akechi Mitsuhide, made the decision to turn on his master. No one knows why for certain, though there is a story about Nobunaga abusing Akechi over some meat and fish which, he said, had gone bad. Or perhaps Akechi was simply ambitious for power. Whether he was acting out of revenge or ambition, now was the moment, because Nobunaga had dealt with most of the opposition. On 19 June, Nobunaga lodged in the Honnō-ji, a temple in Kyoto, on his way westward. Akechi, staying in a nearby castle, led his 13,000 troops to the Honnō-ji, ostensibly, he said, to be inspected by Nobunaga before joining him on campaign. Only his close accomplices knew the real purpose.

In the Honnō-ji, troops armed with arquebuses surrounded Nobunaga's quarters. The opening rounds told him all was lost. 'Treason!' he shouted. 'Who is the traitor?' His aide told him. Nobunaga grabbed a bow, then a spear, and fought his attackers, until, with the building burning round him and wounded in an arm by an arquebus ball, he retreated into a back room and committed suicide, making sure his body would be consumed by fire.

There followed eleven days of chaos – Nobunaga's heir Nobutada also dead by *seppuku*, his third son deserted by his troops, a cousin killed as a suspected traitor – until Nobunaga's senior ally, Hideyoshi, defeated Akechi, took his head and presented it in the burned-out ruins of the Honnō-ji. He confirmed his status by staging a grand funeral for his lord, and then crushed opposition from within Nobunaga's family. By mid-1584, Toyotomi Hideyoshi, Japan's future unifier, was master of central Japan, and in an uneasy truce with his main rival, Ieyasu, who would seize the nation for his own dynasty and secure its enduring unity.

*

But how come Ieyasu, Nobunaga's other staunch ally, had escaped? He had been in Sakai, just south of Osaka and only some 45 kilometres from Kyoto, at the time of Nobunaga's murder. A messenger arrived with the dire news. Appalled, Ieyasu said his duty was to avenge his lord, but with such a small force that was impossible. The only other course was an honourable suicide in Kyoto. He was under way with several advisers, when one of them suggested that Ieyasu would serve his dead master better by returning to his base in Mikawa (today's Aichi prefecture), 150 kilometres to the east, and there raise a force with which to avenge the shogun's murder. But how to get home across Iga without being intercepted by Akechi's men or set upon by bandits or murdered by ninjas eager to revenge their defeat? A retainer named Hasegawa said he would get him through, because he had been a guide to Oda Nobunaga in the Iga Revolt. They set out (in the vivid if unsourced words of A. L. Sadler, Ieyasu's biographer), with one guard 'brandishing his halberd "Dragon-fly Cutter" in the faces of the rustics with a view to eliciting reliable information about the route', and another 'distributing money with the same purpose'. After 40 kilometres, at the Kizu river, there was no ferry, but they commandeered two brushwood boats, which one of the guards sank after crossing the river by punching holes in them with his halberd. On then for 25 kilometres of 'mountain roads and precipices . . . infested by mountain bandits' to Shigaraki, the small town famed for being briefly the capital back in the eighth century, and later for its pottery. This brought them to the borders of Kōga and Iga, where one of Iga's top men, Hattori Hanzō, heard of their predicament and came to help.

Hattori Hanzō, second in a line of famous samurais, had made his name as a warrior in his mid-teens and helped Oda Nobunaga to victory in a hard-fought battle of Anegawa in

1570, acquiring the nickname 'Devil Hanzō'. Then, as a resident of Iga, he had found himself fighting against his one-time lord in the Iga Revolt. He was one of those who, after Iga's defeat, had fled over the Forty-eight Waterfalls, taken refuge in Ieyasu's territory and been well treated, an act of generosity which turned out well for everyone. Possibly by this time 'Devil Hanzō' was back at his home just west of Iga, which, given his fame, I thought would be a prime tourist site. So I took a taxi with Noriko and went in search of it.

There was nothing prime about it. A few kilometres outside Iga, a winding lane and a narrow alleyway led past a huddle of houses to a flight of cement stairs. At the top, steps roughly cut into the slippery earth gave on to a glade about 50 metres across. A sign said that here were the remains of Hattori's castle, Chigachi. But there were no remains. Other castle mounds are contoured with walls and ditches and entrances. This was entirely flat. Perhaps it had been a house, not a castle. A scattering of bushes made it a pretty spot for a picnic, except that no one had been there for months and spiders had taken possession. Noriko did not like the webs, but she was no arachnophobe. 'This spider,' she said, peering at a yellow-legged beauty, 'is *jorigama*, a Prostitute Spider, so-called because she eats the male as well as the flies.' Several engraved stelae, standing about like tombstones, com-memorated the significance of the place: 'This is the birthplace of Hattori Hanzō,' claimed one, 'but he left here when he was 18 to work for Tokugawa Ieyasu.' Another prayed for peace for the souls of those who died in the Iga Revolt.

It was strange: trees had been cleared, the memorials set up, yet who ever came here to disturb the spiders? The taxi was waiting, but the question was worth a few minutes more. Back down below, we braved a barking dog and exchanged bows with its owner, and of course cards. Tsukii Katsuya, a lean, sharp-featured fifty-something with laughing eyes, was a potter, and a master of his craft, specializing in the local ware. Inside, beside his kiln, he showed me a rectangular vase to explain the subtleties of Iga-style pottery: the deliberately coarse texture, the way the black merged into charcoal and then a soft yellow, a technique which he called 'rained on'. I remembered something I had been told a few days before: the great English potter, Bernard Leach, came to Iga once. He loved the ware for its colours, its roughness, its simplicity. Apparently there were examples in his studio in St Ives. I had never been. I promised myself I would go, if and when I was better prepared. There was a chance here to be inducted into the mysteries of great art – perhaps, who knew, to acquire a . . .

No. This was foolishness. I didn't have the time to go off on such tangents. I explained my interest in Hattori Hanzō. Were there many visitors here, Japanese, locals perhaps, keen to reconnect with their history? 'Maybe one or two a week. Of whom,' he added, 'twenty per cent are foreign.' How did he know? Did he talk to them all? And what did this statistic mean? But the taxi was waiting, and we were out of time.

If Hattori was at Chigachi as Ieyasu approached Iga, he would have been only some 14 kilometres from Ieyasu's party, a day's ride north over the hilltop where Iga and Kōga families used to meet to sort out their problems. Now, under Hattori's direction, 200–300 men from Tsuge, a village on Iga's northern border, and another 100 from Kōga came to Ieyasu's aid.

Which route to take? This was going to be tricky. There was, of course, a well-established road, of sorts, leading eastwards – the Tokaido. But it was crowded with people from far and wide, some of whom would surely be on the lookout for Nobunaga's successor, while others would be quick to oppose Hattori and take revenge on an ally of Nobunaga who had been with him during the conquest of Iga.

The answer, probably, was to head for the hills, back the way Hattori had (perhaps) just come. The route is still there today. Shigaraki, with its arrays of ceramic figures crowding the front of shops, drops away behind you. The road winds up through forested hills. Back then, of course, it would have been nothing but a one-horse track, levelling out at the top with a view through the trees down to the flat lands of Iga. Today, it is no more than a pretty little road leading past an upmarket country club, but it has a claim to historical significance because it was on this crest, Otoge, that the leading families of both sides, twelve from Iga and ten from Kōga, used to meet. Besides, of the half dozen roads between the two, this is the smallest and most tortuous. Local officials are in no doubt, as a newish wooden post proclaims: 'Tokugawa Ieyasu came this way to Iga.'

I can believe it, because there was one other piece of circumstantial evidence. At the bottom of that wooden post was another sign, broken off, with a grim statement. When Ieyasu became shogun in 1603, it read, he appointed police chiefs everywhere and 'in this region, the police force's execution area was here'. It is still there today. A grassy side-track led downhill through cedars, whose tall smooth trunks and high canopies created (in my eurocentric mind) a Gothic gloom, like that of a medieval abbey. Branches brought down by the recent typhoon littered the forest floor, and the still air was damp from mouldering foliage. The cedars opened on to a small clearing, where, in a glow of light from above, two small stone memorials turned the place into an open-air chapel. They were flanked by vases of fresh flowers. Each stone bore an engraving.

'Buddhist chants,' said Noriko. 'To make sure the souls of those executed here rest in peace.'

'What do they say?'

'*Nam yo horen*...' she said, peering at the first. 'It's

Sanskrit. I don't know. Don't ask a priest. His answer will last for hours.'

How many died here? Were they criminals, or perhaps local ninjas who continued the fight against Ieyasu, 20 years after the defeat of Iga? Anyway, this mournful place suggested a narrative: Ieyasu's placeman imposes his master's will by condemning locals to death, and then faces a problem: where to hold the executions. Ieyasu himself sends a message – go up the road to the top of the rise, and you will find a suitable spot. Kill them there, privately, far from any unruly warrior farmers.

He could suggest the spot because he came this way himself, if the sign is to be believed. Perhaps. No one can ever be certain, as Ieyasu himself intended. He would not have risked anyone but his closest and most trusted advisers knowing his whereabouts. How could he have done this? By copying the measures adopted by countless rulers from the First Emperor of China to Saddam Hussein. Not that there is a mention of this in the sources, but local historians have no doubt. Yoshihisa Yoshinori, as driver for the Kōka Tourist Board, knew what was said. 'There is no document telling us his route, but there could have been two or three different ones, because his lookalikes would have had a choice.'

'He had a *double*?'

'Yes. All lords had lookalikes, to avoid assassins. Perhaps his lookalikes had more guards than he did himself, so that villagers here and there would all claim to have seen his procession.'

'How would they know, or think they knew?'

'They would not show their faces. They would all be wearing his armour and helmet and colours. They would all look the same, with no way to tell which was the real one. So he could come along this road in safety.'

It worked. Hattori Hanzō and his 300 hundred or so

warriors guided Ieyasu along Iga's northern borders into Ise. How dangerous the journey was emerged when Ieyasu's ninja escorts caught and beheaded a notorious bandit, Ikkihara Genda, and his gang, while one of Ieyasu's retainers, taking a different route, was murdered by a different gang.

So, after a further week's travel, they came to the coast at a little place called Shiroko, a port on Ise Bay now little more than a railway station on the line running north to Nagoya. Here they hired a merchant willing to take their charge across the bay and home (though Sadler adds an unsourced and unlikely tale about Akechi's men searching the boat and Ieyasu being hastily hidden under cargo and the searchers poking about with spears, one of them wounding Ieyasu, who had the presence of mind to wipe the blood off the spear as it was withdrawn to avoid giving himself away).

The success of this mission made a terrific impression on Ieyasu. He showed his gratitude by rewarding top ninja aides with gifts of swords and commendations. And the ninjas, never previously known for their loyalty to an outsider, stuck by him. Ieyasu's initial generosity; the ninjas' guidance; Ieyasu's rewards; the ninjas' declaration of loyalty – all worked together to create a powerful bond, with many ramifications. Ieyasu would, 20 years later, emerge as the leader of the nation and impose a peace that would define its destiny for the next 250 years. But the peace would also mean that the ninjas, the products of centuries of war, would be barred from their traditional roles as spies and specialists in covert warfare. It was Ieyasu who would provide them with a new if diminished role in the new, peaceful Japan.

12

THE FINAL BATTLES

*Fighting among yourselves can always happen, [so] always
decide on a sign for your warriors beforehand.*

Ninja instructional poem

IEYASU, JAPAN'S THIRD UNIFIER, WOULD HAVE TO WAIT 20 YEARS
before assuming dictatorial rule of all Japan. Under him, the
ninjas would enter a long decline, debilitated by peace, killed
by kindness.

Meanwhile, under Japan's second unifier, Hideyoshi, the
ninjas could pretend for a while that the world had not
changed, and play a traditional role, not in Japan, but overseas. Hideyoshi, the 'Napoleon of Japan', completed
unification and dreamed of regaining Japan's old empire in
Korea, a first step in a much grander vision: to conquer all
China. The invasion in 1592 included a 100-strong unit of Iga
ninjas, who saw action in the assault on the castle guarding
Seoul. But it all came to nothing. The Japanese army was cut
from its roots by the Korean navy, and at home Hideyoshi

bogged himself down with lavish entertainments. In the summer of 1598, Hideyoshi, 63, became ill and, in the words of common metaphors, took the dark road to the Yellow Spring and became a guest in the White Jade Pavilion. His heir was a five-year-old, watched over by a council of regents. Factions formed, tensions grew, war threatened.

Ieyasu, the most powerful of the regents, had been awarded the Kantō region (the central eastern provinces of Japan's main island, Honshū). Having never been part of the Korean campaign, he had been busy building his base in the little fishing village of Edo (which eventually grew into today's Tokyo). It was he and his implacable foe Ishida Mitsunari who now held the fate of Japan in their hands.

There followed a campaign, which, like a game of chess on a massive scale, involved the taking of many castles vital for the control of the great roads, the coastal Tokaido and the inland Nakasendo. The campaign ended in the biggest battle ever fought on Japanese soil: Sekigahara, on the Nakasendo road about 100 kilometres northeast of Kyoto.

By the time it occurred, on 21 October, the time and place were so obvious that people gathered to watch, setting up with teapots and luncheon boxes on a nearby hilltop. They would have a good view, because the battleground was hemmed by hills, except that the morning started foggy. Some 160,000 men fought that day, in an action too complex to describe here.

For ninja-philes, there are two points.

Firstly, Ieyasu won, largely because he managed to persuade several commanders to switch sides.

Secondly, one of the losing commanders introduced a novel ninja-like tactic. The commander was one of the Shimazu clan from Satsuma, on the southern tip of the southerly island of Kyūshū. Satsuma was famous for the fertility of its volcanic soils; hence the oranges named after it. It was also notoriously independent, firstly because it was isolated by ranges of mountains and secondly because it possessed the superb harbour of Kagoshima, a natural window to the world beyond Japan, to the Pacific, China and all points south. The Shimazus were among the first to appreciate the advantages of the firearms introduced by the Portuguese. Recently, they had developed the use of guns by snipers, whose job was to lie low – playing dead, perhaps, or hiding – if their army retreated, and pick off enemy combatants. This they did at Sekigahara when their main contingent came up against the 'Red Devils' of one of Ieyasu's top commanders, Ii Naomasa. Like all samurai, Ii's men were easy to spot, because they wore brilliantly coloured armour and carried silk banners and flags and ribbons identifying their rank, affiliation and name. 'All armour, harness, saddles and stirrups to be red' ran one of their regulations. Ii himself was on horseback, turned into a bull's-eye by his standard, 5 shaku (about 1.5 metres) long, four widths of silk wide, bearing the first character of his name in gold. A Satsuma sniper shot at him, close up, not very accurately, because the bullet passed through his horse's belly and shattered Ii's right elbow. The horse collapsed, Ii was carried from the field, and a ninja officer in his service gave some medicine – evidence that ninjas did indeed acquire medical skills when they did their Shugendō training. After victory was declared, Ieyasu personally bound Ii's wound, but some say he never fully recovered. He died two years later.

That left Ieyasu as Japan's virtual dictator, confirmed when he had the emperor proclaim him shogun in 1603, the start of the Tokugawa government that would last for the next 265 years. He moved fast to consolidate his power, executing some of his main opponents,[1] forgiving others, confiscating

[1] Sadler reports a story about the death of Ishida Mitsunari, loser at Sekigahara. On his way to execution with his colleague, Konishi Yukinaga, he asked for a cup of tea from his captors. He was offered a persimmon, but

fiefs here, dispensing them there, controlling enemies, securing allies, and starting the immense task of making Edo into the capital.

One of his acts was to reward the ninjas who had come to his aid with such spectacular success 20 years before. Iga was at peace under its new lord, Tōdō Takatora, with the local ninjas returning to their lives as farmers. Kōga, his ally during the Iga Revolt, was allowed to continue its self-governing traditions, on the understanding that there would be no challenge to his authority. But he knew better than to allow any resentment to fester, and to this end gave 200 ninjas positions, and a significant income, as security guards in Edo.

To secure peace in this way demanded a rare combination of ruthlessness, vision and generosity. If Oda Nobunaga was like Genghis Khan in rising from nowhere to become a national leader, Ieyasu was like him in that both did what autocrats are notoriously bad at: looking after the succession in good time. In 1605, Ieyasu made his third son, Hidetada, shogun, ensuring continuity and stability, while retaining power behind the scenes for the next eleven years.

There remained Hideyoshi's heir, Hideyori, now a grown man of 21, living in his great fortress of Osaka, and eager to make a comeback. Tens – possibly hundreds – of thousands of samurai, resentful of Ieyasu's seizure of power, were willing to join him. The potential revolt was centred on Osaka castle, Japan's most impressive castle after Edo itself. Built by Hideyoshi in 1586, it stood on the site of the Ishiyama Hongan-ji temple destroyed by Oda Nobunaga. Its base was

---

refused it, saying that it would not be good for his digestion. 'It seems hardly necessary to consider one's digestion just before decapitation,' said Konishi dryly. 'How little you understand,' was the retort. 'You can never tell how things will turn out . . . while you have breath in your body you have got to take care of yourself.' That's the samurai spirit: always look on the bright side of death.

a platform of immense stones, the provision of which had been a matter of intense competition between rival lords. They are still there today, some of them weighing up to 75 tonnes. This, combined with some 15 acres of walls and palisades and three moats and arrays of guns, should have made it very hard to take. For that reason, the ninja officer who had attended to Ii during the battle of Sekigahara, Miura Yoemon, went to Iga – to the Nabari area, not far from the Forty-eight Waterfalls – to hire ninjas, who were still keen to make use of their skills after a decade of peace.

In the winter of 1614, Ieyasu arrived with his army to begin the siege. On one occasion, the ninjas used unorthodox tactics that saved lives. A force led by Ii's son, Ii Natada, attacked across a dry outer moat, using a fog bank to hide their approach, when a hail of bullets from the walls ahead drove them back. Such was the confusion of fog and fighting that Ii could not make himself heard to order a retreat. On the bank, Miura, busy removing arrowheads from wounded soldiers, ordered his ninjas to lob arrows *at their own men*. That got their attention. They turned to face this apparent new threat, and 'advanced' away from danger, to safety.

The winter siege proved too much for both sides. Ieyasu's guns – 17 European cannons and 300 home-made ones – undermined morale: a cannonball smashed a tea cabinet while Lady Yodo, Hideyoshi's ageing consort, was entertaining, and another felled a pillar on top of two of her ladies. Sleep was impossible. For the besiegers, so was the cold. Neither side, though, was ready to give up. The result was a peace treaty which neither intended to take seriously. Hideyori promised never to rebel again. Ieyasu promised to back off, but got the better deal, because the treaty allowed him to fill in the two outer moats. He then departed, proclaiming eternal peace, leaving the ladies in Osaka to return to their beds and tea ceremonies.

Peace after war is either imposed by the victor or based on trust. In this case, there was no victor and no trust. Both sides prepared for another round. Osaka repaired its defences, Ieyasu regathered his forces. Miura returned to Iga to persuade the ninjas to rejoin. It could not have been easy. They had only just got home, and now it was spring – time to start preparing the rice fields. But they were after all mercenaries, and they responded when the price was right. In the two months of fighting that followed, the only ninja action recorded was when they were ordered to fire on an unruly crowd of camp followers and locals who were impeding operations. The crowd quickly dispersed, leaving two or three dead who were under the command of Tōdō Takatora, Iga's new lord and owner of the newly built castle that still crowns Iga-Ueno's central hill. He would not have been a popular figure among the sturdily independent inhabitants of Iga. It sounds as much like a by-mistake-on-purpose act as a piece of crowd control, but was soon forgiven and forgotten amidst the many other actions that involved uncounted deaths, suicides, heads taken and displayed on poles and eventually, in early June, the surrender of the castle.

It must have seemed to the ninjas that they would never fight again, until 20 years later, when trouble broke out in the southern island of Kyūshū. It stemmed from the persecution of Christians, which came about because over the previous century Catholic missionaries had won a core of some 300,000 converts that seemed to challenge the shogun's authority. In 1612, a campaign of persecution started, which reached a peak of ferocity in the 1630s. Tens of thousands of converts recanted, while those who didn't were subjected to tortures that would have delighted a Grand Inquisitor: a forced recantation might involve being drowned, tossed into snake pits, sliced with sharpened bamboo, roasted alive, branded, boiled in hot springs or immersed in icy water. Tens of thousands died, hundreds fled the country (despite a law forbidding flight abroad), leaving a hard core of Christians in Kyūshū, most of them in the Amakusa Islands off the west coast. The final straw, literally, was the behaviour of a tyrannical local lord, who liked to punish recalcitrant peasants by dressing them in straw capes, such as the locals wore against rain, dowsing them with oil and setting them on fire. In December 1637, driven beyond endurance by oppression and a harvest failure, peasants and Christians on the mainland rebelled, killed a dozen officials and attacked several castles, before taking ship across the Ariake Bay to the Shimabara peninsula and rebuilding an abandoned stronghold called Hara. There was nothing sophisticated about their work: no great stone platform, simply earthworks and trenches topped by a scaffold of tree trunks, with planks from their ships as firing platforms and piles of rocks to drop on attackers. But the location was good, with cliffs on one side and a marsh on the other. No one knows how many there were inside – some say 20,000, others 50,000, but anyway they included women and children.

Morale was high, because, as Christians, they believed they were bound for Heaven, not that it would come to that because their leader, appointed as a figurehead by a general, was a charismatic Catholic teenager named Amakusa Shirō. The arrival of a Redeemer had been much prophesied by Kyūshū's put-upon Christians. In the words of a poem written some years before:

> A God will come into this world, a boy aged twice times eight.
> The youth, endowed by birth with every gift,
> Will effortlessly show forth his wondrous power.

Lo, he appeared when needed, a boy of 16, able (it was said) to attract birds like St Francis and walk on water.

To end the rebellion, the local governor sent a 3,000-strong force, which endured the humiliation of failing to break into Hara. The Tokugawa government in Edo sent an army of some 50,000, which tried again at the beginning of January 1638, this time using cannon bought from the Dutch, who joined in the bombardment from the sea. Among the government forces was a contingent of Kōga ninjas.[2] They surveyed the earth walls, moat and approach roads, and drew plans that were forwarded to the shogun in Edo, further proof that ninjas were skilful in much more than secret operations. Later that month, they launched a raid to seize bags of provisions that were crucial for the defenders.

A week later, the Tokugawa commander, wanting to know the conditions inside the fortress, called for ninja volunteers to break in, warning them that only two or three could expect to survive. Five answered the call, at least two of whom were from families listed as ninjas prior to Ieyasu's invasion in the 1560s and 1570s, further proof that ninja skills were passed down the generations even after the defeat of 1579–81. A contemporary account runs: 'We dispersed spies who were prepared to die [or "were a suicide squad", in an alternative translation] inside Hara castle.'

An assault followed, a special operation intended to spread fear and confusion and gain information. The ninjas, dressed in plain clothes like the defenders, planned to attack at night before the moon rose, which would mean climbing walls that were well lit by flaming torches. With the infiltrators in place, a contingent of gunners fired their arquebuses, at which the defenders, fearing a conventional attack, doused all the torches, leaving the place in starlit darkness. 'Then,' the

[2] These details are mainly based on Turnbull in *Ninja*.

record continues, 'we raided at midnight.' Entry was not as tricky as climbing a stone platform, like those typical of many castles, with a broad base sloping up to a vertical top. Earthworks can be climbed in relative silence, with spiked shoes and knives to act as pitons.[3] Still, it was dark enough for one of the ninjas to fall into a pit of some sort. Perhaps it was this that alerted the defenders. Torches were relit, the moon rose, and the ninjas just had time to haul their comrade clear and make their escape, taking a Christian banner with them as a souvenir. As they climbed back down the wall, the moon made them targets for volleys from above, which wounded two of them. They suffered 'for forty days', says the record of the raid, after which (presumably) they recovered.

The siege continued for another three months, by which time the defenders were down to a few bushels of rice and soy beans, with some reduced to eating seaweed, scraped from rocks beneath the cliffs. In mid-April the government forces, now increased to 125,000, at last managed to breach the walls, and the rebellion ended three days later. Many of the defenders committed suicide, hurling their families and themselves into burning buildings, and most of the others – men, women and children – were slaughtered in one of the greatest massacres in Japanese history. In the words of Ivan Morris in his magisterial analysis, *The Nobility of Failure*: 'Vast ditches were filled to overflowing with severed heads, and heads were strewn thickly over the fields, with 10,000 stuck on wooden spikes and 3,000 loaded on to ships for mass burials in Nagasaki.' Among the dead was 'the Japanese messiah', Amakusa, who has since become one of Japan's 'heroic failures', those beloved for their sincerity and bravery who die in a hopeless cause.

---

[3] The assault is portrayed in the Akizuki Museum (cf. Turnbull's *Strongholds of the Samurai*, pp. 131–2 and 180–81, and his *Ninja*, p. 88).

That was the end of resistance against Tokugawa rule, the end of all fighting for both the samurai and ninjas, the end of any hopes for Christianity, and the beginning of the two and a half centuries during which Japan became a 'closed country'. For the ninjas, it also marked the beginning of a new phase: an end to a life in the shadows, the beginning of self-promotion; and the beginning of reinterpreting the past – or, to put it bluntly, of spin, gloss, fantasy and myth-making.

13

SHADOWS IN RETREAT

Every single thing is decided by your own mind and by the way you think. Never let your guard down nor fail to observe your state of mind.

Ninja instructional poem

SHIMABARA MARKED THE END OF THE NINJAS' FIGHTING ROLE, but they had already been playing a role in keeping the peace for over 30 years. Ieyasu owed a debt of thanks to the ninjas of Kōga and Iga, who had, under the direction of Hattori Hanzō, seen him safely across hostile territory in 1582. As soon as his great castle in Edo was ready for occupation, he took on about 100 ninjas each from Iga and Kōga as bodyguards and guards. Hattori himself was given a residence there, with a salary of 8,000 *koku* (a measure of rice, one *koku* being enough to feed a peasant for a year). A low-level samurai cost about 20 *koku*. Hanzō's Gate remains as a reminder of his presence. The ninjas' job was to patrol the buildings, and keep the peace by ensuring that no one wore a sword inside the castle. They were expected to be masters of unarmed combat, able to disarm anyone with their bare hands or with a rope.

That wasn't all Ieyasu did for them. He employed other ninjas as spies to keep an eye on lords whose loyalty could be in doubt. In short, they became his secret police. And later in his reign he asked some of his lords to do what they could for the ninjas by employing them.

Now, 200 ninjas employed as guards, a few dozen others as shogunal spies and another few dozen employed by other *daimyos* was hardly equal to the numbers who had acted as ninjas previously. Most of them returned to their main occupation as farmers and family men, as craftsmen and doctors. But there was no denying that for those still hoping for employment, opportunities all but vanished. With no more battles to fight, no one wanted mercenaries. Peace meant a loss of status and self-image.

One answer was to keep on practising those skills that had been so useful in the past, and teach them, and make it as clear as possible how important they were for personal development, self-control and strength of body and character. That was why the ninjas broke with tradition and recorded their secrets.

When I was eleven, I was in a small, private boarding school for boys. That summer, the class was seized by a mania for 'strength'. We avidly discussed our merits. We flexed biceps, and wrestled, and wondered how to gain strength. Was it an inbred talent? Could it be cultivated? If so, how? One day, in a magazine, I saw a tiny advertisement showing a man stripped to the waist with giant biceps and pecs like beached whales. He made a promise that I too could have a body like his, if I bought his body-building system. It was called 'Dynamic Tension'. I had no idea what that meant, but suddenly I realized that, if I had the money, I had access to something that would turn me from a weed into an oak. To my classmates, I let slip that I knew the secret of strength. This was an explosive claim. Instantly, I was surrounded. They demanded that I share my knowledge. I was astonished to discover I was in possession of a secret that was, in its way, as strong as my body would be become after I had studied, swallowed, injected or otherwise absorbed 'Dynamic Tension'. Obviously, the whole point was to keep the secret, or I would end up simply making all the others as strong as me. I refused. They threatened. They said there were ways of making me talk. I said there weren't, which was foolish. They tortured me. They sat on my head, they boxed my ears, they gave me Chinese burns – which for the uninitiated means counter-twisting the flesh on the forearm. I cried, but kept silent. In the end they gave up, pretending they didn't care. But they did, and I was able to capitalize on my knowledge by telling two allies, swearing them to secrecy. For a brief, sweet while, I had a cocoon of friendship and security. It didn't last, because soon afterwards, we forgot about strength, and became obsessed with the little coloured glass balls known as marbles. It was a lesson, though. Strength would have been good; but almost as good was the secret of how to acquire it. A secret that others want confers power.

The ninjas had status partly because they were good at what they did; but also partly because they kept it secret until the late 16th century. This makes it hard to say anything definitive about pre-1600 ninja fighting skills, the body of knowledge and activities wrapped up in the term 'ninjutsu'. To publicize their skills would have undermined the very purpose of their existence. Masters took care to pass on their skills to one chosen heir. If you were not on an inside track, you had to make up your own set of techniques. So there arose a general body of skills, and many subgroups, 'schools' or *ryu*, perhaps as many as 80, developed all over Japan, though focused on the prime areas of Kōga and Iga, and all of them secret. Occasionally, a master or scholar recorded the details of a *ryu*, to be kept safely under lock and key. But the country was at war, and writings were hard to preserve. So, little documentation survives from the 15th and 16th centuries.

That takes us up to 1638, at which point conflict came to an end permanently, and the ninjas, like the samurai, lost the fundamental point of their existence, which was war. They might then have vanished. But there were traditions, and some had a job of a sort to do. What they could not do was go out and infiltrate castles, spy and assassinate. How in this changed world could they preserve themselves? One answer was that they could retain a sense of identity by clinging to their teachings and making them available to a wider public, while maintaining the myth that war was still a fact of everyday life.

There are several summaries of ninja knowledge and techniques, all of them dating back no further than the late 17th century, when the ninjas' great days were over. One is the *Shoninki*, which forms the three 'How to' chapters in the early part of this book. It is the most literary and succinct of the manuscripts. Another is the *Ninpiden, The Secret Ninja Tradition*, perhaps written by a Hattori, but at least in the possession of the Hattoris, the famous ninja family from Iga. A third is the *Gunpu Jiyoshu, The Collected Way of the Samurai Military Arts*, so called because Ieyasu thought all samurai should read it; it's 59 paragraphs of severely practical advice on tactics and equipment. Finally, there is the encyclopedic *Bansenshūkai*, which intrigued me because it was the only one of the four not translated into English,[1] and because of its size.

*

[1] It is now. The 180,000-word translation by Antony Cummins and Yoshie Minami is due for publication in autumn 2013.

The hotel in Kōga was of the traditional sort, built around little Zen-style courtyards of gnarled trees and stones, with corridors of sliding doors and paper screens leading to steamy mineral baths. One moved to the tinkling twitter of caged grasshoppers, which call with the sound porcelain would make if it could sing. My room had fitted, off-white *tatami* matting, and that was all, the futon being still stored away.

'There's nowhere to sit or lie down,' I complained.

'You can sit or lie *anywhere*,' said Noriko.

But I couldn't. It seemed odd to lie on the floor, and it hurt to kneel or sit cross-legged. Compared to the kimono-clad lady of the house, who could drop to her knees and rise again with ease and elegance, I was a graceless lump, unworthy of the hotel's charm.

Besides that, though, the hotel had one overwhelming advantage. The owner, Tsuji Kunio, was a member of the local historical society, and among his many books he had a multi-volume copy of the most famous of ninja books, often called its Bible, *Bansenshūkai*. The Japanese like four-part titles and phrases, like the 19th-century political slogan *Son nō jō i* (Revere the Emperor, expel the Barbarians). *Ban Sen Shū Kai* – though usually transcribed as one word – is one of them. It means 'Ten Thousand Rivers Merge (Into) the Sea', which I take to be a metaphor meaning that 'countless elements make a single philosophy' (i.e. ninjutsu). So it was here, with *Bansenshūkai* spread out on the table, that half a dozen local amateur historians met to tell me about the ninja response to redundancy. I was in awe: here, apparently, was a copy of the most impressive of ninja records. I was about to touch the very roots of my subject.

Why, though, would some ninja authors choose to reveal their secrets at all?

It was the elderly Toshinobu Watanabe who explained, he who had taken me round to various ninja sites in Kōga. For the first 20 or 30 years after the Iga Revolt, the ninjas found gainful employment with the shogun as guards, and twice as spies and soldiers in the last great actions, in the siege of Osaka and the Shimabara Rebellion. Then all was quiet. They were in the uncomfortable position of not being needed any more; worse, actually, because they had fallen in status, and were ordinary farmers, much put upon by the taxman. Like the samurai, they were at best gradually turning from active to passive, from soldiers to bureaucrats, dependent (if they could claim samurai status) on stipends of rice to feed their families. Soon, perhaps, they would be out of a job altogether. They would age, and die, and, because they had been so secretive, no one would remember them or their great deeds. They had to show what they were made of, the skills they had, and the importance of passing them on from generation to generation. Nor was it just the practitioners of ninjutsu: all specialists – in archery, sword-fighting, firearms in all their different schools – felt the need to record details of their ways.

'In fact the ninjutsu experts came to this view quite late,' said Toshinobu. 'Around 1670, specialists from Iga and Kōga got together and said, "My goodness, we had better do something about this, or we will disappear." So that's how *Bansenshūkai* came to be written, along with several other works on ninjutsu.'

To focus on *Bansenshūkai*: this is a ten-book record of ninja ways, in some 20 to 26 chapters or 'volumes', depending on the edition. It was compiled by an ex-samurai called Fujibayashi Yasutake and completed in 1676. 'He wrote it as a combination of the Kōga and Iga ninjutsu,' said Toshinobu, 'because his house was on the border between the two.' It is, in effect, an encyclopedia of ninjutsu, a manual of covert operations which includes fighting techniques, weaponry, strategy, spying, astronomy (because the stars pointed the

BANSENSHŪKAI: THE CONTENTS[2]

1. Introduction
Preface and Prologue; Guiding philosophy of successful warfare; Historical examples; Index; Questions and Answers

2. Correct Mind/1
Sincerity, motivation and moral strength of intention; Correct approaches to life and death

3. Correct Mind/2
How to manage a ninja organization; Successful use of ninjas; Considerations for stopping enemy agents; Methods of entering the enemy's base

4. A Guideline for Commanders/1
Methods for discovering the enemy's intentions; Continuous observation by agents placed during peaceful times; Location of agents after war breaks out; Observing the geographical layout of the enemy's territory; Observing the enemy's numbers, capabilities and other strengths; Observing the enemy's strategy and positioning; Agents specializing in watching and listening

5. A Guideline for Commanders/2 and 3
An agreement between lord and ninja; The three prohibited matters in ninjutsu; Two points on secret letters; Two points on letters sent tied to arrows; Four points on signals; Secret letter with occult power; Six points on making an agreement; Three qualifications for a commander; Two ways to guarantee a ninja's safety; The reasons for hiring a ninja
(Part 3: missing)

---

[2] Adapted from Antony Cummins, with thanks.

6. A Guideline for Commanders/4
How to protect against the enemy's tactics/1: Five reasons for not hiring the enemy's ninja; On disciplining your force

7. A Guideline for Commanders/5
How to protect against the enemy's tactics/2: On watch-fires; On passwords and secret signs to identify allies; On watch guards; On patrolling night guards; On listening scouts; On tools for defending against enemy ninja

8. Infiltration/1
Preparation; Planting an undercover agent; The same in a tense situation; Female ninja; Using locals; Turning a local into a spy; Serving the enemy to betray him; False letters to make an enemy retainer look like a traitor; Winning over an enemy ninja; On defecting falsely; Ninja–commander relations

9. Infiltration/2
On passwords; On secret signs; On infiltration at a distance; On disguise; Infiltration during a night attack; Sporadic infiltration; 'Turning' a prisoner; Making an enemy commander seem a traitor by forging letters to his family

10. Reconnaissance
Reconnaissance: Investigating mountains and valleys; Further points on the same; On seashores and rivers; On the depth of rice fields; On the depth and width of a moat; On discovering how well a castle is fortified; Estimating topography, distance and elevation; On estimating the strength of the enemy; On estimating enemy numbers; On the numbers of an enemy formation; Estimating numbers of an enemy on the march; Scouting a castle or camp from without; Likely mistakes when scouting at night; Judging if the enemy is advancing or retreating from camp or castle; Judging if the enemy is taking up a position or retreating; Assessing if there are ambushes; Judging

if the enemy is about to cross a river; Judging the enemy by observing flags and dust

11. Secret Infiltration/1
Ten points to consider before the mission; On the art of taking advantage of gaps; On taking advantage of the enemy's negligence

12. Secret Infiltration/2
Where you should infiltrate from; On the art of choosing tools; On infiltrating when allies arrive; Infiltrating by consecutive raiding; On the art of the 'invisible cloak'; On arson

13. Secret Infiltration/3
Distinguishing seasonal sleep patterns; Detecting if people are asleep or not by age, disposition and behaviour; Dealing with dogs; Ways of walking; Hiding your shadow and making no noise; On appropriate nights for action; On the appropriate place for action; On listening to snoring; On observing the enemy; On hiding; How to arrange your men when infiltrating a house; On how to be cautious; On using the sword-cord; On traps to injure the enemy

14. Secret Infiltration/4
Preparing to open doors; On feeling for locking sticks; How to undo locking sticks; Feeling for hooked latches; How to undo hooked latches; Finding bolts; Undoing bolts; Discovering wooden latch-pegs; Releasing wooden latch-pegs; Identifying padlocks; Opening padlocks

15. Secret Infiltration/5
On scouting; On outfits for night raids; On instructions during night raids; Tactics before night raids; On the right time for night attacks; On ninja night attacks; On burglary raids; On taking captives

16. The Time of Heaven/1
The divination of time; How to know the right times and directions; On the *Five Precepts* and times of day; On knowing a lucky day by consulting the *Five Elements*

17. The Time of Heaven/2
Astronomy; Predicting wind and rain; Knowing the time of moonrise and moonset; On tides; Knowing the direction on moonless nights; How to tell the time

18. Tools/1
Climbing tools: illustrations of eight kinds of ladder, hooks, grappling irons, the 'dragon-climbing aid', flying tools and ninja-sticks

19. Tools/2
Illustrations of bridges, reed rafts, pot rafts, basket rafts, 'water-spider' floats, flippers, marsh-shoes, the 'cormorant', war-boats

20. Tools/3
Tools for bypassing locks

way at night), psychology, explosives, basic chemistry, and guidance for survival in warfare (see box for details).

Since working as a ninja involved having a 'correct mind', there is also much esoteric lore, some of it in Chinese (or rather Kanbun – Chinese adapted for Japanese), with many quotes from Chinese sources, because so much of the theory – strategy, tactics, divination, the calendar – came from China, and because using Chinese conferred authority on the text. For example, the sections 'Determining Direction and Location from the Stars' and 'Divination' include much in Chinese about Chinese divination that was standard knowledge among Japanese generals – 'They are not to be trusted,' says the *Bansenshūkai*, 'but the knowledge of them is useful when conducting warfare against a general who believes in them.' Practical matters – burglary, infiltration, espionage, tools, explosives – are mostly in Japanese.

It's a puzzle. It looks like the proud product of the ninja heyday, when they were living secure, happy and active lives. But if that were so, the secrets would never have been written down. The very existence of the *Bansenshūkai* suggests insecurity, unhappiness and inactivity – an attempt to make sure that later generations would know their birthright, and be able to apply it if necessary.

In its original form, it was no literary masterpiece, as the edition in front of me proved. It was a Xerox of a hand-copy of an original, which has been lost. Noriko had been wondering about the calligraphy. It seemed to her to be pretty sub-standard. She guessed this because her father is an eminent historian, Katsuhisa Moriya,[3] and as a child she was used to seeing good-quality calligraphy and printing of all ages around the house. Later, Professor Katsuhisa expressed his own opinion, in no uncertain terms. On the basis of this copy, the original must have been the work of an educated commoner, which was not saying much. 'A samurai with an education in Kanbun would never write rubbish like this!'

True, but a little harsh, because Fujibayashi was indeed a low-level samurai, who would not be expected to be a master of Kanbun. As Antony Cummins pointed out to me, 'The fact that he could write Kanbun at all is totally amazing.'

At some point, a century after it was written, when the former ninjas needed even more help, the *Bansenshūkai* was

[3] Former dean of Human Environmental Science Department and now emeritus professor of Japanese history, Mukogawa Women's University. Author of several books on Japanese history and contributor to *Traditions Unbound: Groundbreaking Painters of Eighteenth-Century Kyoto* (in English).

recopied in better calligraphy to become a plea to the shogun for recognition, in effect an extended job application. The sub-text of this later, improved edition was: Appreciate our skills! Employ us! Make sure our masters are able to pass on our secrets from generation to generation!

'That's the one that is in the National Archives today,'[4] said Toshinobu.

'Did it have an effect?'

'Not at all! Nothing changed!'

So much for the ninjas' hopes for employment. And what of my hopes of touching the roots of ninja culture? How accurate are the copies? How well did the long-gone original represent the realities of ninja life, given that it was written a century after the true ninja lifestyle came to an end? Extremely well, according to the Koka historians and to the *Bansenshūkai*'s translator, Antony Cummins. 'An outstanding manual,' he told me. 'One hundred per cent correct. No doubts here.' And the proof? The *Bansenshūkai* and the *Shoninki* both record 'the same set of skills and reflect each other'. That's what shows this to be 'one of the all-time survival and guerrilla warfare manuals'. Which in turn implies those who dismiss the *Bansenshūkai* as shoddy and unreliable are expressing deep-seated prejudices against ninjas, deriving from samurai traditions about the supreme value of calligraphy and scholarship and display and death-defying bravado.

By the time the *Bansenshūkai* was written, the ninjas were on their way into the realms of make-believe. Even the *Bansenshūkai*, with all its supposed authenticity, has its share of doubtful information. It prints a 'ninja code' made up of mock-Chinese signs that makes no sense, it suggests that

---

[4] It is known as the Ohara Kazuma version, after the Kōga man who presented it.

ninjas could transmit information by training a horse to walk in certain ways, it insists that a good ninja can live 'off snow and hail', it gives a recipe for pills to counteract thirst (pickled plums, crystallized sugar and wheat).

Over the next century, the ninja began to acquire his modern traits as a superman in black, able to perform magical feats. An illustration of an 1802 romance shows a black-clad figure crossing a moat by climbing along a rope held to a castle wall by a grapple.[5] A similar rope-climbing figure appears in a sketch done around 1814 by the great artist Hokusai. Several other black-robed ninjas appear regularly in 19th-century prints, though the range of subjects was limited by the censorship of the Tokugawa shogunate, which was sensitive about anything that suggested secret opposition. In one of a grisly series entitled '28 Scenes of Murder', Tsukioka Yoshitoshi portrays a hero on the point of committing suicide, with the shadow of doom looming over him – a shadow that is a ninja in silhouette. It was done in 1866, and the ominous shadow might well symbolize the fate of the Tokugawa shogunate. The strongest image of a latter-day ninja appeared only after the end of the shogunate in 1868. It is a woodblock print created in 1883 by Toyonobu Utagawa, of an attempt on the life of Oda Nobunaga in 1573 by an assassin named Manabe Rokurō. The print shows him as the archetypical ninja, dressed in black, thrashing about with his sword with a servant woman on his back, while the shogun looks on coolly (see picture section).

Of the many strange ninja transformations, the strangest is the one that changed the 12th century's great hero Yoshitsune from a tragic failure into a glorious success. After the (apocryphal) incident in which he is smuggled through

---

[5] *Ehon Taikō-ki* by Takenouchi Kakusai. Details are in Turnbull's *Ninja*, Chapter 12, 'The Floating World'.

the Ataka Gate by his loyal servant Benkei, Yoshitsune was defeated in battle and committed suicide. Or did he? Folklore does not like its great men to vanish. So it suggests an alternative fate in which he finds a destiny suitable to his greatness. In this legend he does not die, but escapes northwards, to the island of Hokkaido where the local aborigines, the Ainu, welcome him as a leader. Then what? Obviously he cannot die. So he travels on, ever northwards, across the island of Sakhalin, to the mainland, then westwards to Mongolia, where he re-emerges as the world conqueror Genghis Khan.

This is utter rubbish, of course. Yoshitsune killed himself (or vanished) in the battle of the Koromo river in 1189, at the age of 30. Genghis became the founder of his nation in 1206, which presumably acted as the legend's foundation stone, because the intervening 17 years offer enough time for Yoshitsune's transformation. As it happens, the two were about the same age. But the storytellers were ignorant of the fact that at the time of Yoshitsune's death or disappearance, young Genghis – Temujin, as he was still called – was already busy uniting Mongolia's feuding tribes. Not that this could have been widely known in Japan, but it is clear enough in both Chinese and Mongol sources. Actually, the whole thing is batty. It ignores distances, problems of travel, language and cultural differences. But legends grow by avoiding inconvenient facts. The real question is how and why the story arose.

It started at least in the early 19th century, because it was first recorded by the all-round German scholar and scientist Philipp von Siebold, who visited Hokkaido in the 1820s. The legend gained a new lease of life soon after the revolution of 1868, which ended the shogunate and brought the Meiji government to power. During the revolution, rebels had set up a short-lived republic in the northern island of Hokkaido. Crushing the rebels focused the attention of the new regime on the island. They remained there, mainly because they were afraid the Russians would seize it. In the ferment of nationalism, some Japanese needed to see a future building an empire on the mainland. All the better for the future if there was a precedent. Here it was – an empire had been built by Genghis which included all of China. Obviously, ran the argument, no Mongol could have done this, because the Mongolians, as everyone knew, were mere barbarians. Therefore Genghis, genius that he was, could not have been Mongolian. And since he conquered China, he could not have been Chinese. So, by iron logic, he must have been Japanese. This was the lunatic rationale of a Japanese author named Oyabe Zenichiro, whose book on the subject was published in 1924. It became a bestseller, and the idea acquired a certain respectability, with the result that it is constantly recycled as part of Yoshitsune's story, itself part of the process that was fast taking the ninjas away from reality into the realm of myth.

Yet a seed of reality remained alive, and was about to re-bloom in the most unlikely circumstances.

14

THE NAKANO SPY SCHOOL

When you are on night patrol or have to stand guard in an emergency, you should keep quiet so that you can hear any sounds.

Ninja instructional poem

THE NINJAS LIVE ON IN MANY DISTORTIONS OF A DISTANT REALITY, but they also live on in one man, Onoda Hiroo, who survived in the Philippines for 30 years after the war's end. It is a famous story. Onoda, 90 as I write and still going strong, was as loyal to his country as any samurai to his lord, but kept himself alive with techniques and an attitude that owed more to the ninjas than the samurai. His attitude in particular: where the samurai accepted, or sought, or ensured a 'glorious' death, Onoda was a dedicated survivor.

We'll get to Onoda himself in Chapter 16. First, we should look at the roots of his ethos, which he shared with a small band trained in covert operations. They were a remarkable group. All alumni of or instructors in a 'spy school' devoted to intelligence-gathering and guerrilla warfare, these few, 2,500 in all, might have been examples of expansionist, imperialist, militaristic Japan at its most extreme. In fact, they were just the opposite: though unshakably patriotic, they possessed extraordinary streaks of creativity, liberalism, idealism and flexibility. One man in particular possessed all these qualities. It is rare for anyone to retain moral integrity in opposition to the beliefs and actions of his nation. Fujiwara Iwaichi was such a man. He would not have put it in these terms, but he was a 'shadow-warrior', in the tradition of those few ninjas who tried to balance loyalty, action and morality.

He and Onoda owed their careers to the Nakano Spy School,[1] the roots of which go back to Japan's emergence on to the world stage in the late 19th century. The emperor had been restored to full power in 1868. The samurai vanished. Japan's new modern armed forces went from strength to strength, defeating China (1895) and Russia (1905), joining the Allies in World War I, then in the 1930s building an empire in Manchuria, with ambitions for a greater one in Siberia, Mongolia and China. But brute military strength was not enough. Inner Asia was a complicated place, with China torn by warlords, nationalists and Communists, Soviet armies strengthening their grip on Siberia, and Mongolians eager both for independence and for Soviet support. The Japanese army saw it needed to help conquest along with subversion and covert operations. Spies posing as Buddhist missionaries or businessmen built intelligence networks that produced maps and information on opposing armies.

As Japan's military machine grew in strength in the 1930s, the army saw that something rather more professional was needed in terms of covert warfare. In 1937, focusing

---

[1] Officially, the Nakano *Gakko* Military Intelligence School.

principally on the threat from the Soviet Union, the army began to develop the tools and techniques of 'shadow warfare': secret inks, cameras hidden in cigarette lighters, explosives disguised as canned food and coal, couriers reporting on what they saw while travelling on the Trans-Siberian Railway, an intelligence unit of anti-Soviet Russians, a counter-intelligence agency. Finally, in summer 1938, it was decided to formalize training in a 'spy school', which the following year acquired an HQ in Tokyo's Nakano district.

The Nakano Spy School, a compound of nondescript buildings with a forest of telegraph poles, had once been a military telegraph unit, and – according to a deliberately deceptive sign – was no more than an 'Army Communications Research Institute'. It was run at first by the brilliant and unconventional Akigusa Shun. Fluent in Russian, with round glasses and a gentle manner, Akigusa drank no alcohol, preferred coffee to tea, and took his students to the Imperial Hotel, designed by Frank Lloyd Wright, to improve their Western manners. He selected his students with care, preferring reservists and disdaining army officers drilled in absolute obedience and rote learning. From 600 candidates, he chose just 18, all notable for their intellectuality, internationalism and fitness. They were an élite, and acted the part, sporting fashionable haircuts and wearing smart suits.

From the first, they were taught a new type of covert warfare that would help establish the Japanese empire, or as they termed it the Greater East Asia Co-Prosperity Sphere. The 20th century, as World War I had shown, was an age of total war. But, they learned, full-frontal assaults were of less importance than intelligence, with which one could undermine the enemy by fomenting religious strife or class conflict. A single spy, said one teacher, could be more valuable than a division of soldiers. 'Shadow warfare', ninja-style, was the thing – but adapted to the modern world. They studied psychology, aviation, marine navigation, pharmacology. They were taught how to handle explosives and time bombs. They read up on German strategy, American politics and the campaigns of Lawrence of Arabia. They learned how to photograph documents surreptitiously, to disguise themselves, even (with known criminals as teachers) to crack safes. In an introduction to biological warfare, they were shown how to use special pens designed to release bacteria into water supplies. Everything, of course, was top secret. No one was to expect public honour. All should accept that they might die for their country without recognition. Nothing could have been more different from the samurai ethos, nothing more in line with that of modernized ninja-ism: dedication, patriotism, flexibility, thorough-going professionalism in 'shadow warfare'.

And spirituality, Japanese-style. A shrine at the front gate was dedicated to Kusunoki Masashige, the great 14th-century general who fought for the emperor Go-Daigo in the early years of the 60-year civil war between the Northern and Southern Courts, the one who oversaw the defence of several 'hilltop' castles in Yashino, who escaped from one castle by pretending to have committed suicide, who defended another with an army of mock figures, and who obeyed his imperial master by going into battle (Minatogawa, 1336), even though he knew it meant his death, and who, dying by committing *seppuku*, became the paragon of loyalty.

On this basis, the first students were supposed to take on board two root concepts: integrity and spirit, *makoto* and *seishin*. 'Success in clandestine activity comes from integrity' was a key phrase, while 'spirit' meant a fervent patriotism. These attitudes might have evolved into modern versions of the gung-ho, arrogant, 19th-century samurai cry of *Son nō jō i!* 'Revere the Emperor, expel the Barbarians!' One of Akigusa's subordinates, Major Ito Samata, almost put this

OF ARMS AND ARMOUR

Besides swords, the ninja armoury consisted mainly of farming tools. But ninjas were not merely farmers. Many were samurai, and adapted samurai fighting traditions. Since ninja operated in secrecy, they could not wear exotic samurai armour. If they had armour at all, it was chain mail, which could be worn beneath clothing. Many suits of ninja armour exist in museums, and some are still held privately.

Above: *Ueda Masaru runs a restaurant by the Forty-Eight Waterfalls, an ancient training ground for both Shugendō students and ninja. He also owns the ninja armour below.*

Left: *Ueda's ninja armour, inherited from his grandmother, is made of dark chain-mail, ideal for night-time operations.*

Above: *Ninja armour in the ninja museum in Takayama.*

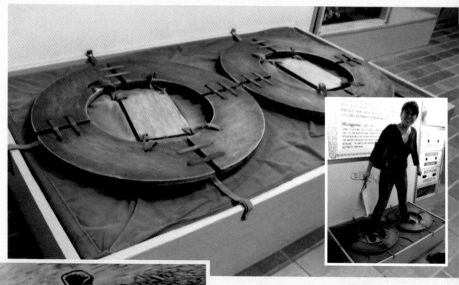

These puzzling objects in Iga Ueno's ninja museum are called 'water-shoes', 'mud-shoes' or 'water-spiders'. Supposedly they were for crossing moats. Some say you walked on them, as shown above by my guide Noriko – but how were they attached? Besides, they don't work on water, only mud. Some also claim they were used as portable boats (left).

Below: In Kōka's ninja museum, Hukui Minogu displays two throwing stars (shuriken).

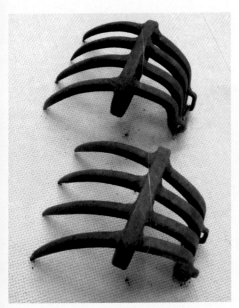

Above: *The fearsome tekko-kagi (hand-armour hook) was supposedly attached to the hand as an extreme form of knuckle-duster.*

Above: *Throwing stars (shuriken), the most famous of ninja weapons, come in many different forms – though how they were used in warfare is controversial.*

Above: *Caltrops, scattered to wound the feet of pursuers, were usually made of iron – but they might also be natural: those at the back are water-chestnut seeds, which are iron-hard when dried.*

Right: *The sickle-and-chain (kusarigama) derived from a farming tool. You disable or ensnare your opponent with the weighted chain, then kill him with the blade (or in the case of this one in the Iga-Ueno ninja museum, with the double blade).*

James Bond, the Spy Who Brought the Ninjas West

Some call James Bond a Western ninja: secret agent, loyal to a fault, adept with specialist weaponry, master of unarmed combat, the ultimate survivor. So it was appropriate for Bond (or rather his on-screen persona, Sean Connery) to give the ninjas their first big – if inaccurate – PR boost in Europe and the US, in *You Only Live Twice* (1967).

Above: *Not so much a ninja as a traditional master of martial arts, Connery trained at staff-fighting (bōjutsu) with the American martial-arts expert Donn Draeger.*

Left: *Sean Connery with a Japanese hair-do.*

Above: *Connery in a more standard PR shot in front of the seventeenth-century Himeji castle.*

As these on-set shots show, the film's 'ninjas' were martial-art extras. They were armed with swords and staffs (above), wore protective clothing (right), and in the climax – the invasion of the villain's mountain lair – operated as a team of commandos (below) ready to die rather than individuals dedicated to survival.

STREET NINJAS, FANTASY NINJAS

Ninjas have long since been removed from reality to become fantasy figures, toys and tourist items – mutant turtles, comic-book heroes and villains, and stock characters to entertain visitors in Iga-Ueno and Kōka, the towns that were home to the historical ninjas

Above: *The four Teenage Mutant Ninja Turtles are young heroes who owe their success to other non-ninja archetypes – musketeers, Robin Hood's Merrie Men and Peter Pan's 'lost boys'.*

Right: *In the manga Basilisk, ninjas have turned into mutants with diabolical powers. This one is the shape-shifting Rousai Azuki.*

Above: *Outside the Iga-Ueno ninja museum, a guide in ninja clothing adopts a killer pose.*

Above: *In Iga-Ueno, even the trains are dressed as ninjas, though in an endearing baby-pink rather than threatening black.*

Right: *A cheerful ninja sign in Iga-Ueno advertises a tourist shop.*

THE LAST OF THE 'LAST OF THE NINJAS'

Though he does not claim the title, Onoda Hiroo (as he is in Japanese) deserves to be called the last of the ninjas, having held out for thirty years on the Philippine island of Lubang. For much of this time he was alone, relying on ninja-like skills – self-sufficiency, loyalty to his masters and a determination to survive at all costs.

Onoda emerges from the jungle (above left), salutes Major-General Rancudo of the Philippine Air Force (above right), to whom he presents his sword (below). The central figure is the leader of the search party, Akihisa Kashiwai.

Left: *Onoda's account of his time in the jungle was published in 1974, the same year in which he returned to civilization.*

idea into action by planning to raid the British consulate in Kobe, to search for evidence of bribes offered to Japanese politicians and financiers. In the event, this plan, made in classic ninja tradition, was discovered, Ito court-martialled, and his boss, Akigusa, reassigned to Berlin. After that, Nakano avoided such 'cowboy' schemes, preferring well-thought-out projects. Covert ninja-style operations were all very well, but they would need a clear military and political purpose.

That same year, 1939, world events and a setback on the mainland rewrote Japan's plans for imperial conquest, and gave the Nakano School its true agenda. In inner Asia, Japan's advance came to a sudden halt when their army was crushed by a joint Russian–Mongol force. In Europe, Hitler signed a non-aggression pact with Russia and invaded Poland, inspiring Britain and France to declare war. War in Europe offered a chance for Japan to end European imperialism in Asia by driving out the British, French and Dutch – and then, in June 1941, with Hitler's invasion of the Soviet Union, a new opportunity to seize the Soviet Far East, even all Siberia. What a vision for an ambitious young power, to become the force to free Asian peoples from Western rule, to reverse centuries of humiliation! By 'Western', Japanese meant both European and American, since it had been the US, more than any other nation, that had forced Japan to open itself to the world in the mid-19th century, and turned the Pacific into its own backyard. Surely no Asians, from Siberian hunters to native Hawaiians, from British-ruled Indians to Filipinos, could possibly object to a war of 'liberation' by fellow Asians?

In pursuit of these goals, the ethos of Japan's new ninjas was very different from that commonly associated with the Japanese military. As Stephen Mercado puts it in his history of the school: in an army that 'inculcated unquestioning execution of orders and a fiery patriotism, the Nakano School began encouraging its shadow warriors to think creatively. They were to know the enemy, not simply to fight him. Such knowledge would be the strength underlying whatever technical skills in martial arts, safe-cracking, or the like in their covert quiver. From such knowledge, too, would flow empathy. A competent intelligence officer must, whatever his personal beliefs, be able to grasp the basis of his opponent's beliefs and actions.' In brief, Nakano trainees were to develop a combination of private initiative and group 'spirit'.

Purists in today's 'ninja community' argue that the Nakano graduates were not true ninjas. Quite right, in the sense that ninjas and ninjutsu evolved in historical circumstances that had vanished. No one could be loyal to a lord any more, because lords no longer existed. And in purist terms, a ninjutsu specialist could only learn his expertise from a master, which had to be passed on man to man, not learned in a group. But several aspects of ninjaism justify the use of the term here. The man who claims to be the inheritor of the ninja tradition, Masaaki Hatsumi, lists 18 fundamental areas of expertise, 11 of which were echoed in Nakano's training: spiritual refinement, unarmed combat, swordsmanship, fire and explosives, disguise and impersonation, stealth and entering methods, strategy, espionage, escape and concealment, meteorology and geography. Seven others were not exactly mainstream in modern warfare: stick-and-staff fighting, throwing blades, spear fighting, halberd fighting, chain-and-sickle weapons, water training and horsemanship. But there was enough in common between traditional ninja training and Nakano's to call these men modern ninjas. The two shared enough: loyalty, secrecy, a sense of duty, a sense of integrity. As Onoda puts it:

In what then can those engaged in this kind of warfare put their hope? The Nakano Military School answered this question with a simple sentence: 'In secret warfare, there is integrity.' And this is right, for integrity is the greatest necessity when a man must deceive not only his enemies but his friends. With integrity – and I include in this sincerity, loyalty, devotion to duty and a sense of morality – one can withstand all hardships and ultimately turn hardship itself into victory.[2]

Well, it may be a challenge to you and me to justify the deception of friends or a nationalist, militaristic agenda as moral, but secret services the world over have no problem in believing it. And many Nakano graduates and teachers were able to maintain their personal integrity by opposing or avoiding the worst aspects of Japanese wartime behaviour.

How the entrance examiners found men with the right qualities was as much a matter of gut reaction as analysis. A corporal arriving for the interview was ushered into a room where half a dozen high-ranking officers started to fire questions at him. 'You,' said one, 'd'you like women?' The corporal was totally nonplussed, unable to answer yes or no. Afterwards, he asked the assistant commandant Ueda Masao if the questions were planned. No, came the reply, nor did it matter: whatever the question, it was the way the interviewee answered that mattered, not what he said. The interview was not an examination but a personality test to see how the candidate responded to pressure. In this case, apparently, confusion was seen as a perfectly appropriate response.

When the war broke out in Europe, Nakano graduates

---

[2] Onoda's words in this and the next chapter are from his book, *No Surrender: My 30-Year War.*

focused on British-ruled India and the rest of southeast Asia. They scored some extraordinary successes, thanks to a team of agents under the remarkable Fujiwara Iwaichi, a one-time lecturer at the Nakano School and at the outbreak of war a captain in the army's Eighth Section, which handled intelligence. At first glance, he seemed a conventional type. Akashi Yoji, the translator of his memoirs, met him after the war: 'The lanky general with his short haircut, tight lips and hawkish eyes gave me the impression that he was a man of strong will and principle . . . something like the old-fashioned samurai with all the virtues attributed to that class.' But there was much more to him than that; indeed, he impressed everyone with whom he came in contact during and after the war – Malayan, Indian, even British – everyone except his own benighted superiors.

In September 1941, Fujiwara was given the task of leading covert operations in Malaya. He was supposed to contact Indians in the British Indian Army and in the independence movement, and Malay and Chinese anti-British groups. He had five Nakano graduates, each 'sound in thought and pure in heart' – in his own positive, *always* positive, words – but utterly naive. Fujiwara was 'dumbfounded by the unexpected order', firstly because he (like his team) had no experience of espionage, and secondly because he was very different from regular soldiers and officers. He was the opposite of everything Japan would soon come to stand for: arrogance, xenophobia, brutality. Fujiwara was loyal and patriotic, of course, but also generous, flexible and idealistic. In addition, he was highly emotional, often weeping at crucial moments, contrary to the chilly stoicism usually associated with Japanese officers. All of this made him one of those rare romantic figures in Japanese history. He knew it, too, comparing himself to Lawrence of Arabia (not the only Nakano graduate who did so, as we will see).

In Fujiwara's view, operations so far had been 'devoid of a principle that would inspire the cooperation of alien nationals'. What was needed was 'an ideology based on noble and universal political principles', which ought to involve 'an understanding of the Asian peoples' aspirations for freedom and liberation'. After a sleepless night agonizing over these ideological differences, he accepted his task, telling himself he would do what he could to revolutionize attitudes in the imperial army. In that, he failed; but he made a pretty good start.

He called his young officers to his home, had his wife prepare a supper of sea bream, and gave them a pep talk of shining idealism and – by hindsight – staggering naivety:

Keeping in mind His Majesty's concern for benevolence that extends not only to our troops but also to enemy soldiers, we must impress his concern about indigenous peoples and the enemy, especially prisoners of war, and build, by inducing them to cooperate with us, the foundations for a new friendship and peace out of the ashes of war ... We must impress on them that this war is a war of righteousness aimed at freeing indigenous people and POWs and helping them to achieve their national aspirations and happiness ... We should be modest and moderate, refraining from being loud-mouths, political bullies or swaggerers. Men of such arrogance will not achieve anything.[3]

It's a message he repeats several times. 'We were inexperienced, ill-prepared and ill-equipped to challenge the Western colonial powers. For us, the only way to break through this citadel of colonialism was to respect national aspirations with love and sincerity and win their hearts.

[3] Fujiwara's words here and later are from his book, F. Kikan.

Sincerity could move even heaven.' Seldom has an officer been so out of tune with the spirit of his government and its top military brass; and seldom so prescient.

The Fujiwara *Kikan* (Agency), as it was called – *F. Kikan* for short – set themselves up under cover in Thailand. At the heart of several nations and colonies all about to be at war with each other, Bangkok had suddenly become a centre of international espionage. Fujiwara's account makes the city sound like the set of a farce, with German, French, Japanese, Chinese, American and British agents all sneaking around trying to avoid being followed, constantly changing rickshaws and doubling back on their tracks.

Fujiwara made surreptitious contact with Pritam Singh, a young, fragile-looking Sikh, the leader of the Indian Independence League, banned as subversive by the British. He was ushered furtively up to Fujiwara's hotel room. 'I have come to help you realize your high ideals,' Fujiwara told him, as excited 'as if meeting a sweetheart'. Other meetings followed, one in a smelly warehouse that appeared to be a pickle factory, where Fujiwara promised to help the cause of Indian nationalism if Singh provided information and spread anti-British propaganda among Indian military units. Fujiwara and Singh agreed that Indian soldiers who surrendered to the Japanese would be returned to the frontline, where they would help undermine the morale of Britain's Indian troops.

When the invasion came, Fujiwara's operation rapidly moved from its covert, ninja-style roots to something overt, large-scale and very political, with important consequences. Indian units in Malaya, outflanked, overrun and cut off, surrendered by the hundred – some 2,500 of them by mid-January 1942. Fujiwara was so impressed by one of the prisoners, Captain Mohan Singh (there are many Singhs in this story), that he organized a lunchtime banquet for him and his officers, with Singh acting as master chef. Singh was impressed by Fujiwara's readiness to embrace Indian ways, eating with his fingers, trying curry for the first time, so different from the racial superiority and aloofness of the British. Singh was bowled over by Fujiwara's qualities, reeling them off in a foreword to Yamashita's memoirs – shrewd, tactful, well-informed, calm, cool, unruffled, sympathetic . . . It seemed a match made in heaven: 'Mentally, emotionally and spiritually, we had become one.' A few days later, Fujiwara agreed to back Singh as commander of an Indian National Army.

When Singapore fell on 15 February, Fujiwara and Singh had thousands of Indian prisoners from which to build the Indian National Army. Two days later, in a terrific propaganda coup, Fujiwara spoke to 45,000 of them in Singapore's Farrer Park, his words translated first into English then Hindi. Japan was waging a war of Asian liberation, and had no designs on India, he said, to much cheering. 'When I told them of my conviction that the fall of Singapore would provide a historic opportunity for Asian peoples who had suffered under the yoke of British and Dutch colonialism to liberate themselves from bondage, they went into a frenzy. The Park reverberated with such echoes of applause and shouts of joy that I had to stop my speech until the tumultuous commotion had subsided.' Japan was their friend, Fujiwara went on. She recognized their freedom struggle. She would help. The prisoners need not remain prisoners, if they chose to join the struggle to free India. With 'continuous applause, flying caps and waving hands', tens of thousands surged forward to pledge themselves to the cause of national liberation.

That was Fujiwara's moment of triumph. But his success drew the appalled gaze of those in power. Almost immediately, higher echelons of the government and army took over from Fujiwara, with a very different agenda. Disagreements arose with Indian nationalists over the timing, size and leadership of the INA. Japanese racism surfaced. Indian leaders, believing they would be treated as equals, made demands that the Japanese saw as unreasonable. Indian prisoners were used as mere labourers. Resentment grew. In March, having been in office only four months, Fujiwara was replaced by Iwakuro Hideo, a founder of the Nakano School, but lacking Fujiwara's idealism. In December 1942, the Japanese, fearing revolt, disarmed the INA and arrested its commander, Mohan Singh.

But this new Indian army was too important an asset to be allowed to die. The key to what happened next lay in Berlin, where the leading nationalist militant Subhas Chandra Bose – wealthy, brilliant, charismatic – was in exile. Bose had courted Hitler and Mussolini in the 1930s, had an Austrian wife, and in 1941 had fled house arrest in India through Afghanistan, where he was given a false passport by the Italian ambassador, completing his journey to Berlin through the Soviet Union three months before Germany invaded. In Japan's conquests, Bose saw his chance. The day after Singapore's surrender, Bose met Japanese diplomats in Berlin and begged to be allowed to command the Indian prisoners in Malaya, in effect to re-form the Indian National Army. Tokyo agreed, Hitler agreed, and Bose sailed by U-boat to Madagascar, there to be transferred to a Japanese submarine and taken via the Dutch East Indies to Tokyo, and finally to Singapore. There he revived the INA as the army of his Provisional Government of Free India. It fought with the Japanese against the British and Commonwealth forces in Burma throughout the war, until March 1945, when the British advance into Burma totally undermined its morale. In the words of one account, as Lt General William Slim's 161st Brigade drove south, 'it rounded up parties of dispirited INA, whose only anxiety appeared to be to find out where to "report in"'. Some 20,000 of the INA troops were repatriated to India, where they were to be tried for treason, making them a focal point for those striving for freedom from British rule. Protests turned to demonstrations and riots. As it happened, it was Gandhi's pacifism not Bose's militancy that came to dominate Indian politics, but it remains true that, in totally unpredictable ways, the decision to set up the Nakano School in 1937 played a significant role in Indian independence ten years later. Fujiwara played the most crucial part, for 'without him it is doubtful whether the INA [Indian National Army] would have existed'.[4]

Fujiwara chalked up another success in Malaya with a man whose story makes a remarkable footnote in the history of Japanese covert warfare. His name was Tani Yutaka, and he became famous as a bandit-leader known in Malaya as Harimau, 'the Tiger'. Just before World War I, his father, a barber, had come to work in Malaya with his wife, bringing baby Tani with him. When he was 12, his parents had another child, a girl. At the age of 20, Tani returned to Japan to do his military service, but failed the physical, because he was too short. He stayed on in Japan to work. By then, Japan had started to build her mainland empire, carving Manchukuo from northern China, and earning the hatred of Chinese everywhere, with catastrophic results for Tani and his family. Back in British-ruled Malaya, local Chinese took out their anger on the Japanese community. Among the victims were Tani's family: his father's barbershop burned and his sister, now eight, killed.

Tani returned to Malaya, radicalized by the tragedy and

---

[4] Louis Allen, author of *Burma: The Longest War*, in what he called the 'Postface' to Fujiwara's *F. Kikan*.

consumed with hatred both of the Chinese and of the British, who had (in his view) failed to protect his family. In his anger, he turned to crime, for which he was well qualified as a Malay speaker with intimate local knowledge. He gathered a band of Malay and Thai bandits – actually, a small army of between 1,000 or less, or 3,000 or more (estimates vary) – who specialized in robbing trains as well as routine theft. As his notoriety grew, he acquired his nickname: Harimau, 'Tiger'.

As the Japanese prepared for expansion, his skill in mounting what were in effect commando-style raids brought him to the attention of Japanese intelligence. An agent made contact, appealed to his sense of patriotism, and recruited him into the Fujiwara Agency. Come the invasion, 'Tiger' Tani gathered intelligence and led raids on British units, which included derailing a British supply train outside Kuala Lumpur. Unfortunately for him, life in the Malayan jungle gave him severe malaria.

Fujiwara finally met the Tiger, between bouts of malaria, just before the fall of Singapore. 'Harimau of Malaya, who had rampaged through Kelantan at the head of several hundred bandits, was, contrary to my expectations, a fair-skinned young man of small stature. His appearance was so gentle and timid that he hardly gave me the impression of being Japanese.' A few days later, Fujiwara sent Harimau, now much weaker, to a military hospital in southern Malaya, then on to another in Singapore, where Fujiwara visited him, bringing flowers and some good news. 'He was lying in bed amongst a row of other Japanese soldiers. Outside his bedroom were five Malays sitting on their haunches, as if they were servants attending a noble. Their eyes were bloodshot due to sleepless nights of looking after their master . . . I told him: "Tani, today I talked to General Manaki of the military government requesting him that you be appointed an officer of the military administration. General Manaki has agreed to it." His joyful reaction was so overwhelming I was quite taken aback.'

Harimau died a few days later. Fujiwara had him commemorated in Tokyo's Yasukuni Shrine, set up after the Meiji Restoration in memory of those who died for the emperor. Then – well aware of the ex-bandit's propaganda potential – he convinced the newly established Japanese movie company Daiei that his story had commercial possibilities. *The Tiger of Malaya* appeared the following year.[5]

One of Japan's greatest strategic problems – indeed, a prime reason for war – was oil. Japan had a few small fields in Niigata prefecture, but nowhere near enough. Without more, the carriers, battleships, planes, factories, the tanks and trucks in Manchukuo – all would be useless. There was an excellent source within reach – the oil wells of Palembang, in the swampy, jungly interior of Sumatra, in the Dutch East Indies (which became Indonesia in 1945). The Dutch had every reason to fear an assault, and were prepared. Not that their small defences would be a match for the Japanese war machine, but, given the difficulty of a 100-kilometre advance either up a small river or through the jungle, they would have ample time to blow the wells up before they could be taken.

What to do? The Nakano School was given the job of finding an answer.

Assistant commandant Colonel Ueda Masao devised a plan: paratroopers would swoop down in advance of an

---

[5] Not to be confused with General Yamashita Tomoyuki, who commanded the invasion of Malaya, was hanged in 1948 after a controversial trial, and is also known as the Tiger of Malaya. A 2003 play of this name, by Hiro Kanagawa (Japanese-born Canadian actor, playwright and screenwriter), is about the general, not the bandit. The two Tigers were linked through Fujiwara, one his boss, the other his employee.

up-river assault. But no one knew anything much about oil fields, and anyway Japanese paratroopers had no experience of jumping into them. Nakano's commandant commissioned a small team who spent a month researching newspapers and journals, visiting the Niigata fields, and persuading Japanese companies that had been operating in the region to hand over information and pictures. After a few practice jumps, the paratroopers – six from Nakano, another half dozen army men, all 'barely old enough to shave' – set off in mid-January 1942, hopping from southern Japan via Taiwan, Vietnam and Cambodia to their jump-off point on the Malay Peninsula.

One Nakano man, Lt Hoshino Tetsuichi, with only a few parachute drops under his belt, left a dramatic account of what happened next, one of the most successful paratroop operations ever, wonderfully retold by Stephen Mercado.

Hoshino and his five companions had assumed they would jump in the first wave. Instead, they were told they were relegated to the second. They were incensed. That evening Hoshino accosted an officer to protest, arguing that his group knew the terrain and the facilities better than anyone, while he himself had studied Malay. Moreover, he lied, he had actually scouted Palembang. It worked, sort of: he was given a place on the first jump, though his five Nakano companions were not. That night, he tossed and turned with nerves, wondering if he could possibly hope to win over the locals, round up the technical personnel and disarm the demolition charges in time. Next day, 14 February, he was on his way, complete with currency and propaganda leaflets proclaiming in Malay: 'People of Indonesia are our friends. We have come down from the skies. Everyone, please put your minds at ease.' Below was Singapore, smoking under the Japanese assault, one day from surrender. As they approached their drop zone, the leader called him to the door and pointed to the refinery 3,000 metres below, and yelled: 'You follow me!'

So Hoshino, with no previous experience in action, found himself second in the invasion. He landed safely, and ran through a refinery gate with some others. Seeing some Indonesians in an air-raid shelter, he passed out some of his leaflets and questioned them (so his Malay was up to the mark): 350 troops, no tanks or armoured vehicles. He raced on to other shelters, found three captive Dutch technicians and learned there were no demolition charges, which he confirmed by checking key points. By evening, his group had secured most of Palembang. Next day, the second company of paratroopers – including Hoshino's five Nakano companions – arrived, as did the main force advancing up the Musi river. The Dutch retreated to Java, and Japan had the oil it needed to fuel its war.

Hoshino was left to spread more propaganda, prepare the way for occupation by troops and petroleum engineers, and to play a later part in the story of Nakano alumni, which will emerge in due course.

Japan's involvement with Burma might have worked out well, if only the high brass had listened to the leader of its covert operations, Major Suzuki Keiji. Suzuki, whose agency employed many Nakano School graduates, was another sort of Lawrence of Arabia figure – more hands-on than Fujiwara, though equally idealistic, equally romantic – as devoted to the Burmese and their independence from British rule as Lawrence had been to the Arabs. As the historian of his exploits puts it, 'he devised unorthodox and audacious schemes which left people in astonishment'.[6] And like Lawrence, Suzuki was seen as 'wild' and sidelined by a conservative and fearful establishment, dedicated not to Burmese independence, but to military rule, with dire

[6] Tatsuro, *The Minami Organ*.

consequences for Japanese interests in Burma. This is Suzuki's story.

By 1940, British-ruled Burma had become a problem for the Japanese military, because they wanted to control all China, and Chinese nationalists and Communists were fighting back, Chiang Kai-shek's nationalists in particular being supplied by the British from Burma along the 700-mile Burma Road, newly built by 160,000 Chinese across the eastern Himalayas, which included an infamous 24-bend zigzag descent into China. The way to close the Burma Road was to support the Burmese struggle for independence, headed by Aung San, famous father of a now famous daughter, the pro-democracy activist and Nobel peace prize laureate, Aung San Suu Kyi. His organization, the Thakin ('Master') Party, had of course been banned by the British. In March 1940, Suzuki, a specialist in Anglo-American affairs, then an obscure backwater of intelligence operations, was told to come up with a plan to cut the Burma Road.

Suzuki, with a piercing gaze and 'fierce' moustache, seized this chance to make his mark. He entered Burma posing as a journalist under the name Minami Masuyo.[7] Hearing that Aung San and a group of companions had escaped Burma to evade arrest, he used private funds to have Aung San sent to Tokyo, where the two men met. Suzuki, eager to show his fighting spirit, boasted to his guest of killing Russian civilians, including women and children, in Vladivostok when in 1918–22 Japanese troops joined Allied forces to oppose the Communist revolution; the Burmese, he said, should fight with equal ferocity against the British, with Japanese help.

Suzuki's wildness spurred his superiors into action. In February 1941, they authorized Suzuki to head his own

[7] Minami means 'south', the direction in which the Imperial Japanese Army was heading.

network, a joint army–navy operation known as the Minami Agency after his nom-de-guerre. His boss was a Nakano instructor, Oseki Masaji, and his team included five Nakano graduates. Working in Bangkok, their task was to back Aung San by smuggling arms into Burma and training Aung San's group to become guerrillas – 30 of them, known later as the Thirty Comrades, one of whom was Ne Win, Burma's future military dictator.[8] The uprising was to be in June, after a few months of training in a secret camp in Hainan island off China's south coast.

It didn't happen. The Burmese didn't like the authoritarian training regime, nor did they like being made to bow every morning in the direction of the imperial palace in Tokyo. And the Japanese army changed its mind on independence, because they were now planning the assault into southeast Asia. June passed, with no action. The Thirty Comrades found themselves taken from Hainan to Taiwan. Only in December, after the attack on Pearl Harbor, did the high command turn to Burma. Aung San and the Thirty Comrades were brought to Bangkok, where Suzuki put together a volunteer force, the Burmese Independence Army (BIA), with some two dozen Nakano 'advisers' – all to no avail. The imperial army did not want anything to do with the un-predictable Suzuki and his irregulars. Sidelined into a separate mini-invasion, they entered an area of minority groups hostile to the Burmese and pro-British. Suzuki did his dashing best, riding a white horse, leading assaults on local police, railways and offices of colonial administration. In a separate BIA operation, Ne Win headed a small group, including two Nakano graduates, into Rangoon. But all hopes of immediate independence vanished when the Japanese army, unwilling to relinquish Burma with British

---

[8] Ne Win ('Brilliant Sun') was his alias. His real name was Shu Maung.

India on the doorstep, set up a military administration, promising independence at some unspecified date in the future. Suzuki, his Minami Agency, Aung San, Ne Win – all, like Lawrence and the Arabs, learned the hard way that 'imperial interests trump ideals of liberation' (in Mercado's telling phrase).

Suzuki pestered his army bosses to distraction, until they saw him as a rogue element who had 'gone native'. But he still had influence, directing the BIA, now a force of 30,000 well stocked with captured arms, with considerable combat experience against the retreating British. In May 1942, Burma fell. In a chaotic retreat, British, Burmese and Chinese fled over the northern borders, just before the monsoon struck. On 11 June, Japan's army ordered the dissolution of Suzuki's agency and scattered his staff to new appointments (some to the Dutch East Indies, with results detailed in the next section). Aung San, with no political role, was graciously allowed command of the Burma Defence Army, a 10-per-cent rump of the BIA. He, Ne Win and the other Thirty Comrades were part of an impotent puppet force, subject to Japanese 'advisers' and under surveillance from the dreaded military police, the Kempeitai. Suzuki was transferred to Tokyo, where he spent the rest of the war organizing military transport.

So ended Burma's dreams of independence under the Japanese. Under Suzuki and his ninja-like operation, what had started with such high and liberal hopes foundered on the rocks of Japanese military and political conservatism. Independence of a sort came in 1943, but under a puppet regime. Japan's decision to treat Burma as an occupied nation rather than an ally virtually guaranteed that when events turned against Japan, Burma's nationalists would turn back to the British and lead a behind-the-lines revolt against those who had once seemed their liberators. In early 1945, the

BNA's 8,000 men started to fight the Japanese, something that Aung San was keen to do before the British arrived in order to lay the foundations for independence from Britain.

The shadow warriors of Nakano staged one other mission of high drama, because it involved raiding Australia itself just at a time when Japan was on the way to losing the war – high drama, a few comic elements, and absolutely zero significance. So it goes with covert operations. There's no telling what they may lead to.[9]

In February 1943, the army decided to reconnoitre northern Australia from its base in the Dutch East Indies. Not that they lacked information, because they had very detailed reports from naval intelligence. The problem was that the reports were too good to be true. They suggested an on-the-spot source, and there was none. In the main base of Ambon, the Nakano School graduate Yamamoto Masayoshi decided to check for himself, using his own people and also eight from Suzuki's Minami Agency, who had been redeployed from Burma. Setting up his HQ in Timor, some 400 miles off the Australian coast, he contracted two boats from some reluctant Japanese fishermen, who were nervous of being blown out of the water by the Australian navy. That might happen anyway, Yamamoto told them. Better to have a gun aboard and rely on us to rescue you. But there was another problem: Japanese Nakano alumni did not look much like Australians, whether white or native. So Yamamoto decided to use Timor locals to go ashore, providing a sort of life insurance for them by building huts for all the families.

By the time the operation started, Yamamoto had a little

[9] This section is based on Louis Allen: 'The Nakano School'. See Bibliography. Allen cites no source for this account, but gives the impression it is based on a personal communication from Suzuki Hachiro.

society of some 300 men, women and children, all on his pay-roll. It was proving an expensive business. To pay for it, Yamamoto approached a colleague who was running his own agency, none other than Hoshino Tetsuichi, the same Hoshino who had parachuted second in line to seize the Palembang oil wells. Yamamoto had been Hoshino's senior in Nakano, and he tried pulling rank. Surely Hoshino hadn't used up all his funds? Surely he could use some to help pay for Yamamoto's operation? Surely Hoshino, as the junior, was in the position of a son, and owed Yamamoto help out of some sort of filial duty? Surely imperial funds should be used in the most effective way, whoever controlled them? Hoshino saw the force of these arguments, or perhaps lacked the authority to counter them, and did his bit.

The time came for action. There was a rumour of an Allied naval base being built in King Sound, the 50-kilometre-wide bay on the coast of Western Australia. The Japanese navy wanted the rumour checked out. They couldn't risk it themselves, because Australian planes would sink them. One of Yamamoto's fishing boats would be much more suitable. But, Yamamoto complained, a fishing boat would also be much more vulnerable. Never mind, he was told. This was an order.

The boat, the *Shōei Maru*, was made ready, with an anti-tank gun fitted to the bows and three heavy machine guns aboard. A light bomber would keep watch above, and for much of the way the crew would be in contact with base by radio. But once near the coast, a radio signal would give the game away, so crew and landing party – four Japanese and 25 locals – would rely on 40 pigeons for land-to-sea communication. At midnight on 10 January 1944, the No. 1 Australian Expeditionary Intelligence Unit set off over rough seas.

Come the dawn, the wind died. The boat approached a speck of an island just over halfway across the Timor Sea. High above, Captain Suzuki Hachiro (nothing to do with 'wildman' Suzuki who ran the Minami Agency) in the light bomber spotted a shocking sight – an Australian submarine on the surface, with men preparing an attack. No one on the fishing boat had seen the danger. Suzuki ordered his pilot to open fire, saw the crew race for the conning tower, and, as the sub began to dive, aimed a bomb that struck the bows. An oil slick spread across the surface. On the fishing boat, the crew and landing party, finally aware of the threat, waved in relief and delight as the bomber turned for home to refuel.

Next day, Suzuki was back, and saw the fishing boat moored in the lee of Browse Island, some 160 kilometres offshore and 320 kilometres northeast of their destination, with the landing party relaxing on the sandy beach, for movement during the day would have been fatal. Seeing there was nothing more to be done, Suzuki headed home for the last time. That night, the boat completed its journey, and entered King Sound. By dawn, it was moored inshore, its superstructure well camouflaged, and the landing party was ashore, searching for the rumoured base.

They found absolutely nothing. There was no base. They shot some film to prove it, then made for home. That was the extent of the Nakano School's covert operation in Australia, and the only time that Japanese troops actually landed there.

Back home, the Nakano School faced a stark new reality. Japan's advance had stalled, then been reversed. By late 1943, Guadalcanal, lynchpin of the South Pacific, was lost. New Guinea, the base from which Japan had planned to invade Australia, was held by a small group of irregulars, the 18th Army's Special Volunteer Corps led by Nakano-trained Lt Saito Shunji. He and two other Nakano men commanded three squads each, 135 men in all, many of them aborigines from the mountains and jungles of Taiwan, famous for their stamina and hunting abilities. In September 1943, carrying explosives, hand grenades and incendiaries, they made a night attack on an Australian camp, seizing several machine guns and 5,000 rounds of ammunition, and killing some 60 and wounding 80 without a single loss. Later assaults on other villages and camps killed 300, again without loss.

When briefed on the results, military intelligence drew the obvious conclusion. Intelligence and subversion were no longer enough. The empire needed to focus on unconventional warfare. Since no one could contemplate defeat, it seemed clear that Japan would be at war for a long, long time, and to maintain a foothold in its fading empire it needed commandos not only to undertake guerrilla actions, but also to survive behind enemy lines, gathering intelligence, until the moment came when they could help in reconquest.

The result was the opening of Nakano's new commando training centre at Futamata (today part of Tenryu, some 200 kilometres southwest of Tokyo). Here, in an intense three months, students were taught reconnaissance, infiltration, demolition, propaganda, map-making, the military government of occupied territories, and guerrilla fighting techniques, keeping fit with kendo and karate. Much of the training was similar to ninja techniques, and some of it derived directly from them, like the practice of walking close up against a wall to avoid casting a shadow. One of those who taught there was Fujita Seiko, a shadowy figure who claimed to be the last of the ninjas – of which there have been quite a few, as we will see – and specifically the last of the Kōga ninjas, no less.

One of the 220 at the opening ceremony on 1 September 1944, was Second-Lieutenant Onoda Hiroo, later to become Nakano's most famous graduate. He had worked in China, spoke Chinese and had then served in China as a soldier, perfect background for commando training. He was surprised by what followed:

It was certainly very different from the officers' training school. Military forms and procedures were observed, but without excessive emphasis on regulations. On the contrary, the instructors kept stressing to us that in our new role as commando trainees, we should learn that so long as we kept the military spirit and remained determined to serve our country, the regulations were of little importance . . . They urged us to express our opinions concerning the quality of the instruction and to make complaints if we felt like it. We had four hours of training in the morning and four in the afternoon. Classes lasted two hours each, with fifteen-minute breaks in mid-morning and mid-afternoon. When the time for a break came, everyone piled out of the classroom windows into the yard to have a smoke. There were 230 of us, packed like sardines into one small barracks, and the break was not long enough for all of us to leave and return in orderly fashion through the door. At officers' training school, if anyone had dared leave by the window, the punishment would have been swift and severe. At Futamata it was routine.

In an unimposing collection of wooden buildings, half a dozen expert instructors, all with international experience in diplomatic missions, stressed not only the need for individual initiative and a willingness to develop critical views, but also something totally opposed to the samurai tradition of courting or choosing an honourable death rather than face the humiliation of defeat. That tradition was still alive, not in the expectation that defeated soldiers would commit suicide by cutting their bellies, but in other ways. Officers returning from the defeat by Russian and Mongolian troops in eastern Mongolia in 1939 were presented with pistols. In Mercado's words, 'Left alone with the weapon, the repatriated officers did what was expected by committing suicide to expiate their "shame".' Later, when the war turned against Japan, soldiers would choose a final suicidal charge rather than surrender. The tradition would, in October 1944, find renewed expression in the suicide bombings of the kamikaze pilots. But none of these was the Nakano way, which derived directly from the ninja tradition: first and foremost the mission, only to be fulfilled by staying alive.

At the end of his three-month training, Onoda and his fellow trainees were deployed to where Japan's next and perhaps final battles would be fought: on home ground in the south, in Okinawa, Tokyo, and the far north, and overseas in Vietnam, Indonesia, Burma, Taiwan, Korea and the Philippines, which was where Onoda and 20 others were to go.

By 1944, Japanese authority in the Philippines was facing widespread resistance. The Japanese, welcomed as liberators by many in 1942, had squandered all goodwill by their arrogance and brutality. This was not a liberation but an occupation. Often, soldiers slapped local men in the street for not bowing to them. They shot those suspected of being sympathetic to the US, raped and stole. Mercado quotes one Futamata/Nakano commando's rueful assessment: the Spanish had brought Christianity in their 300-year-rule, the Americans had brought roads, cars and movies in their 50 years, but all the Japanese had done in their two years was take. As a result, American guerrillas, preparing the ground for the US return, proved very effective, but inspired ever more brutal responses from the Japanese military police. Into this stew of regular, guerrilla and covert operations came some Nakano graduates, 24 of them by September 1944, even as Japanese losses in the Pacific mounted. In October the navy lost four carriers and the super-battleship *Musashi*. Kamikaze pilots made the fight more brutal, fearful and bitter, but would not restore Japan's fortunes. Japan lost airfield after airfield, and mounted daring, often suicidal raids to retake some of them, crash-landing transport planes wheels up, firing machine guns and dropping bombs from parachutes, bayoneting sleeping Americans, all to no avail. Next would come the American invasion of Mindoro, then Luzon, the Philippines' main island. Onoda and his fellow graduates were supposed to do whatever they could to disrupt the advance. In all, there were 98 shadow warriors in the Philippines, of whom a third survived the war.

On 17 December, Onoda and 21 others from Nakano flew into Clark airfield on Luzon, and were taken to Manila. Five then travelled on to divisional HQ in Lipa, an overnight drive away, with Major Taniguchi Yoshimi, boss of covert operations, who had both trained and taught at Nakano. He briefed the five men. Four were to lead groups on Luzon and Mindoro islands, while Onoda was told he was to lead a garrison in guerrilla warfare on Lubang island, 50 kilometres to the southwest of Luzon. This was the first he had heard of Lubang. Only 25 kilometres long, it was dominated by a jungly spine of mountains, and had an airfield and pier, which Onoda was to destroy to slow the American invasion of Luzon.

In the presence of a visiting lieutenant-general, Onoda was also briefed by his division commander, Lt-General Yokoyama, who re-emphasized one of Nakano's main lessons:

With his eyes directly on me, he said, 'You are absolutely forbidden to die by your own hand. It may take three years, it may take five, but whatever happens, we'll come back for you. Until then, so long as you have one soldier, you are to continue to lead him. You may have to live on coconuts. If that is the case, live on coconuts! Under no circumstances are you to give up your life voluntarily.' A small man with a pleasant face, the commander gave me this order in a quiet voice. He sounded like a father talking to a child . . . [In another version of the same occasion, it is the lieutenant-general, Chief-of-Staff Muto Akira, who delivers the pep talk, but with the same message: 'Let me repeat, suicidal *banzai* charges are absolutely forbidden.'] I vowed to myself that I would carry out my orders. Here I was, only an apprentice officer, receiving my orders directly from a division commander! That could not happen very often, and I was doubly impressed by the responsibility I bore. I said to myself, 'I'll do it! Even if I don't have coconuts, even if I have to eat grass and weeds, I'll do it!'

One of his comrades, Yamamoto Shigeichi, born in the same prefecture and also a graduate of Futamata, was told he would be leading 50 men in an attack to retake the airfield at San Jose. He said he expected to die soon. He nearly did, because his group was torn apart during the assault. But he survived, vanished into the jungle, and re-emerged eleven years later, in 1956, as a sort of curtain-raiser to Onoda's much more extended experience.

As Onoda prepared to disappear into the jungles of Lubang, his comrades back home were preparing for the ultimate victory-or-death battle, a sort of mass, ninja-style Armageddon. The army was building a massive underground shelter for the emperor in Matsushiro, in the mountains of Nagano (nothing to do with Nakano) prefecture, a natural fortress in central Japan which would be the heart of the empire's last stand. Industries, too, were shifting into the area. Mitsubishi had two whole cities ready for the construction of its Zero fighters and other weapons. In all, some 600 other factories had set up in Nagano by the summer of 1945.

All would be defended to the end by shadow warriors coordinated by the Nakano School. Now that the Philippines was lost, the next line of defence would be Okinawa and the other Ryūkyū islands that led, like stepping stones, north-wards to Japan's heartlands. In the Philippines, the army had learned that to meet the invaders on the beaches or in open combat was not merely suicidal: it was futile. In Okinawa, there was no hope for victory over a vastly superior force, the greatest armada in history. The only aim could be to make the price too high for the enemy to pay, with suicide boats, suicide planes and troops dug into the mountains, exacting losses that would force the Allies to negotiate, and thus avoid the humiliation of unconditional surrender.

On every one of the myriad small islands, the military posted lone shadow warriors who were supposed to organize locals to resist. Eleven were from the Nakano School, who were in the guise of teachers. One of them, Sergeant Sakai Kiyoshi, arrived in Japan's most southerly point, a coral island named Hateruma, with a large orange crate filled with his uniform, swords, pistols, hand grenades, explosives, and even one of those pens designed to release bacteria into the water supply if the Americans landed. After school, he taught martial arts, exhorted his students not to fear death, even giving hand grenades to young girls with the order to use them on themselves if capture seemed imminent.

As it happened, lone individuals could play hardly any role and commando units only a small one in a battle that was the most deadly and costly of the war. In three months – twice as long as planned – Japan's so-called 'typhoon of steel' led to the death of some 100,000 Japanese soldiers and 120,000 civilians. One thousand five hundred kamikaze attacks sank over 30 US ships and damaged 400, to no avail. In mid-June, Okinawa was lost, and the Nakano men could begin their real missions – except that it was too late. On Hateruma, Sakai managed to evacuate many of his charges to a neigh-bouring island, where many died of malaria. On Okinawa itself, Murakami Haruo, commanding the Third Raiding

Unit, planned to use his local Okinawan auxiliaries as terrorists, posing as refugees until they received the order to attack. No order came: the US dropped its two atomic bombs, Japan surrendered and Murakami led his commandos into captivity. In the far north of the Ryūkyūs, where islanders were angry at their leaders for taking them into war in the first place, they denounced their 'teacher' to US soldiers.

Next line of retreat – the next site for yet another 'final battle' – was Kyūshū, the most southerly of the four islands that make up the Japanese heartland. This would be even tougher for the Americans to take, and might, if it was too tough, force a negotiated settlement. The plan was to have coastal defence units sacrifice themselves by delaying the invaders on the beaches, and then stopping them in the forested hills of the interior, where fortifications lay far beyond the guns of the US warships. Douglas MacArthur's assault would throw 350,000 men on to the beaches, but they would contend with 2,000 suicide planes, 1,100 conventional aircraft, and 700,000 troops. In this, the greatest invasion in history, the Americans might lose 250,000.

Then, given victory of sorts, there would be the un-conventional forces, the guerrillas, trained by some 100 Nakano men, intelligence people from Manchukuo, China, Southeast Asia. The prime mission was to teach guerrilla warfare to civilians – attacking airborne troops, setting ambushes, con-ducting night raids, sabotaging – a task undertaken by a group of shadow warriors known as the Kirishima Unit, named after a local shrine and a mountain range. By the late summer, they had trained about 5,000 soldiers and 10,000 veterans and civilians. These were the latter-day ninjas who would pick off Americans floating down on parachutes or threading their way in single file through paddy fields.

On the home front, students and staff travelled by train,

truck and even ox cart to a new HQ in Tomioka, near the emperor's underground shelter in Matsushiro. They would lead the population in mass, nationwide resistance, demolishing facilities, infiltrating, and mounting assaults. Across the nation, Nakano School shadow warriors began drilling everyone – reservists, civilians, men, women and children – for the coming invasion. For most, there were no weapons except bamboo spears with which to attack American foot patrols. Members of the so-called Izumi (Spring) Unit, one of the Nakano School's most secret programmes, had undergone intensive training from June, focusing on the use of explosives, hiding out in mountains and valleys, where they would be linked by runners rather than radio. When the time came they would throw off their civilian roles and bring assassination and terror to bear against Allied forces and collaborators. Resistance in the Tokyo area would be handled by the Yashima Unit, after an old name for Japan, whose commander, Arai Fujitsugu, had stocked hill caves with radios, weapons, clothing and food, much of it taken from downed B-29 bombers. Ten Nakano graduates commanded 100 men, who would organize civilians to mount attacks behind enemy lines. But in early August Arai was told to shift his operation to the coast, which would mean certain death when the invasion came. Arai was appalled, and complained to his army HQ.

Why throw away his men in vain? 'What's the point of having them die a dog's death before fighting?' he asked.

'Is life so precious to you?' came the blinkered reply. 'The kind of tactics you're talking about aren't written in the Military Academy textbooks.'

Of course, Arai and his men did not have to fight and die after all. Ten days later, Japan surrendered.

In the far north, too, in Hokkaido and beyond, Nakano men prepared for battles that never came. Here, they had to consider another possible enemy. Russia and Japan were (and are) old rivals in both the island chains that almost link Japan to Russia – principally the long thin island of Karafuto (the Japanese name) or Sakhalin, and the Chishima (or Kuril) group. In December 1944, an old Nakano acquaintance of ours resurfaced – Suzuki Keiji, mastermind of the Minami Agency and minder of Burma's Thirty Comrades, of whom Aung Sang Suu Kyi's father had been the leading light. Suzuki had been sidelined after objecting too vociferously to Japan's refusal to back Burmese independence. Now here he was on one of the Chishima islands, Etorofu (Iturup in Russian). The island, a 200-kilometre spine of volcanoes looming above fir forests, had one good feature, a bay which provided fine anchorage. There was a brief operation to train 25 officers, 14 of them from Nakano, to attack enemy ships and their shore-based HQ, but it lasted only a couple of months, and the focus shifted to Hokkaido, just in time for the surrender.

Not that their presence would have amounted to anything. When, three days after the atom bombs were dropped, the Soviet Union invaded Manchukuo, Japan's puppet nation on the mainland, Stalin already had Allied agreement that he could, as a reward, have the Chishima Islands. Today, as southern Sakhalin, they are still in Russian hands.

Nakano men were meant to be different, more creative, more flexible than their regular army counterparts. In building their new empire, all were supposedly 'liberating' their Asian brothers and sisters. The training made some shadow warriors less arrogant, less xenophobic, willing and occasionally eager to put the interests of other peoples and cultures before their own. But there was nothing in their training that taught respect for the enemy. Of course, almost all governments and almost all high commands like to see their troops hating their opponents, lumping them together as the embodiment of evil. You can't have your men fraternizing with the enemy, because they might then not kill them with quite such abandon. But most wars have been against neighbours, and in most wars ordinary fighting men know that the enemy are also ordinary fighting men doing a job they dislike for some greater cause. In World War I, British and German troops referred to each other as Tommy and Jerry, with a certain affection. In World War II, some commanders won grudging admiration from the other side. But in the war with Japan, not even shadow warriors were touched by such humanity. All believed that the Americans would kill and rape and maim indiscriminately, and did their best to make civilians believe it too.

(Their attitude had its mirror image. Ordinary American fighting men who watched kamikaze pilots diving to their deaths concluded they were up against some new and perverted form of the human species. It was remarkable, given the horror and inhumanity of the conflict, that in victory American troops often surprised Japanese civilians with their lack of vindictiveness.)

There were, of course, atrocities on both sides. Nakano graduates were on occasion as atrocious in their behaviour as any. One particular incident stands out. This occurred outside Fukuoka, which guards Hakata Bay on the southern island of Kyūshū. Fukuoka, 16th Area Army HQ, had been pounded to rubble by American bombers. Four days after Hiroshima and Nagasaki vanished under mushroom clouds, the HQ learned from foreign radio stations that surrender was imminent. Some shadow warriors decided to take out their rage and frustration on American prisoners. These men were airmen, and were considered criminals for their indiscriminate, indeed deliberate bombing of civilian areas (let alone the atom bombs of Hiroshima and Nagasaki, the great fire-bombing raid on Tokyo of 9 March 1945 killed or injured 120,000 and destroyed 250,000 homes).

On the evening of 10 August, Captain Itezono Tatsuo summoned over 20 shadow warriors, Nakano graduates who had not yet seen combat, and told them that they were to participate in the execution of eight American POW airmen. Permission had been given to practise guerrilla and martial arts training on them, this being a form of execution that had been widespread since 1937. They could use hands, bows and arrows, and swords. It would, Itezono said, boost the morale of his men.

If this was sadism, it was also sanctioned by the culture. Until late in the 19th century, samurai swordsmen had honed their skills by beheading the corpses of prisoners. It was, after all, something they might be called upon to do if they had to participate in *seppuku*, when a man who commits suicide by cutting his belly would be finished off by a coup de grâce from an aide.

The next morning, the prisoners were taken to Aburayama, a forested hill just south of Fukuoka. The prisoners were stripped. One was made to kneel. Itezono asked for volunteers. While others warmed up, practising karate strokes, a lieutenant took a sword, and, when given the go-ahead by a colonel, Tomomori Kiyoharu, beheaded the prisoner with one stroke. Four others were also beheaded. Then came the martial arts exercises. One of the men struck the fifth prisoner several vicious karate blows, and another volunteer beheaded him. Another two died in the same way. The eighth prisoner was forced to sit, while a Futamata probationary officer shot at him with a bow and arrow. The third shot pierced the man's head above his left eye. He was then beheaded.

Colonel Tomomori said that for his men the experience would be valuable for the decisive battle to come.[10]

---

[10] Later, 40 were tried for war crimes. Nine death sentences were handed out, but commuted on retrial. Twelve were condemned to life imprisonment, 15 to prison sentences of 20–40 years.

*

That battle never came, of course. Japan surrendered instead, nine days after the A-bombs fell. Already the Nakano School, in its new buildings in Tomioka, was dead, condemned by orders to close it from its new commandant, Major-General Yamamoto Hayashi. Across the empire, its hundreds of operatives obeyed orders to cease fighting. Though some, meeting in Tokyo, were for rebelling against the decision to surrender, they backed down after a major, Hata Masanori, an expert on Germany, pointed out that Hitler's determination to fight to the bitter end was disastrous for his people. Better to obey the emperor, he said, and focus on reconstruction. Even those who planned to continue the war underground as members of the secret Izumi Unit never put their plans into effect. As one American liaison officer and an expert in Japan commented, 'When the Japanese were told by the emperor to stop, boy, they stopped.' It was an attitude that, once conveyed to General MacArthur, helped ensure there would be no direct military rule by the US, but indirect, relatively benign rule through a Japanese government.

On 13 August, burning documents, weapons and communications gear sent clouds of smoke billowing over the school's buildings. Two days later, at an assembly in the school's courtyard called by Yamamoto, the staff heard the emperor's voice on the radio calling upon his subjects to 'bear the unbearable'. Then, wracked with emotion, Yamamoto set fire to the Nanko Shrine, the one dedicated to Kusunoki Masashige, which had been brought from the school's original buildings to Tomioka. A few remained to bury weapons in case of a future uprising. That was the school's formal end. Futamata, its specialist commando branch, closed ten days later.

Other than the small memorials that mark the sites, the Nakano School shadow warriors shared a considerable legacy. In the words of Louis Allen, historian of the war in Asia, 'In the long perspective, difficult and even bitter as it may be for Europeans to recognize this, the liberation of millions of people in Asia from their colonial past is Japan's lasting achievement.'

Fujiwara would have been gratified by Allen's words. His story makes a telling postscript to that of the Nakano School, and adds a personal footnote to Allen's conclusion. At the end of the war, he was in Fukuoka, recovering from malaria contracted during the Burma campaign. A few months later, he was back in India, subpoenaed to help defend the first three of almost 20,000 INA officers being tried for treason by the British. The upcoming trial inspired protests, then riots. The British backed down, the men were released, British prestige plummeted, independence became a certainty. But Fujiwara was kept in India, to face accusations that he, like countless other Japanese, was a war criminal. He spent three months in Changi prison, in grim conditions. Handcuffed, half-starved, shoved about by guards, Fujiwara was appalled that his agency could be confused with the imperial army. He defended himself vociferously. Transferred to Kuala Lumpur prison and re-interrogated, he was cleared of all charges. At the end of his incarceration, he was given a final interview, in a totally different atmosphere. The tall, balding colonel was puzzled. How was it that Fujiwara and his colleagues, who were really no more than naive amateurs, had proved so successful? His answer is worth quoting, because it captures the essence of the ideals of a tiny minority, which were the complete reverse of the ethos that dominated the Japanese military.

I was at my wits' end when I was given this difficult assignment shortly before the war, when we started out with nothing and with an extremely poorly trained staff. Then I became aware of one thing. The British and the Dutch had made remarkable achievements in the development of industry and in the construction of roads, schools, hospitals and houses, in their respective colonies. They were, however, developed and built for their own benefit, not for the welfare of the indigenous people . . . The [colonial powers] made no pretence to understand native national aspirations for freedom and independence, but suppressed and emasculated them, [and] had no love for the local people . . . I made a pledge with my men that there was no other way but to put into practice our love and sincerity. The indigenous people who were hungry for love reached out for the mother's milk that we offered. I believe this is the reason for our success.

This was the attitude that infused Japan's wartime shadow warriors. Yes, it's naive, even childlike in its simplicity. It never had a chance to grow up, because the *F. Kikan* and the other covert agencies were quickly opposed by the Japanese leadership. On the other hand, Fujiwara would perhaps always have remained a Peter Pan idealist, because he saw his role as making independence possible, not engaging in the complex, difficult, compromising business of creating new governments. Love and sincerity can remain pure and simple, if not tested by reality.

15

TO JAPAN, WITH LOVE

If you always assume you are facing the enemy, you will never drop your guard in any way.

Ninja instructional poem

ON 6 DECEMBER 2011, THE *GUARDIAN* PUBLISHED A REPORT INTO the violence that broke out in London and other cities in August. The report, 'Reading the Riots', was based on 270 interviews with participants. It revealed that the rioters were young and poor, and felt so alienated from society that they felt no shame at trashing stores and stealing the contents. In many areas, as word spread of coming violence, few saw any connection between their actions and the individuals on the receiving end. Almost all shops were fair game, especially big stores and those selling clothes and electronic goods. A major factor in the spread of the riots was the slow response by the police. The explosion of violence, the absence of immediate police action, the rage, the heady sense of freedom, the feeling of power and of entitlement – all combined into a toxic mix.

One 19-year-old from Battersea described how he plundered shops at least 12 times, stashing the stolen goods in a hiding place: 'I felt like I was a ninja, on a mission . . . like I was jumping in all the shops, using front rolls, yeah, run in there, get a bag out there quick . . . tie it up, put it back on my back, roll out, run to my little road that I know no one else knows.

'I felt like I was a ninja.' Here is a young man untroubled by morality, whose sole purpose at that moment was theft, which had to be done surreptitiously; and this, he imagines, was what ninjas did.

That pretty much sums up today's popular image of the ninja. The man in black whose task in life is to break, enter, steal and kill (luckily our young rioter did not come up against opposition). He felt like he was 'on a mission', but the only mission was self-serving theft. No sense of family or a cause. He was not part of a gang. He was not gathering information that would help others. In brief, other than being a loner, his use of the word 'ninja' bears no relationship to the historical ninja. Where did it all go wrong?

As for the international appeal of the ninjas, it's largely the fault of Ian Fleming, creator of James Bond. Bond is, in any case, a Western ninja: dependent on, and utterly loyal to his boss, M; a master of unarmed combat and of fighting with a variety of exotic weaponry; an infiltrator, gatherer of information, assassin, and above all a survivor. Fleming does not make the comparison himself, until the last Bond book before his death, when Bond actually becomes a ninja.

The idea seems to have come to Fleming as the result of a trip to Japan in 1959, when he went for three days to research an article for a *Sunday Times* series entitled 'Thrilling Cities' (subsequently republished in a book of the same name). That was enough to introduce him to martial arts, then re-emerge from the shadows at the hands of enthusiasts. His guide was 'Tiger' Saito, editor of an annual magazine on Japan produced by the Japanese Embassy in London. 'Tiger' was 'chunky, reserved, tense . . . he looked like a fighter – one of those war-lords from Japanese films'. Together, they shared a 'cheerful and excellent luncheon' with the writer Somerset Maugham, who had by chance just arrived on a visit. Fleming claimed they were friends, their friendship being based on the fact that 84-year-old Maugham 'wishes to be married to my wife, and he is always pleased to see me if only to get news of her'. The real link was that Maugham had been a spy in Russia, an experience reflected in the fictional adventures of Ashenden, the archetype of the secret agent and much admired by Fleming. Maugham referred to Ashenden's boss by his initial (C.), a device copied by Fleming, who named Bond's boss M. Anyway, the three went off to watch a display of jujitsu. No mention of ninjas.

But five years later, Fleming set his twelfth Bond novel, *You Only Live Twice*, in Japan, and built on the subject of martial arts. The novel has some rather dark themes. Bond's wife has been murdered by the master-criminal Ernst Stavro Blofeld, founder of SPECTRE, the Special Executive for Counter-Intelligence, Terrorism, Revenge and Extortion. Bond is depressed, drinks too much, gambles too much. Later, his girlfriend (Kissy) gets pregnant. There are subtexts about the decline of empire, Britain's lack of moral fibre, and the rise of America to world domination. He is given one last chance. The real-life Tiger Saito becomes Tiger Tanaka, head of the Japanese Secret Service. Bond's job is to get from him vital information about Soviet plans to destabilize the world by testing nuclear weapons and then using them as a threat. In exchange, Tanaka sets a challenge for 'Bondo-san' (as Fleming points out, Japanese prefer to end words with a vowel).

A certain Dr Guntram Shatterhand, a Swiss multi-millionaire and amateur botanist with impeccable credentials, has created a castle estate, which includes a pool of piranhas and several death-dealing volcanic fumaroles, and in which he grows numerous fatally poisonous plants. It's a wild premise, but made credible because Fleming lists the plants, all 22 of them, with their effects, and classes them in six categories of poisons. This 'Castle of Death' attracts would-be suicides, for, as is well known, Japanese seeking to restore honour do so by committing suicide. Hundreds have entered Shatterhand's estate and chosen to die horrible deaths. This is an embarrassment to the government. Shatterhand, who protects himself from poison by wearing armour, has committed no crime and is immune to prosecution. Bond's task is to take on the role of St George, to redeem Britain's tarnished image, to enter this 'Castle of Death and slay the Dragon within'. Success will qualify him to receive the information he seeks.

As part of his training, Tanaka plans to take Bond to his 'Central Mountaineering School' near Kyoto:

It is here that my agents are trained in one of the arts most dreaded in Japan – ninjutsu, which is, literally, the art of stealth or invisibility. All the men you will see have already graduated in at least ten of the eighteen martial arts of *bushido*, or 'the ways of the warrior,' and they are now learning to be ninja, or 'stealers-in,' which has for centuries been part of the basic training of spies and assassins and saboteurs. You will see men walk across the surface of water, walk up walls and across ceilings, and you will be shown equipment which makes it possible for them to remain submerged under water for a full day. And many other tricks besides. For of course, apart from physical dexterity, the ninja were never the super-humans they were built up to be in the popular imagination.

So it is. The school is a castle where ninjas – dressed in black, of course, with their heads hooded – stage a mock invasion of the Castle of Death. They skim across the moat on wooden floats, and scale the immense wall. One weakling falls to his death. Inside, attackers and defenders whack each other with staves, leaving many unconscious or groaning in pain, but none the worse, apparently, for blows to the groin. Bond sees ninja armament: throwing-stars, caltrops, hollowed bamboo for breathing underwater – all the paraphernalia of ninja tourist museums.

Later, relaxing on a pleasure steamer, Tanaka tries to interest Bond in haikus, quoting some of Bashō's. 'Do me a favour, Bondo-san. Write a haiku for me yourself. I'm sure you could get the hang of it. After all, you have had some education.' Bond admits to some rusty Latin and Greek, and tries his hand at one.

> You only live twice:
> Once when you are born
> And once when you look death in the face.

Tanaka applauds the sincerity, but really it's a disaster – too many syllables, and an odd first line implying many lives. But it provides the novel with its title.

Bond asks how the ninjas can take stave-blows to the groin. 'That might be of some practical value to me instead of all this waffle about poetry.' Tanaka explains:

You know that in men, the testicles, which until puberty have been held inside the body, are released by a particular muscle and descend between the legs? ... Well, by assiduously massaging those parts, [the warrior or sumo wrestler] is able, after much practice, to cause the testicles to re-enter the body ... Then before a fight, he will bind up that part of the body most thoroughly to contain these vulnerable organs in their hiding-place. Afterwards in the bath, he will release them to hang normally. It is a great pity it is now too late for you to practise this art. It might have given you more confidence on your mission. It is my experience that agents fear most for that part of the body when there is fighting to be done or when they risk capture. These organs, as you know, are most susceptible to torture for the extraction of information.

Only now does Tanaka brief Bond about his target. Wonder of wonders, Shatterhand is none other than his wife's murderer, Ernst Stavro Blofeld. Suddenly, this is no longer an official assignment. It's personal. Bond wants revenge. 'And with what weapons? Nothing but his bare hands, a two-inch pocket knife and a thin chain of steel.'

First, though, Bond has to get to the base of the castle wall. He will do this from an island which is home to the Ama people, who make their living diving for *awabi* (abalone) shells. For this he becomes a ninja, adopting the persona of an anthropologist coming to live with the Ama. He goes out to sea with the daughter of his hosts, accompanied by her pet cormorant, which is trained to catch fish. The girl is, of course, his next love, Kissy Suzuki, who was briefly in Hollywood, and therefore English-speaking, before returning to her island life. After a few idyllic days, she insists on swimming with him across the half-mile of ocean to the castle. It's night. He climbs in, dressed in his ninja gear, which is 'as full of concealed pockets as a conjurer's tail-coat', with numerous useful bits of equipment. He finds a base in a garden shed, makes a stealthy survey, identifies sulphurous fumaroles and the piranha pool, witnesses two suicides, hides and sleeps through the day.

That night, he breaks into the castle, is captured, and placed above a geyser that erupts under tight control at regular intervals. Interrogated by Blofeld, Bond manages to strangle him, upset the timing mechanism of the geyser and escape, using, of all things, a balloon (over the top, even for Fleming). The castle is blasted to bits by volcanic action. But, while escaping, Bond is wounded in the head and loses his memory. Kissy rescues him, nurses him for weeks, reignites his dormant sexuality, and is soon pregnant.

Meanwhile, back home, it's assumed he has died. M writes his obituary in *The Times*, with a witty reference to 'a series of popular books written around him by a personal friend and former colleague of James Bond. If the quality of these books, or their degree of veracity, had been any higher, the author would certainly have been prosecuted under the Official Secrets Act.' The book ends with Bond, unaware of Kissy's pregnancy, wondering about his past, intrigued by the word 'Vladivostok' which he sees in a scrap of newspaper. It suggests another name: Russia. 'I have a feeling that I have had much to do with this Russia,' he says, and determines – with Kissy's broken-hearted consent – to go there in pursuit of his memories and his past life.

Fast-forward three more years to the film version. The dark themes are ditched in favour of action, gimmicks and a few 'sex' scenes so unbelievably coy it hardly counts as sex these days. The plot-line is irredeemably ludicrous, even more so than Fleming's. So is the script, as the writer, Fleming's friend and children's book author Roald Dahl, well knew. Blofeld is set on igniting a war between the US and the Soviet Union. This he does by launching a spacecraft that gobbles up the satellites of both powers and miraculously vanishes with them, turning both sides towards war. Blofeld's castle is replaced by a volcano, inside which is a space centre, source of the cannibalistic spacecraft. The crater floor slides back when the rockets take off and return. Today, it is about as convincing as the original King Kong. But it made its budget back four times over. One thing the film kept was the idea that Bond should work with ninjas, who overwhelm Blofeld and his evil empire in the climax.

The film needed a consultant. In the West, there were none. The most obvious choice was Donn Draeger, ex-US marine, veteran of the Pacific and Korean wars, founder of the US Judo Federation, expert in many martial arts, and prolific author, but as yet no expert in ninjas.

There were, however, ninja experts in Japan – not many, because all martial arts had been banned in 1945 by the Supreme Command Allied Powers (SCAP) as symbolic of Japanese militarism. Besides, many – perhaps most – Japanese themselves looked upon all martial traditions as part of the folly that had led them into war in the first place. The ban was repealed in 1948, with martial arts undergoing a steady renaissance in the following years, and increasing popularity in books. A favourite theme was suggested by the Nakano Spy School. Japan found its equivalent of James Bond in Ichikawa Raizo, who appeared in six spy films, waging desperate battles against both foreign spies and regular officers of the Japanese Army. In the martial arts, the revival was led by the few who had kept the old traditions intact through the war years. The most famous of these was Fujita Seiko, the self-proclaimed 'last of the ninjas', head of one of the 53 Kōga family schools of ninjutsu – but he died in 1966, as filming of *You Only Live Twice* got under way.

So while in Japan coaching Sean Connery in martial arts techniques, Draeger recruited Masaaki Hatsumi, who was seeking to establish himself as a ninjutsu master with his teacher, Toshitsugu Takamatsu,[1] who had his own claims to

---

[1] Because both these two are known internationally, their family names are usually placed last, following the Western tradition.

fame. He lived in Kashihara, near the Forty-eight Waterfalls, the heartland of the Iga ninjas. As a young man in the early 20th century, he travelled through Mongolia, taught martial arts in China, and was bodyguard to the last Chinese emperor, Puyi. One of several 'last of the ninjas', he is said to have won 12 fights to the death and gouged out the eyes of one of his attackers, while somehow avoiding the attention of the police for murder. Both were great self-publicists, and both involved in the Japanese film *Ninja Band of Assassins* and its many sequels. Soon Hatsumi was on set, waiting to offer advice. Apparently, he was not called upon much, though he did get a walk-on part as the photographic assistant to Tiger Tanaka.

Perhaps he expressed surprise when he saw the so-called ninjas in action. Bond arrives alongside a castle by helicopter. It is in fact Himeji in Hyūgo castle, a fine example of a restored 17th-century keep, all grey-tiled roofs and upturned eaves, with a maze of interlocking walls and gates. Blofeld's rocket has just consumed a Russian satellite. Tiger Tanaka and Bond greet each other with information known to the other, which is normally banned in Hollywood scripts. But Dahl was not going to throw away the chance of a good line:

TANAKA

Bad news from outer space.

BOND

Yes, I heard. This time the Russians are accusing the Americans.

TANAKA

Next time it will be war.

BOND

We'll have to get down into that volcano.

TANAKA

I agree.

BOND

We'll also need a company of first-rate men. Do you have any commandos here?

TANAKA

I have much, much better. [A beat] *Ninjas!* Top secret, Bond-san.[2] This is my ninja training school.

Instant cut-away to several dozen iron-hard men in judo gear punching, wrestling and hacking away at each other with staves. This top-secret operation is conducted in full public view, in brilliant sunshine, to a chorus of ferocious yells. Bond is a little slow, which gives Tanaka a chance to define ninjas, over a cacophony of grunts and screams.

BOND

Ninjas?

TANAKA

The art of concealment and surprise, Bond-san.

Perhaps Bond – or Dahl – is being ironic, for there is nothing ninja-like about these very unconcealed fighters. They are martial art experts and, as their assault on Blofeld's space centre shows, commandos, expert in mass assaults,

[2] Not 'Bondo-san', as in the book. Fleming liked authenticity. Mass-market movie-makers don't much care.

abseiling and modern weaponry. Also, like samurai, they are quite prepared to die. They are the very opposite of shadow warriors. Real ninjas, operating in small numbers at night, don't make for huge, expensive, rip-roaring set pieces.

No matter. It was the film more than the book that popularized the term 'ninja' in the West.

The film also gave Hatsumi a terrific leg up into the role he has played ever since as the latest, greatest exponent of his branch of ninjutsu, Togakure. In his hands, ninjutsu became a martial art with an impressive pedigree. He established Togakure as a *ryu*, a school, of which he is the 34th head. He is the founder of an international martial arts organization, the Bujinkan, and the author of many books. He says he inherited his title of *soke*, or head of his *ryu*, from Takamatsu, behind whom – writes Hatsumi – 'eight centuries of history and tradition stretch all the way back to the founder of our system, Daisuke Nishina of Togakure Village' in Nagano prefecture. Hatsumi backs these impressive claims by listing all the 33 preceding Togakure heads and by referring to 'ancient ninjutsu documents which I inherited from my teacher', one of which supposedly lists the 18 'levels of training' of ancient ninjutsu.

All this and more is repeated as fact in many websites and books. And for all of it the only source is Hatsumi himself. No one else has confirmed the existence, let along the contents, of the 'ancient scrolls'. The result is that a few sceptics began to wonder about Hatsumi's authenticity. As one ninja expert told me, 'Nobody ever said there was a ninja martial art until Takamatsu came along. He taught it to Hatsumi. I think he made it up.' Scepticism has spread to Wikipedia, which flashes up warnings: 'factual accuracy is disputed', 'needs additional citations', 'has multiple issues', 'needs attention from an expert'.

This controversy is a minefield. The ninjutsu community seethes with claim and counter-claim on the subject of authenticity. The reason for these high passions lies in the way that skills and authority are passed down the generations, from master to pupil, in direct line of succession, rather as authority is passed in Islamic tradition, or the authenticity of a Shugendō mountain established by tracing its traditions back to the revered priest who 'opened' it. Coming to Hatsumi as a pupil, an outsider like me would be impressed by his actual teaching: does he teach the skills he claims to? But for martial artists, authenticity lies more in the lineage. Tracing it back a couple of generations is not good enough; 800 years carries conviction. But if it's a made-up tradition, there are those who will feel betrayed, as if, in the words of my rather-not-be-named expert, 'they have been rolling around on the floor for the last twenty years for nothing'.

Though Bond did his bit to popularize ninjas in the West, in Japan ninja-lovers had no need of him. There, a boom was already under way in film, TV, books and the graphic novels known as manga, with effects that show little sign of fading. This was fertile ground, because there had been a mini-boom in ninja fiction earlier in the century, in the form of the fictional Sarutobi Sasuke, boy-hero of children's literature between 1911 and 1925, resurrected in 1950s manga.

Another boost came in 1958, when the novelist Yamada Fūtaro published a tale with pseudo-historical roots: *Kōga Ninpōchō* (*The Kouga Ninja Scrolls* – Kōga becomes Kouga because in some transliterations all macrons are represented with a *u*). The context is the unification of Japan in the early 17th century, the geographical setting Iga and Kōga. That's pretty much it as far as history is concerned. Kōga and Iga, far from being allies, have been at each other's throats for 400 years. But at present they are held apart by a truce arranged by Hattori Hanzō. Yamada's ninjas, cut off for centuries in their mountain fastness, have interbred and evolved into magical beings, monsters or beauties who can fly, shape-shift, and deploy outlandish fighting skills. One can spurt blood from every pore, another is a slug-like creature without limbs, a third has a body like jelly that can absorb sword-blows and squeeze through the narrowest spaces.

Here's a sense of the fairy-tale quality of the stories, taken from the beginning of the first and most successful book. Two ninjas from Kōga and Iga are fighting five warriors each, before turning on each other. Shōgen, the Kōga ninja, is a hideous creature with bumpy forehead, hollow cheeks, long grey limbs bloated at their ends, a humpback and red dots for eyes. He climbs a wall, backwards, with one hand and two feet, the other hand still wielding his sword. He spits a glob of thick, sticky mucus, which blinds his five opponents. Meanwhile, the Iga ninja Yashamaru is a beautiful youth, with cheeks the colour of cherry blossoms and shining black eyes.

> He drew out a black ropelike object. This 'rope' had immense power. It was incredibly thin, yet had the strength of steel wire. Even a direct chop from a sword could not cut it. During the day it shone with dazzling brilliance. But once the sun went down, it became completely invisible . . . The rope had been forged through a special technique: Black strands of women's hair had been tied together and sealed with animal oil. A mere touch of the rope upon human flesh had the same effect as a blow from an iron whip. As the rope coiled around the thighs and bodies of the defeated soldiers, their skin burst open as if sharp swords were slicing them. Several dozen feet long, the rope moved like a living creature, spinning, twisting, striking, encircling, and amputating the limbs of its enemies.

The book's plot centres on the question of who will succeed Japan's unifier, Ieyasu, now 73. Which of two grandsons should he choose? A monk provides the answer. Ieyasu should decree an end to the truce. Let ten ninja warriors from each side fight each other, until one side is exterminated. The clan of the survivors will decide on the succession, with the added advantage that the top ninjas will have exterminated each other. Two scrolls – the scrolls of the book's title – record the names of the warriors. Meanwhile, in Kōga and Iga, two young people have fallen in love, Gennosuke from Kōga – a graceful, intelligent boy with long eyelashes – and Oboro of Iga, whose beauty shines through her veil. This is the story of two houses, both alike in dignity, and of star-crossed lovers. Can romance heal a 400-year rift? Or are they doomed? Doomed, as it happens: all 20 die, the lovers being the last to go.

The story, with its magical elements, burrowed into Japanese culture. Yamada wrote another 23 ninja novels over the next decade, many of them being turned into films. A five-volume manga adaptation of the first book is available in English. In 2005, almost 50 years after it was first published, the story became a feature film, *Shinobi: Heart Under Blade* (the subtitle recalling the hidden meaning of the *kanji* sign), all gorgeous landscapes, beautiful people – though with five warriors per side rather than ten to make things simpler – and much magical fighting.

Other novels, manga, films, TV series and video games are too numerous to mention, with two exceptions.

No account of modern ninja literature can omit *Naruto*, the multi-volume manga series by Masashi Kishimoto. This is pure fantasy, with no pretence at any historical roots, and phenomenally successful, easily the best-selling manga of all time, with almost 60 volumes – 113 million copies – sold in Japan. The *anime* versions (220 episodes in Japanese, 209 in English) and video games and novels and card games and on and on and on have all had equivalent success.

Secondly, with even less connection with reality, is the brilliant, bizarre phenomenon of the *Teenage Mutant Ninja Turtles*. The idea sprang as a parody of several different comics from two young artists, Kevin Eastman and Peter Laird. In the late 1980s, their rough, self-published seed grew overnight into a cultural and commercial beanstalk, with comics, TV series, films, toys, games, songs, and a parody of its own (*Adolescent Radioactive Black Belt Hamsters*).

And a backstory:

Once upon a time in Japan, a handsome young ninja master named Yoshi, who had a pet rat called Splinter that copied his every ninja move, loved a beautiful girl named Tang Shin. He had an evil rival called Saki. Rather than risk a fight between the two rivals, Shin persuaded Yoshi to flee to America, plus rat. They settle in New York. But one day Shin and Yoshi are murdered by Saki, leaving the rat, now a ninja master, to fend for himself in the sewers. There Splinter finds four baby turtles in a puddle of radioactive slime. They are mutants. They grow, and speak. He names them after Italian artists: Leonardo, Raphael, Donatello and Michelangelo.

What is this all about? Teenagers certainly, especially New York teenagers, who are, as parents know, mutants, if not aliens, with a language of their own. But there are many other possibilities, principally assimilation *v*. non-assimilation.[3] The turtles are immigrants who modify their traditions to fit in with the American way. Rat and turtles bond, just as the 'poor and dispossessed' on the Statue of Liberty are supposed to do. They love pizza, which they slice with ninja weapons. They have nicknames. They are street-wise, slang-talking, powerful individuals, yet bonded by their code into a

[3] The idea is well explored by Nora Cobb (see Bibliography).

Democratic Brotherhood. They like girls, in the form of their mother-figure April O'Neil (god forbid the turtles should fancy each other). They oppose the evil Saki, who is a criminal non-assimilator in black kimono and preys on vulnerable child dropouts. In brief, they are archetypes, with echoes of the Four Musketeers, Robin Hood and Peter Pan, but with something very reassuring to middle America and a little disturbing for the rest of us: they are separate, they cannot truly assimilate, they cannot reproduce, they cannot threaten the old white, dominant culture.

What it's not about is ninjas, except in terms of weapons and their dress, which keeps them together, yet apart from mainstream society.

Fantasy, it seems, is crucial for the survival of ninjas in today's world. It certainly was for the man who all this while had been surviving in the jungles of the Philippines, but fantasy of a totally different sort.

16

THE LAST OF THE NINJAS

If guiding and planning the way whilst moving position, the essential information you must bring are the mountains, the rivers and the distance from the enemy.

Ninja instructional poem

ONODA'S STORY OF SURVIVAL IS EXTRAORDINARY ENOUGH. Anyone able to live alone for 30 years, close to civilization but apart from it, deserves admiration. But in what follows perhaps the most extraordinary thing, not so much admirable as simply astonishing, is his motivation, his mindset, his determination to cling to his mission, a commitment based on his unshakable belief that the war was not over.

That belief derived from his training not just as a shadow warrior, but as the product of a society in which loyalty had been the very stuff of life for centuries, loyalty to one's lord and to the semi-divine emperor, a loyalty so powerful that it suggests evolutionary or IT metaphors: 'inbred', 'hard-wired', 'part of the DNA'. 'Programmed' is a better analogy. Onoda's loyalty was to his division commander. Once programmed with his mission, only his commander could de-activate him with new orders. For 30 years, no new orders arrived. Therefore everything that happened had to be interpreted in the light of the old ones. For those 30 years, Onoda's mind ran a program that treated all evidence contrary to his world view as a virus to be rejected. Those who suffer from such programming are often too far removed from reality to be considered sane. But Onoda was perfectly sane, and his programming was not *totally* rigid. He recognized reality when he was finally able to see it clearly. Given the right 'input', his old world view collapsed, freeing him to adopt a new one, pretty much in line with one that we call normality.

But where, we have to ask, did his loyalty come from? Whence this extraordinarily rigid belief that orders from a superior must be obeyed, absolutely? Of course, most armies train most of their fighting men to obey instantly, without question. But Onoda's training as a shadow warrior had specifically told him that orders could be questioned, that he had to remain flexible in his responses.

He was a living paradox. Programmed to be creative and show initiative, he deployed his creativity and initiative in proving to himself that the world was not as it seemed, but as he wished it to be. For comparable examples of faith carried to extremes, you usually have to look to closed systems: churches, dictatorships, cults, lunatic asylums. But Onoda was and is unique: tough and dedicated, of course; but also as humane and moral as a fighting man can be. Today, at 90, he works for his own children's charity.

Onoda arrived in Lubang with a cargo of explosives aboard a motorized sailing boat whose captain kept making the dangerous crossing because he made money importing cows from the island. He, a newly trained lieutenant, was supposed to lead about 200 men divided into army, radar, intelligence and naval sections. But he had no authority to command. He could only lead if others followed, and they didn't. They had high hopes of leaving Lubang, and objected to an attack on the airfield because it would be needed when – not if – Japan started to win. Nor would they agree to guerrilla war. They were true Japanese! They would repulse the enemy or die fighting! With little help, Onoda shifted his explosives to a base at the foot of a mountain, and fell into an exhausted sleep.

Two days later, on 3 January 1945, a yell from the mountain top summoned him. There, through his binoculars, he saw an astounding sight: the US fleet heading north, battleships, aircraft carriers, cruisers, light cruisers, destroyers, some 150 troop transporters and more landing craft than he could count. The invasion of Luzon was about to begin. It was perhaps Onoda's coded short-wave radio message – perhaps, because no one is certain, even now – passed from base to base, that triggered the Japanese response: waves of kamikaze pilots, who sank 25 US ships. It was the beginning of a long, hard campaign, for the Japanese had already withdrawn into Luzon's interior, where they would continue resisting until almost all were killed.

On Lubang, Onoda failed to fulfil the first part of his mission. He had set charges on the pier, but they didn't work. He could not get the other men to help destroy the airfield. Besides, he soon realized that blowing holes in the runway would delay landings by no more than a day or two. But he did what he could. He recalled the story of how the great Kusunoki Masashige, defending Chihaya castle in 1333, set up straw men to draw the fire of the enemy (the incident detailed in Chapter 5). Kusunoki's statue, remember, stood outside the Nakano HQ.

I decided to take a leaf out of Masashige's book. With Lieutenant Suehiro's assistance, I gathered up pieces of airplanes that had been destroyed and laid them out to look like new airplanes, taking care to camouflage them with grass. As I think back on it, the scheme sounds rather childishly simple, but it worked. After that, when enemy planes came, they invariably strafed my decoys on the airfield. At that time, they were coming over every other day, and we utilized the other days to put together fake airplanes. I considered it good guerrilla tactics to make attacking planes waste as much ammunition as possible.

A suicide group turned up, 70 of them, with boats laden with explosive, expecting to be fed. But food could come only from the locals, and they were unwilling to help. The Japanese did what so many of them did: they stole, and further alienated the locals. 'My heart was sinking,' Onoda writes. 'What can you do with a bunch of idiots?'

At the end of February, American troops arrived, with a sea and air bombardment, followed by a battalion-strong landing. All Onoda could do was retreat into the hills to avoid detection while the others, 'babbling about dying for the cause', succumbed to disease or got shot. At one point, he helped 22 sick men prepare charges to blow themselves up when the US troops appeared. 'Later, I came back to the place and found no trace of either the tent or the 22 corpses. Nothing was left but a gaping hole in the ground. I just stood and stared at that awful hole. Even the tears refused to come.' After three months, only three dozen remained alive, with him as the only officer. They decided to split into groups. Onoda was left with just two others, living on iron rations for the next six months, shooting a cow for meat now and then, keeping in occasional contact with the other groups.

In mid-October, they found a leaflet in Japanese: 'The war

ended on August 15. Come down from the mountains!' None of them believed it, because only a few days earlier one of the groups had been fired on. How could that happen if the war was over? This was a delusion embraced by all, but already Onoda was in a class on his own. He decided he would go on with his self-selected task, to keep clear of the other 'disorderly, irresponsible soldiers' and 'to study the terrain so that I could be useful when the Japanese army launched its counter-attack'.

At the end of 1945, they saw their second surrender leaflet, dropped by a B-17 bomber. It was an order to surrender signed by General Yamashita Tomoyuki, the 'Tiger of Malaya', conqueror of Singapore and ex-commander of the 14th Area Army. Nothing could have carried greater authority. But Onoda was in the grip of his faith. He pounced on an obscurity in a sentence, which said those who surrendered would be given 'hygienic succour' and 'hauled' to Japan, whatever that meant. Also it said that Yamashita was responding to a 'Direct Imperial Order', which neither Onoda nor anyone else had heard of. 'I could only conclude that the leaflet was phoney. The others all agreed with me. There was no doubt in our minds that this was an enemy trick.'

In 1946, many of the Japanese surrendered, while the others were all short of food, and kept begging Onoda for his carefully limited supplies. He told them sternly, 'You men made pigs of yourselves when you had rice, so now you don't have any. Don't come asking me to give you any of ours. I was sent here to destroy the airfield, and I still plan to do it. We're eating as little rice as possible. If we give you rice, we'll all be in trouble.'

There were more leaflets urging surrender, and Onoda heard people calling in Japanese. Those who had surrendered also left pencil-written notes. But still he and his three companions refused to believe the war had ended. 'We thought the enemy was simply forcing prisoners to go along with their trickery.'

They were now the only ones holding out on Lubang, and formed a tight-knit group: Corporal Shimada, the oldest at 31, tall, fit and cheerful; Private Kozuka, 25, very reticent, rarely speaking unless spoken to; Private Akatsu, 23, a shoe-maker's son, and the weakest both emotionally and physically, in a word a liability; and 24-year-old Onoda, who kept them together not by giving orders but by persuasion, always taking care to match the workload with the strength of the men. Each had a knife, a rifle, with several hundred rounds, a bayonet, two hand grenades and two pistols.

They established a routine: moving around the mountains, steering clear of local groups coming up from the plains and coasts to work, entering campsites in search of rice, always examining signs – ashes, leaves, tree stumps, footprints – to assess how long the workers had been there and whether they would be returning, sometimes taking rice, and if so always moving to a new location, staying only a few days in any one place, working in a rough circle.

In all this, Onoda's training was of little use. Guerrilla warfare was almost impossible. It took all his time and energy just to survive. He needed to know how to make fire without much smoke, how to make a net, how to hunt for food, how to sneak bananas from plantations, how to kill and butcher cows (more on this important subject later).

So life continued for another three years. Eventually, Akatsu, the weakest link and the least trustworthy, could not take it any more. 'Unlike me, he had no assignment, no objective, and the struggle to keep alive here in the mountains may well have come to seem pointless to him.' So he disappeared, presumably to surrender. As it happened, he was on his own for six months before giving himself up, not that Onoda knew it at the time. But the following year, he found a note left by Akatsu saying that Filipino troops had greeted him as a friend.

Soon after Akatsu vanished, the three survivors heard a loudspeaker telling them in Japanese they had 'seventy-two hours' to surrender, or a task force would come after them. Again Onoda found a reason to doubt. Japanese didn't refer to three days as seventy-two hours – 'still more proof that the war had not ended'. Anyway, he could not contemplate surrender, for a very good reason:

> I had come to this island on the direct orders of the division commander. If the war were really over, there ought to be another order from the division commander releasing me from my duties. I did not believe the division commander would forget orders that he had issued to his men. Supposing he had forgotten. The orders would still have been on record at division headquarters. Certainly somebody would have seen to it that the commander's outstanding orders were properly rescinded.

After that, Onoda speeded up the trips around their circuit, firing on locals whenever they saw any, for 'we considered people dressed as islanders to be enemy troops in disguise or enemy spies'. Their confidence grew, for they knew the whole area intimately. It would take a battalion or two to find them. Patrols of 50 or a 100 were no threat. Far from it – Onoda relished the challenge. They were only three men, but healthy, motivated and fit. 'We were making a force of fifty look silly. That is the kind of warfare I had been taught at Futamata.'

They got used to their life, and even had times of content-ment, sitting in a shelter, listening to the familiar sounds of the forested hills, talking about the old days in Japan. Shimada would describe his daughter ('I guess she must be old enough to like boys now'), wonder if the child his wife had been expecting was a boy or a girl, reminisce about dancing at a festival.

In February 1952, a small plane circled overhead, calling their names through a loudspeaker. It dropped leaflets, including letters and photographs from the families of all three men. One was from Onoda's oldest brother, Toshio. It mentioned the man who had brought the letter to the Philippines, said the war had ended, told Onoda that his parents were well – all proof enough, surely, that the war was over and that the men could surrender at last with their integrity intact.

Not a bit of it. 'My reaction was that the Yankees had out-done themselves this time. I wondered how on earth they had obtained the photographs. That there was something fishy about the whole thing was beyond doubt, but I could not figure out exactly how the trick had been carried out.'

In this way, Onoda shored up his illusory world, an illusion that could be sustained not simply by remaining committed to the ethos of wartime Japan as promulgated by the Nakano School, but also by becoming an ever-more-expert shadow warrior, indeed far more expert than any other. He was the ultimate ninja, the man with a mission who would do any-thing to survive, and fulfil it.

A month later, they heard another loudspeaker. This time it was (supposedly) a journalist, from *Asahi Shimbun*, wanting an interview. He kept repeating that he was Japanese, and ended by singing a Japanese war-song.

'They're at it again,' commented Onoda, and the three remained hidden.

Later, they scouted out the area where the man with the loudspeaker had been, and found a newspaper. Circled in red was a story about a lieutenant-colonel coming to the Philippines to persuade the government to stop its 'punitive missions' to capture Japanese soldiers on Lubang. The three men read the newspaper. Well, it looked genuine. Equally obviously, it was a trick. The enemy must have gone to a lot of trouble inserting a *false* article in a *genuine* newspaper. But it just wasn't good enough. 'Punitive missions' indeed! If they were punitive, the war must still be going on. And there was something funny about the broadcasting schedules. Too many light entertainment programmes. Poisoned candy, said Onoda. 'It looked good, but it was deadly.'

June 1953: in an exchange of fire with some fisherman, Shimada was shot in the right leg. Onoda carried him into the forest, and bound the wound with cow fat as a poultice. It took him four months to recover, but he walked with a limp, and was not his old self. It was like a premonition, which almost a year later, was fulfilled. They spotted a search party of 35 down on the shore, and retreated, but then argued about whether to stay or move across the island. They stayed, and sliced up some fruit which they put out to dry. A little later, Onoda saw something move nearby. An intruder. Onoda fired, and the man dived for cover. Shimada stood still, aiming. A shot rang out, and he fell forward, killed outright by a shot between the eyebrows. Onoda and Kozuka fled.

Ten days later, near the spot where Shimada was killed, a plane dropped leaflets, and a loudspeaker called, 'Onoda, Kozuka, the war has ended.' This merely angered them, for they were now utterly gripped by their own version of reality. 'We wanted to scream out to the obnoxious Americans to stop threatening and cajoling us. We wanted to tell them that if they did not stop treating us like scared rabbits, we would get back at them some day, one way or another.'

Later, back in the same spot, Onoda recalled Shimada's friendship, which had lasted almost ten years. 'I vowed that somehow we would avenge Shimada's death . . . I wiped my cheek with the back of my hand. For the first time since I came to Lubang, I was crying.' With powerful emotions added to his peculiar brand of loyalty, what could ever convince him that the world was not as he believed it to be?

Not, for instance, a flag he found on which the names of family members had been written. But why were they *slightly misspelled*? He pondered until the explanation occurred to him. It ran as follows: his bosses would obviously be trying to contact him to help reoccupy the airfield; they wanted the Americans to know this so that they (the Americans) would shift troops away from other areas; so the flag was allowed to fall into enemy hands; and the enemy were now using the flag to entice Onoda out; knowing they would do this, the Japanese had deliberately made a mistake in the spelling of the names in order to warn him not to take the message seriously. 'Today all this sounds ridiculous, but I had been taught in Futamata always to be on the lookout for fake messages.' Moreover, Onoda had taught Kozuka to be equally sceptical. The two supported each other in their paranoia.

As leaflet followed leaflet, each was interpreted as a fake. Here was a picture of Onoda-san's family. But why the presence of a non-family member? Why the honorific *san*, if the picture was intended for him alone? And here was Kozuka's family *in front of a new house*. 'How do they expect me to believe this?' he scoffed, unaware of the Allied bombing raids and the shattered cities. And the leaflets were on poor-quality paper; which meant they were being mass produced; which meant they were being dropped all over the Philippines; which meant there must be hundreds if not thousands of guerrillas out there; that explained the honorific *san*, quite suitable if the picture was being seen by non-family men; all of which meant the war was still on. And the non-family person in the family picture? Obviously a warning not to take any of the leaflets seriously.

'With both sides sending all sorts of messages like this,' said Onoda to Kozuka, 'the Japanese counter-attack must be coming soon.'

In the absence of what they considered hard information, anything and everything fed their fantasy that the Japanese were fighting back, regaining what had been lost. Bombs that were dropped in target areas by the Philippine Air Force must have been to stop Japanese guerrilla units from landing. A loudspeaker announcement claimed to be from the former chief-of-staff of the Naval Air Force. A *naval* man coming to look for *army* men? Transparently ridiculous! Believing that a landing was imminent on Lubang's south coast, the two determined to keep it safe by scaring away locals. All attempts at contact, of which there were many, were simply seen as enemy agents blocking them from contacting other Japanese agents. Each time they heard a loudspeaker, they moved away.

The fact was that after fifteen years the two of them were so fixed in their ideas that they were unable to understand anything that did not fit in with them. It's a common human condition, the *idée fixe*. Once programmed into the mind, it acts as a lens that either distorts all that passes through it to fit the image, or else rejects what cannot be made to fit. Such obsessions have had horribly real consequences. Witness the witch-hunts of the late Middle Ages, which caused the burning of hundreds of innocent women. Self-delusion is a staple of comedy and drama in theatre, film and fiction. Malvolio is made to believe that Olivia loves him, cross-gartering and all, and is judged mad as a result; Jed Parry in Ian McEwan's novel *Enduring Love* interprets every rejection by Joe, the object of his obsession, as a come-on. So it was with Onoda. 'If there was anything that did not fit, we interpreted it to mean whatever we wanted it to mean.'

*

In 1959, reality almost broke through. A loudspeaker called: 'This is your brother Toshio. Kozuka's brother Fukuji has come with me. This is our last day here. Please come out where we can see you.' At first Onoda thought it was a recording. He crept closer, and was amazed to see what really seemed to be his brother. Yes, 'he was built like my brother, and his voice was identical'.

Then he had second thoughts. 'That's really something. They've found a prisoner who looks at a distance like my brother, and he's learned to imitate my brother's voice perfectly.'

The man began to sing a student song that both of them knew from school, which almost had Onoda convinced, but then went off key. Onoda laughed. The impersonator couldn't keep it up. He had given himself away. Onoda and Kozuka remained hidden, watched as the search party sadly left, then slipped back into the jungle. (Soon after this, in December 1959, Onoda was officially declared dead, along with Kozuka. They had supposedly been killed five years before in a clash with Philippine troops.)

The search party left behind a stack of newspapers and magazines, with countless articles about life in post-war Japan. Fakes! When Onoda left Japan, the war was going badly, but the nation had sworn to fight to the last man, woman and child. 'One hundred million souls dying for honour' had been the phrase on everyone's lips. If Japan had lost the war, there wouldn't be any life! Everyone would be dead! If they weren't, Japan could not have lost the war. Indeed, it seemed to be winning, since it was obviously prosperous. Naturally, 14 years after the end of the war, there was no mention of the flattened cities, the atomic bomb, the surrender, the occupation, the reconstruction – all the developments that might have allowed a truer interpretation of the articles.

Slowly, a new and utterly false picture of the modern world formed in their minds. Sure, Japan was now democratic. But it must still have an empire – its East Asia Co-Prosperity Sphere – because there were good relations with former enemies. If China was Communist, it must be under Japanese auspices. That was how the Americans and English had been driven from China. Presumably the Dutch had been driven from Java and Sumatra. Perhaps Siberia was also in the empire. No doubt the war was still being fought in the outer fringes, for after all Onoda had been taught that it might take one hundred years of war to build the empire.

One article was a particular challenge. It was about him and the school: 'Secret Mission on Lubang: What Did the Nakano School Order Lt Onoda To Do?' Reviewing the history of the school, it said no one was quite sure who had issued his orders. Like a theologian wrestling to reconcile scripture with some alleged piece of evidence, it took Onoda a while to see that this, too, was fake. Of *course* the school knew who had issued his orders. It was all there in the records. This was merely a way for his bosses to send him a message: Hang on, Onoda! We haven't forgotten you.

Hanging on demanded ever high degrees of ingenuity. The solutions they found to the problems of survival would make a fine field-guide to self-sufficiency. They learned to deal with rats, swarms of bees, ants of many species (including five that stung like bees), centipedes with poisonous bites and scorpions. They became superb ecologists, working out how to catch rats and snare jungle fowl. They discovered how best to deal with the steamy, 100-degree heat of May, the July rains, when it pours so hard you can't see 10 metres, the second rainy season in September, the balmy days of October to December, the relative coolness of January and February (though the temperature could still go up to 85°F). A major concern was where to spend the rainy season, during which they couldn't move around. With their tents long gone, they built anew each year. The spot, with a suitable tree to act as an anchor for the hut, had to be on sloping ground for good drainage, safe from intrusion, on the eastern side of the mountains for coolness, not too near a village to avoid their fire being spotted, but near banana fields and coconut groves, all of which had to be planned without knowing exactly when the rains would come. There weren't many such places, and once identified they used the same ones every three or four years. At the first downpour, they would strip the tree of branches, use one for a ridge pole, bind the others to it with vines, and make a roof of palm leaves. Flat rocks made a stove. At the end of the rainy season, they tore the hut down, scattered the site with mud and branches, and again began a nomadic life, sleeping in the open fully dressed. 'During the whole thirty years, I never once took off my trousers at night.' If it rained, they got wet.

Their clothes rotted and split. They needed a needle to patch them. Onoda made one by sharpening a piece of wire, using a hemp-like plant for thread. Occasionally, they requisitioned American goods – canteens, tents, shoes, blankets – from stores made by the islanders. They made sandals from old inner tubes or sneaker soles. They camou-flaged themselves by using fishing line to sew twigs and leaves to their jackets. They ate bananas, ripe if possible, but often bitter green ones, skin and all, sliced and boiled in coconut milk with dried meat to take away the bitterness.

Three cows a year kept them in meat, supplemented by a water buffalo or horse now and then. Onoda gives a lesson in how to kill and prepare a cow. It takes about an hour for two men. Start just before dark when the villagers have gone home. Shoot the cow from no more than 70 metres to fell it, using only one shot, preferably in the rain to muffle the sound. Finish off the fallen cow by smashing its head with a stone and/or stabbing it in the heart with a bayonet. It is lying on its side. Cut off the two upper legs, slice it down the middle of the belly, strip back the skin, turn it over, and repeat. Remove the heart, liver, sweetbreads and other innards, and put them in a sack. After the butchery, with the meat on your back, haul the carcass away as far as possible in darkness and hide it to prevent the villagers putting two and two together. Fresh meat lasted a few days, boiled meat for ten, dried meat – smoked over an open fire – for four months.

Salt they either gathered from brine on the shore or from the islanders' salt pans. There was never a shortage of water, though they feared contamination from cattle and always boiled it. Rice was kept clear of ants in bags placed in five-gallon cans. Coconuts provided copra, milk (for soup) and fibres that made reasonable toothbrushes. At every campsite, they dug a toilet pit, leaving the soil available to fill it in when they left. They used palm leaves for toilet paper. Every day, they examined their shit and urine, modifying diet and activity if anything looked wrong. It worked well. Onoda developed a fever twice in 30 years, Kozuka impaled his heel on thorns twice, causing his leg to swell. Otherwise, no health problems.

Through all this, they remained soldiers, looking after their weapons, hoarding their ammunition, keeping it dry in ammunition pouches made of rubber sneakers. Onoda had several hundred rounds of machine-gun ammunition, which he modified to fire as single shots from his rifle. He carried 60 cartridges with him, just in case of trouble, but used them only infrequently to scare off locals or shoot cows. Faulty and rusty cartridges were opened to release the gunpowder, which was used as tinder, ignited by focusing sunlight through a stolen lens. Spare ammunition was squirrelled away in holes stopped with rocks.

Life improved over time. Their expertise grew, and they learned how to 'requisition' – that is, steal – from locals with impunity. Besides, the islanders were increasingly well off, so Onoda's life improved with theirs. 'Life in the jungle was never easy, but so far as food, clothing and utensils were concerned, it was easier in the later years than in the first five or ten.'

Long-term survival is not all about technique. Underlying the technical skills is emotional and psychological health, as I learned when involved in several media projects on the subject of survival – a TV series and three radio series. There has been a good deal of research into post-traumatic stress disorder, focusing mainly on the malign effects of life-threatening events. I was interested in the opposite: why some seem to come through such events better than others, without ill effects. The plain fact is that some people are better survivors than others, both during and after the event. Naturally, academic research has focused on those who suffer. Those who don't have been less studied. But my interviews suggested to me some guidelines:

- **Have a long-term aim,** an agenda that makes you look beyond your own immediate concerns. This may be no more than a determination to return to a wife, or friends, or beloved children. It may be a whole philosophy or belief system. In German concentration camps, for example, two groups tended to survive slightly better than others: Seventh Day Adventists and Communists. They did so because their experience reinforced their world views. Seventh Day Adventists were certain the Last Days were at hand and that they would be chosen for salvation. Communists, taught that capitalism would collapse, saw around them proof that Marx's prediction was coming true. In brief, these two groups saw themselves as part of a great historical process. The truth or falsity of the belief is not important, because that can only be established in different circumstances. In the extreme and usually brief conditions of an extermination or labour camp, a belief system may help. In Onoda's case, it certainly did. His suffering was for a purpose. He knew why he had to survive.

- **Be wary of faith**. Belief is not always a prop. Those with a naive faith that God is on their side and will be on hand to help are, on the whole, disappointed. In the concentration camps, God was notably absent, and many simply despaired. Despair can do strange things to minds. Take one of my interviewees, Bob Tininenko: he and his brother-in-law were sailing south from Seattle in a catamaran when a storm overturned them. The two were trapped in the hull. Improvising hammocks swinging just above the surface, he set about the task of survival by rationing the remaining stores. But the brother-in-law was a fundamentalist Christian who believed not only that God would save them, but that any attempt to save themselves would be to pre-empt God's intervention. In order to allow God to act in his own time, he actually threw away some of the rations – an extreme example of faith undermining survival (he died; Bob survived). Onoda was not encumbered by a faith in a personal, interventionist god. He knew that no one was going to help him but himself.

- **Accept the possibility of your own death**. This removes a crucial threat – panic, which is one of the prime causes of death in the early days of catastrophe. There is a paradox here: to say to yourself 'I accept that I may die tomorrow' frees you to add a corollary ' – but not today, not yet, not here'. That in turn opens the possibility of survival for an hour, a day, a week, a month, a life. Accept death, find life: that was what Onoda did.

- **Be familiar with your environment.** Two of my interviewees come to mind.[1] The first was a young German woman, Juliane Köpcke, who was on a plane flying from Lima to Pucallpa on the upper Amazon basin when a lightning storm broke the plane apart killing 92 passengers, including her mother, all except Juliane herself. Still strapped in her seat, she fell several thousand metres, hit the forest canopy and woke up, on the jungle floor, with a few bruises and a cracked collarbone. She then walked for some ten days through the jungle, until she came across people. Her big advantage was that she was on home territory. Her parents were zoologists, and she knew what she could eat (in fact, nothing but some cake she retrieved from the crash) and what to avoid, and also knew that following a stream downriver would not only give her fresh water but also lead her to civilization. When I met her, she was back in the same area, researching bats. The second example was a Canadian pilot, Martin Hartwell, who crashed with three passengers in the vast forests of the North-West Territories. He came through the crash with two broken legs. The others died, over a period of time. It was winter. It's a long story with many twists, but the main point is that he survived by making fire and by cooking and eating the frozen flesh of one of the dead passengers. By the time he was found a month later (after a hugely controversial search), he was in remarkably good shape physically. Another few weeks and he would have walked out. Psychologically, he was deeply affected, both by the means of his survival and by a storm of unwelcome publicity. His survival contrasted tragically with the fate of an Inuit boy, who was used to the treeless barrens but was so disoriented and scared by the

---

[1] Both these stories were the subject of many newspaper articles and several books. Both are now well covered by Wikipedia.

surrounding forests that he simply gave up and died. Onoda did not know anything about jungles when he first arrived on Lubang, but his commitment to his mission drove him to learn fast. Pretty soon, he was as practised a survivor as Juliane Köpcke and Martin Hartwell.

- **Establish routines.** Tininenko persuaded his brother-in-law to share formal meals, which in the end amounted to nothing more than a few peas. But the formality gave a shape to the days, a sense of purpose. In the concentration camps, survivors noted that those who withdrew entirely, refused to wash, brush their hair, look after themselves in any way, and became what the inmates referred to as *Musselmänner* (Muslims), did not have long to live. Onoda imposed many small rituals on the two of them, insisting that they brush their teeth every morning, give each other regular haircuts, celebrate birthdays, keep track of the phases of the moon, and mark New Year's Day with a meal of rice and string beans in place of the lentils they used to have at home.

- **Have a secure childhood.** This sounds a bit glib, like the recipe for a long life: have long-lived parents. But it's important. A secure childhood – almost the same as happy, but not quite – builds trust. Mother-love, or at least close human contact; continuity of care; a good supporting network – all of this creates an expectation that the universe is essentially friendly. When things go wrong, you – well-grounded child or adult – believe they can be fixed. When things go *really* wrong, you interpret the catastrophe as an aberration which may make the universe seem more random, but no less friendly overall. Chances are, you can cope as best you can. Whereas the unhappy, damaged, insecure child grows into an adult who sees a disaster as proof of what he or she 'always knew', that the universe is a malign and dangerous place. What follows? Depression, panic, negativity. These are not attitudes with which to deal with disaster. Of course, there is no strict cause and effect in emotional and psychological development. Secure children may grow into panicky adults, insecure and unhappy ones into happy and creative ones.

And there is a danger in childhood security, as I know from experience. As a child, I had all due care and attention from my mother, combined with encouragement to live freely in a safe rural setting – orchards, streams, woods, empty roads. I loved it. It might all have turned out badly, because at eight I was sent to boarding school. There are those who would say this was a parental rejection enough to scar my soul. Not a bit of it. By eight, I was firmly enough grounded to consider school another big adventure. It worked out fine. But there has been a problem: a feeling that the universe is a supportive place induces me to take unnecessary risks, from swimming with piranhas to catching planes with minutes to spare. Sometimes things go wrong. I once spent two weeks in an Ecuadorian jail (it's a long story to do with a rented car and an attempted extortion. A lawyer got me out. I took a taxi to the Colombian border, and escaped into Cali, then the drugs capital of the world and notorious for its murder-rate. I have never been more delighted to see anywhere). So far, so good, but perhaps real survivors don't get into tight spots in the first place.

Always, Onoda looked towards the day the Japanese army would return. To this end, at the start of the dry season they would go to the fields where islanders had been gathering rice on to straw matting. At twilight, when the fields were empty, they would set fire to the rice to make beacons, which would, they hoped, be visible to incoming Japanese and tell them that their agents were still active. To the islanders, this was mere criminality, as was their habit of occasionally

stealing what they needed, or staging hold-ups. To the
islanders, the pair of them were 'mountain devils'. But they
were careful not to antagonize the locals more than necessary.
Once, for instance, they took a farmer prisoner, forced the
terrified man into the mountains at gunpoint, interrogated
him, then told him to go home to bed.

In 1965, they stole a radio. When its batteries ran down,
they improvised with torch batteries, firing at farmers who
dropped the torches as they ran away. The radio, like the
newspapers, should have been enough to show them that they
were living in a fantasy world. But they mainly listened to
crackly shortwave stations with the volume turned down, and
only briefly to conserve power. Some things they could accept
as true, like the Tokyo Olympics and the bullet train. As for
the rest, the two concluded they were listening to tapes put
out by Americans to present American propaganda to
Japanese living abroad. 'I take my hat off to them,' said
Onoda to Kozuka. 'It must be very tricky work.' Tricky work,
indeed, as he realized later, but on his part, not the
Americans', 'tricky for us to read into the news broadcasts
the meanings we wanted them to have'.

Their lives had settled into regular patterns. Year followed
year, often with little to mark the passage of time, with only
occasional dramas: Kozuka's swollen leg from a poisoned
thorn, the time Kozuka's trousers were swept away when they
were doing laundry in a river in preparation for New Year's
Day. But 19 October 1972 marked a turning point. They had
dismantled their rainy season hut and were planning their
usual dry-season 'beacon raids'. Looking out over a field, it
seemed the farmers were preparing to carry away all the rice.
They decided to move quickly, scaring away the farmers with
a shot, guessing that it would take a few minutes for the
police to come, giving them time enough to set a few fires. It
worked. They were on the point of leaving when Kozuka

spotted a pile of sacks under a tree. A pot hung from a branch. Time for one last fire. They laid their guns down, and Kozuka stepped aside to pick up some straw matting to use as fuel while Onoda went to see what was in the pot. At that moment there was a shot, then a volley of shots. The two men dived for their weapons. Onoda saw that Kozuka could not move his arm.

'It's my shoulder,' he said.

'If it's only your shoulder, don't worry! Get back down into the valley.'

Onoda grabbed both guns and fled. Kozuka stood, but did not move. He stood with his arms folded tight. 'It's my chest.' He sobbed. Then: 'It's no use!' Blood and foam spewed from his mouth and he fell forwards. Onoda fired three shots, uselessly. He called Kozuka's name, and shook him by the ankle. No response. There was nothing more to be done. With the two rifles, he ran downhill into a thicket, with the gunfire continuing behind him. 'I'll get them for this,' he yelled, 'I'll kill them all!' He had no idea, of course, that he had been declared dead, and that this clash was the first proof in 13 years to the world outside that they had been alive all this time.

He made his way to a coconut grove where he sorted through his equipment. Nearby he heard voices, saw a small group of people, then later a larger group, but he knew better than to attack. Take it easy, he told himself, now was not the time.

He was alone, and, when he came to consider it, other than being shocked and saddened by Kozuka's death, no worse off materially. For a time, the death hardened him. He would shoot to kill, if only to keep islanders out of 'his' territory. But the search parties and their loudspeakers were closing in. 'Onoda-san, wherever you are, come out!' Then one day, he heard a woman's voice in the distance, though all he could make out was, 'Hiroo, you gave me two, didn't you?' It was his older sister, Chie, referring to a pair of pearls he had given her as a wedding present. Then he heard his brother Tadao's voice, singing a familiar song. This time, Onoda seemed to accept reality, in a way. So it was Tadao. Might as well stay and listen to him. He always was a good talker, and now he talked and talked. Still, Onoda held back, as if suspended between two worlds. Later, he visited the spot where Kozuka was killed, and found a tombstone engraved with his name and a wreath. His hands clasped in prayer, Onoda repeated his oath to his friend: 'I will avenge your death.'

He found newspapers with long reports of Kozuka's death, yet still found reasons to doubt. There was information that should have been included that wasn't. Why? His reasoning was becoming more and more convoluted, because he did not doubt that the search parties were indeed from Japan, somehow operating despite the presumed presence of American forces on the mainland. He concluded that they were here to survey Lubang and win over the islanders. Indeed, since the Americans were having a hard time in Vietnam, the Japanese government could be preparing to woo the whole of the Philippines over to its side. So the appeals to Onoda were simply a cover. If he came out, they would not have time to complete their real task. Only by remaining hidden could he help them. Why, if they really wanted him to come out, all they had to do was leave him a telephone, and he could call them up. They didn't, so the conclusion was clear: 'the pleas urging me to come out really meant that I should *not* come out.'

So it went on, in the face of the evidence, with Onoda almost playing hide and seek with search parties. In his absence, one that included his ageing father found his mountain hut, where his father left a touching haiku:

Not even an echo
Responds to my call in the
Summer mountains.

But to Onoda, his family were just being used by the Japanese High Command for a deeper purpose, to show the Americans that there was a growing threat to Lubang, and thus compel them to keep forces in reserve for the attack that was surely coming. 'So long as I remained in the place, the larger the "search" operations would be – and the more it would cost the Americans in the long run.' Anything he didn't understand, he simply put down to his ignorance. There was much that puzzled him. He wondered if the Filipinos were now allies with Japan. If so, how come they shot Kozuka, and how could he, Onoda, find out what side they were on?

In February 1974, 16 months after Kozuka's death, he checked a favourite banana plantation, and saw a mosquito net. Police, he thought, and prepared for a fight. But no, there was only one unarmed man. Onoda approached, pointing his rifle, and called out. The man, dressed in a T-shirt, dark blue trousers and rubber sandals, saluted and stood his ground, shaking. That was odd. Islanders usually ran off at the sight of him.

'I'm Japanese,' said the man.

'Are you from the Japanese government?'

'No.'

'Are you from the Youth Foreign Cooperation Society?'

'No.'

'Well, who are you?'

'I'm only a tourist.'

Tourist? What could that mean? Onoda was fairly sure he had been sent by the enemy, except Onoda noticed he was wearing thick woollen socks. If he hadn't been wearing those socks, Onoda might have shot him. With the sandals, they made an incongruous sight. He really must be Japanese.

The man said: 'Are you Onoda-san?' and went on to ask him to come back to Japan, because the war was over.

Not for Onoda it wasn't. 'Bring me my orders. There must be proper orders!'

The man offered a cigarette – Onoda's first for years – and said he would like to talk. 'In that case,' said Onoda, 'let's go someplace else.' The man picked up an expensive-looking camera, and followed Onoda across a rice field to a clump of trees. The man talked about Japan having lost the war. But Onoda couldn't believe him, and kept quiet. The man asked if he could take a picture, but it was getting dark, and he doubted the quality of his flashlight pictures. He suggested coming back the following afternoon. Onoda was at once suspicious, and continued the conversation, thinking to trap him. The man gave his name: Suzuki Norio. They talked for two hours. Suzuki finally asked what would persuade Onoda to come out.

'Major Taniguchi is my immediate superior,' said Onoda. 'I won't give in until I have direct orders from him.' Actually, his real commander was Lt-General Yokoyama, but Onoda did not want to mention him without positive proof that Suzuki was not an enemy agent.

So, said Suzuki, if I bring him and 'he tells you to come to such and such a place at such and such a time, you will come, right?'

'Right,' said Onoda, and then suggested staying at Suzuki's camp for the night, as a pretext for keeping him under surveillance.

Back at the camp, Suzuki asked and answered questions, Onoda probing all the time. Suzuki, a university dropout, described his travels – 50 countries in the last four years, during which time, as Onoda's translator Charles Terry says in his Foreword, he had contributed 'to the woes of numerous

Japanese embassies'. When he left Japan, he told his friends he was going to look for Lt Onoda, a panda and the Abominable Snowman, in that order. He had been on Lubang just four days. Onoda warmed to him, telling him how his two comrades died, thinking this would be the best way for the details to reach their families, even if Suzuki was working for the enemy.

The following morning, there were more, and better, photographs and Suzuki left, promising to return. Despite a 1 per cent niggle of uncertainty, despite Suzuki's apparent charm and honesty, Onoda was 99 per cent sure that he should not take him seriously. Taniguchi – who, according to the newspapers, was now a book-dealer – would not appear. There would be no new orders. He still believed Japan and America were at war, because of the size of the 'search' operations, which surely couldn't be just to find him, had to be to survey the island for some future military purpose. So it was his duty to hang on. With the ammunition he had left, he could afford 30 bullets a year for another 20 years. He was 52, but 'I considered my body to be no more than thirty-seven or thirty-eight'. Twenty more years? No problem.

Two weeks later, he heard voices, and found a bag taped to a tree. It contained Suzuki's photos of him, a note saying he had come back as promised, and two orders, one from General Yamashita and a second saying that 'instructions would be given to Lt Onoda orally', presumably by Taniguchi himself.

This was what he had been waiting for, direct, face-to-face, no-nonsense secret orders, for the only way to deliver secret orders was orally. He could hardly guess what he would be ordered to do – keep fighting on Lubang? Start a new oper-ation somewhere else? The only certainty was that he had to get to the meeting point, the spot in the centre of the island where he had met Suzuki two weeks earlier – Wakayama

Point, on a river a good eight hours' walk across the mountains. It might be a trap, of course. But he had to take that risk.

By hindsight, it was no risk. Suzuki had returned to Japan, and reported to the government, touching off what Terry calls 'some of the most extravagant coverage ever provided by Japanese press and television'. They found Taniguchi and flew him to Lubang, with no less than 100 Japanese newsmen. Taniguchi was there as Onoda approached Wakayama Point in the afternoon of 9 March 1974.

He hid in the bushes, intending to wait until the light was right: dark enough to be safe, light enough to recognize Taniguchi. There was no one about. He camouflaged himself with sticks and leaves, crossed the river and climbed a small hill where he could oversee the meeting place. He saw a yellow tent, but no sign of people. He approached warily to about 100 metres, and settled down to wait for sunset. Then, holding his rifle, he thrust out his chest and walked forward. Suzuki was there, standing facing away, between the tent and a campfire. He turned and came forward, arms outstretched. 'It's Onoda!' he shouted. 'Major Taniguchi, it's Onoda!'

As Suzuki grasped Onoda's hand, a voice came from the tent. 'Is it really you, Onoda? I'll be with you in a minute.' He was just changing his shirt. Yes, definitely Taniguchi's voice.

He emerged, fully dressed, wearing an army cap.

'Lieutenant Onoda, sir,' said Onoda smartly. 'Reporting for orders.'

'Good for you!' said Taniguchi, patting Onoda on the shoulder. He gave Onoda a pack of cigarettes with the imperial crest on them, and then, as Onoda took a couple of paces back, said, 'I shall read your orders.' These told Onoda that all combat activity had ceased, that the Special Squadron had no more military duties and that all members, Onoda

being one, should cease military activities and place themselves under the nearest superior officer.

For a few seconds, Onoda wondered if Taniguchi would
follow up with his real orders.

Silence.

Onoda realized at last this was it.

'We really lost the war! How could they have been so
sloppy? Suddenly everything went black. A storm raged
inside me. I felt like a fool for having been so tense and
cautious on the way here. Worse than that, what had I been
doing for all these years?'

The emotion subsided. He took off his pack, laid his rifle
on top of it, and followed the major and Suzuki into the tent,
where, through the night, he gave his report, often blinking
back tears, with Suzuki, a little the worse for drink, snoring
on his bed. With the coming of dawn, Taniguchi slept, but
Onoda, on his first bed in 30 years, could not.

The next morning, Suzuki's beacon fire summoned the rest
of the party, a military escort and Onoda's oldest brother,
Toshio. After spending a day retrieving weapons from the
hills, there followed a meeting with President Ferdinand
Marcos. In a very public ceremony, Onoda, performing his
role of prisoner-of-war, formally surrendered his sword. But
he was no ordinary prisoner. As a mark of respect and as a
sign of reconciliation, Marcos handed the sword back.[2] 'For
a moment, something like the pride of a samurai swept over
me.'

That was just the start of intense, almost hysterical press
coverage. Why did he create such a stir? Nothing like this had
attended the reappearance of Onoda's comrade-in-arms,

---

[2] Another oddity in Onoda's book, perhaps a reflection of the strain he was
under: in the text, he says the ceremony was with General Jose Rancudo, Chief
of the Air Force. But a photograph in the picture section clearly shows him
either handing his sword to Marcos or receiving it back.

Yamamoto, when he emerged from the Philippine jungle in 1956; nor the emergence of an NCO, Yokoi Shoichi, from Guam in 1972. Terry's theory is that Onoda was exactly what Japan needed as an antidote to defeat: a genuine, un-compromising war hero. Also, in Mercado's words, 'his spare frame, intense gaze and goatee gave him the air of a samurai who has seemingly reached Japan in a time machine'. But there was a lot more to him than that. He was intelligent, articulate, strong-willed and stoic.

He was also, incidentally, exactly the opposite to another type of uncompromising Japanese hero – the sort that takes on impossible odds and dies. Such a one was Saigo Takamori, the 'last samurai', who in 1877 led a pointless rebellion against the government of the Meiji Restoration and met an extremely sticky end, vastly outnumbered, wounded, unable to commit *seppuku*; he was beheaded, in true samurai fashion, by a close aide. But who, in a nation recovering from defeat, wants to identify with heroic failure? Onoda was an example of a man who had lived, not died, for his ideals.

Terry, a long-established and well-respected translator of Japanese, was sceptical, until, on TV, he saw Onoda arrive. 'When I saw this small, dignified man emerge from the plane, bow, and then stand rigidly at attention for his ovation . . . I was hooked.' For the next two weeks, the press and TV were full of Onoda's doings, greeting his father, his mother, his friends, having a check-up, eating, travelling to his home-town. He received tens of thousands of letters of praise (though the foreign press looked askance at such adulation heaped on a man who had killed some 30 Filipinos and lived by theft). Naturally, publishers fell over each other offering for the right to his story. He turned all of them down, choos-ing a publisher he admired because of its youth magazines, which he had read as a young man. Here was a man of inflexible will, but also a certain gentleness and nostalgia for the old days. That, perhaps, is what drew him to the open-hearted Suzuki, which in its turn opened the way to his return.

He also had a phenomenal memory. Within three months, he had dictated 2,000 pages of recollections, many of them amazingly detailed. He made sketches of his bases. Articles began to appear in serial form, and editors began work on book versions in both Japanese and English, with Terry as the translator and editor of the English edition.

Onoda was not happy with all the publicity, and the following year he decided to join his brother Tadao in Brazil, where he married a Japanese woman, Machie, joined a Japanese community and started raising 250 head of cattle in a remote ranch on the borders of Bolivia and Paraguay. He was very good at it. In ten years he doubled the size of the ranch and had over 1,000 head of cattle. In 1980, he was shocked by an account of a Japanese teenager who had murdered his parents. Seeing this as a symbol of a decline in youthful standards, he set up a 'nature school' at the foot of Mt Fuji to educate children in boy-scout skills, living off the land.

In May 1996, Onoda returned to the Philippines on a trip proposed by the governor of Occidental Mindoro province, Josephine Ramirez Sato, whose Japanese husband had been a member of one of the search parties hunting for Onoda. Onoda's purpose was to honour the memory of those who had died during his 30 years in the jungle. On Lubang, he laid flowers on the spot where Kozuka had been shot, which had been made into a peace monument in 1981, at the behest of the then Japanese prime minister, Fukuda Takeo, among others. Afterwards, he gave the local mayor a cheque for $10,000 to fund scholarships. There were courtesy calls on Governor Sato and the president, Fidel Ramos. Questioned by reporters and confronted by protesters demanding compensation for murder and theft, Onoda made his message clear. He had acted honourably, as a soldier, for his country. Compensation was for governments. All he could do was help reconciliation by showing goodwill.

The school and the visit seem to be Onoda's answer to his three questions: why had he fought on Lubang for 30 years? Who had he been fighting for? What was the cause?

He had fought to survive; he had survived to do what he could to reconcile old enemies, and to bring the survival skills he had acquired to a new generation. Now, Japan and the Philippines are close business partners. And, in 20 years, some 20,000 children have passed through the school started by the man the children call 'Uncle Jungle', but whom others call the *real* last of the ninjas.

BIBLIOGRAPHY

There are scores, perhaps hundreds, of books that focus on what are supposed to be the ninjas' martial arts, magical skills and esoteric supremacy. There's a great deal of dross out there. The following are the books I found most useful.

Adolphson, Mikael, *The Gates of Power: Monks, Courtiers and Warriors in Premodern Japan*, University of Hawaii Press, Honolulu, 2000.

Allen, Louis, 'The Nakano School', in *Proceedings of the British Association for Japanese Studies* (eds John Chapman and David Steeds), Vol. 10, University of Sheffield, 1985.

Black, Jeremy, *The Politics of James Bond: From Fleming's Novels to the Big Screen*, University of Nebraska Press, Lincoln and London, 2005.

Breen, John and Mark Teeuwen, *Shinto in History: Ways of the Kami*, Curzon Press, Richmond, 2000.

Cobb, Nora Okja, 'Behind the Inscrutable Half-Shell: Images of Mutant Japanese and Ninja Turtles', MELUS, Vol. 16, No. 4.

Conlan, Thomas Donald, *State of War: The Violent Order of Fourteenth Century Japan*, University of Michigan, Ann Arbor, 2003.

Cummins, Antony and Yoshie Minami, *The Book of the Ninja*

[the *Bansenshūkai*], Watkins, London, to be published 2013.

Cummins, Antony and Yoshie Minami, *True Path of the Ninja: The Definitive Translation of the Shoninki*, Tuttle, Tokyo, Rutland (Vermont) and Singapore, 2011.

Cummins, Antony and Yoshie Minami, *True Ninja Traditions: The Ninpiden and the Unknown Ninja Scroll*, Wordclay, Bloomington, Indiana, 2010.

Deal, William E., *Handbook to Life in Medieval and Early Modern Japan*, Oxford University Press, 2007.

Draeger, Donn F. and Robert Smith, *Asian Fighting Arts*, Berkley Publishing Corp., New York, 1974.

Ferejohn, John A., and Frances McCall Rosenbluth, *War and State Building in Medieval Japan*, Stanford University Press, California, 2010.

Fleming, Ian, *You Only Live Twice*, Hodder & Stoughton, London, 1964.

Fleming, Ian, *Thrilling Cities (1)*, Jonathan Cape, London, 1963.

Friday, Karl F., *Samurai, Warfare and the State in Early Medieval Japan*, Routledge, New York and London, 2004.

Fujiwara Iwaichi, *F. Kikan: Japanese Army Intelligence Operations in Southeast Asia during World War II*, trans. Akashi Yoji, Heinemann Educational, London, 1983.

Hatsumi, Masaaki, *Illustrated Book of Warring States Ninpo*, American Bujinkan Dojo, Santa Cruz, 1992.

Hevener, Phillip T., *Fujita Seiko: The Last Koga Ninja*, Xlibris, 2008.

Hitoshi, Miyaka, *The Mandala of the Mountain*, Tokyo, Keio University Press, 2005.

Ishida Yoshihito, *Chūsei sonraku to Bukkyō* [中世村落と仏教], Kyōto-shi, Shibunkaku Shuppan, 1996.

Lamers, Jeroen P., *Japonius Tyrannus: The Japanese Warlord Oda Nobunaga Reconsidered*, Hotei Publishing, Leiden, 2000.

Lidin, Olof G., *Tanegashima: The Arrival of Europe in Japan*, Nordic Institute of Asian Studies Monograph Series, No. 90, Copenhagen, 2002.

McCullough, Helen Craig (trans. and ed.), *The Taiheiki: A*

Chronicle of Medieval Japan, Charles E. Tuttle, Rutland (Vermont) and Tokyo, 1979 (many later editions).

Mercado, Stephen, *The Shadow Warriors of Nakano: A History of the Imperial Japanese Army's Elite Intelligence School*, Brassey's, Washington DC, 2002.

Momochi Orinosuke (百地織之助), *Kosei Iran-ki* (校正伊亂記), 1897.

Morris, Ivan, *The Nobility of Failure: Tragic Heroes in the History of Japan*, Secker and Warburg, London, 1975.

Onoda Hiroo, *No Surrender: My Thirty-Year War*, Transworld, London, 1976.

Peterson, Kirtland C., *Mind of the Ninja: Exploring the Inner Power*, Contemporary Books, Chicago, 1986.

Philippi, Donald (trans. and introduction), *Kojiki*, Princeton and Tokyo, 1969.

Rabinovitch, Judith, *Shōmonki: The Story of Masakado's Rebellion*, Monumenta Nipponica monograph 58, Sophia University, Tokyo, 1986.

Sadler, A.L., *The Maker of Modern Japan: The Life of Shogun Tokugawa Ieyasu*, Tuttle, Rutland (Vermont) and Tokyo, 1937.

Segawa Masaki, *Basilisk* (manga version of Yamada Fūtaro's *The Kouga Ninja Scrolls*), 5 vols, Random House, New York, 2006.

Souyri, Pierre François, *The World Turned Upside Down: Medieval Japanese Society* (trans. Käthe Roth), Columbia University Press, New York, 2001.

Sun Tzu, *The Art of War*, Wordsworth, Ware, 1998.

Turnbull, Stephen, *Ninja 1460–1650*, Osprey, Oxford, 2003.

Turnbull, Stephen, *Japanese Warrior Monks AD 949–1603*, Osprey, Oxford, 2003.

Turnbull, Stephen, *Nagashino 1575*, Osprey, Oxford, 2000.

Turnbull, Stephen, *Osaka 1615*, Osprey, Oxford, 2006.

Yamada Fūtaro, *The Kouga Ninja Scrolls*, Ballantine, New York, 2006.

Zoughari, Kacem, *The Ninja: Ancient Shadow Warriors of Japan*, Tuttle, North Clarendon (VT) and Tokyo, 2010.

ACKNOWLEDGEMENTS

With overall thanks to:
  Noriko Ansell for her help and advice in Iga and Kōka, and her father Moria Hatsuhisa; Antony Cummins, in particular for his help on the Iga Commune and for his translations (along with Yoshie Minami) of the ninja poems that begin each chapter; Tullio Lobotti, SOAS, Shugendō initiate; Dr Gaynor Sekimori, SOAS, Shugendō expert.

In Iga:
  Hiromitsu Kuroi, Iga-Ueno Ninja Museum; Kazuya Kamaguchi, Akame (48 Waterfalls); Momochi Mikio, owner of Momocho Sandayu's house, Iga-Ueno; Morimoto Satoshi, Iga-Ueno Tourist Office; Tomomori Kazuya, Kashihara Castle; Tsuki Katsuya, potter, Chigachi Castle; Ueda Masaru, restaurant owner, Akame (48 Waterfalls).

In Kōka:
Hukui Minogu, Kōga ninja house; Koyama Haruhisa Koga Ninjutsu Study Group; Kōzō Yamada, Shugenja and mountain walker; Sikimoto Jei-ichi, Shugendō priest; Somanosho, priest; Taki Sugao Koga Ninjutsu Study Group; Toshinobu

Watanabe, Kōga Ninjutsu Study Group; Tsuji Kunio, hotel owner; Yoshihisa Yoshinori, Kōka Town Tourism.

My thanks as always to Felicity Bryan and her staff, Doug Young and Simon Thorogood at Transworld, and Mari Roberts for her excellent editing.

Picture Acknowledgements

Every effort has been made to contact the copyright holders. We apologize for any omissions in this respect and will be pleased to make the appropriate acknowledgements in any future edition. All images have been supplied courtesy of the author unless otherwise stated.

Section one

Page 1: Ninja sketch by Katsushika Hokusai (1817). Page 8: Ninja assassin attack on Mori Ranmaru and Oda Nobunaga, Toyonobu (1884) courtesy of Pictures from History.

Section two

Page 9: Ninja armour at the ninja museum in Takayama © Miguel A. Muñoz Pellicer/Alamy. Pages 12–13: *You Only Live Twice* film stills courtesy of www.007magazine.com © 1967 Danjaq LLC and United Artists Corporation. All rights reserved. Page 14: Ninja Turtles image © AF archive/Alamy. Ninja manga drawing from Basilisk 1: The Kouga Ninja Scrolls © Del Rey Books/Masaki Segawa. Page 16: Lt. Hiroo Onoda surrenders his sword to Major General Jose Rancudo

© Bettmann/CORBIS. Hiroo Onoda leaving Lubang Island in 1974 © AP/Press Association Images. Hiroo Onoda salutes to the Philippine Air Force on arrival at a radar site on Lubang Island © AP/Press Association Images.

INDEX

ABOUT THE AUTHOR

John Man is a historian and travel writer with special interests in Mongolia, China and Japan. His books have been published in over twenty languages. His previous books include *Samurai*, *The Great Wall*, *Xanadu*, *Atilla* and the bestselling *Genghis Khan*.